Male Sexuality under Surveillance

Male Sexuality under Surveillance

The Office in American Literature

Graham Thompson / University of Iowa Press / Iowa City

University of Iowa Press, Iowa City 52242

Copyright © 2003 by the University of Iowa Press

All rights reserved

Printed in the United States of America

Design by April Leidig-Higgins

http://www.uiowa.edu/uiowapress

Printed on acid-free paper

Library of Congress Cataloging-in-Publication Data
Thompson, Graham, 1965 –
Male sexuality under surveillance: the office in
American literature / Graham Thompson.
p.   cm.
Includes bibliographical references and index.
ISBN 0-87745-848-0 (cloth)
1. American fiction—History and criticism.
2. Offices in literature. 3. Melville, Herman, 1819 –
1891. Bartleby, the scrivener. 4. Howells, William
Dean, 1837–1920. Rise of Silas Lapham. 5. Lewis,
Sinclair, 1885–1951. Babbitt. 6. Sex (Psychology)
in literature. 7. Sex in literature. 8. Men in literature.
I. Title.
PS374.O34T48 2003
813'.009'355—dc21   2002035378

03 04 05 06 07   C   5 4 3 2 1

For Emma

Contents

ix Acknowledgments

xi Introduction

Part One: Managing Desire

---

3   1. "Dead letters . . . dead men?":
The Rhetoric of the Office in
Melville's "Bartleby, the Scrivener"

21 2. "And that paint is a thing
that will bear looking into":
The Business of Sexuality in
The Rise of Silas Lapham

47 3. "A dream more romantic than
scarlet pagodas by a silver sea":
The Businessman and the Fairy
Child in Sinclair Lewis's *Babbitt*

Part Two: Postwar Unsettlement

---

65 4. "The spirit of work
weaves a magic wand":
From Babbittry to Gray Flannel
via Tropical Incorporation

87 5. "Opaque glass bricks":
    Sloan Wilson's Gray Flannel Man
    in the Queer Organization

109 6. "I ascend like a condor,
     while falling to pieces":
     Fear, Paranoia, and Self-Pity in
     Joseph Heller's *Something Happened*

     Part Three: A Word for Windows
----

133 7. "My own plein-air
     Arnality bared to the sky":
     Shoelaces, Social Energy, and
     Sexuality in Nicholson Baker's
     The Mezzanine and *The Fermata*

165 8. "Frank Lloyd Oop":
     Microserfs, Modern Migration, and
     the Architecture of the 1990s

201 Conclusion

207 Notes

233 Bibliography

245 Index

Some of the material that follows has been printed elsewhere, albeit in somewhat different form. Chapter 1 was published under the same title in the *Journal of American Studies* 34 (December 2000), 395–411. Chapter 2, again under the same title, was published in *American Literary Realism* 34 (Fall 2000), 1–20. Part of chapter 7 appeared in "Shoelaces and Social Energy: Surveilling the Man's World of Nicholson Baker's *The Mezzanine*," *OVERhere: A European Journal of American Culture* 18 (1998): 36–53. A shortened version of chapter 1 was awarded the 1999 British Association for American Studies Essay Prize. An abbreviated version of chapter 8 was published with the same title in the *Canadian Review of American Studies* 31 (2001): 119–35.

This book owes much to the support—intellectual and financial—provided by others. Dick Ellis has proved invaluable in ways for which I will always be grateful. His risky (or desperate) decision to provide me with my first teaching experience after a hurried meeting in a coffee bar was the catalyst for all that has followed. His encouragement gave me the confidence to start the research project out of which this book developed, and his incisive and coherent supervision through the inevitable ebbs and flows of thinking and writing ensured that I finished it. I am also grateful to the people who have read and commented on earlier versions of chapters—David Bell, Ruth Holliday, Phil Leonard, Gregory Woods, Peter Nicholls, and Ann Hurford—and those conferees who have sat through papers and either asked questions or talked with me later. The two anonymous readers of this book for the University of Iowa Press provided not only perceptive and practical criticism but also a degree of generous enthusiasm that was welcome and reassuring. To each author in the bibliography a debt of gratitude is due. Any misinterpretations or misreadings are down to me alone.

I am grateful to the Nottingham Trent University for providing me with a bursary for all but the first year of my work on the project out of which this book developed. For financial help during this period and before I thank my mother, Blanche Thompson.

This book explores in a literary context the interaction between three themes that, judging by recent events, are still of the utmost importance in American culture. Anyone who witnessed the spectacle of Bill Clinton reluctantly exposing the nature of his sexual relationship with Monica Lewinsky will have seen there the intertwining of these three themes of surveillance, the office, and male sexuality. In Congress, in court, and on global television networks, the precise nature of the sexual contact that took place in various offices inside the White House was subjected to an unprecedented level of scrutiny. Personal testimonies were supplemented by sophisticated methods of forensic science to identify Clinton as genetically responsible for the semen staining Lewinsky's dress; White House logs were used to pinpoint the precise times both Clinton and Lewinsky were present in the building; while the intensity of the media coverage placed in the widest possible public arena a sexual relationship which occurred in the first instance behind closed office doors and beyond the sight of all but the two participants. From the confines of the Oval Office, Clinton himself even spoke publicly on television about the incidents.

When finally impeached, of course, Clinton was accused of undermining the integrity of his "office" not because of the sexual acts themselves, but because of his failure to represent truthfully what had happened when subjected to the surveillance of Congress, although the implicit theme of the proceedings was that the true nature of Clinton's character could be revealed in the course of exposing these "inappropriate" sexual acts. The ultimate penalty for this behavior would be his "removal from office." And while the word "office" here clearly carries with it particular constitutional associations, it was precisely the dramas which took place in the physical space of the White House—the material location of constitutional office—which threatened the status of Clinton's hold on constitutional power.

The way men interact with women in offices, then—and this is as true in cases of sexual harassment and discrimination as it is in cases of presidential impropriety—affects their public status and their tenure in offices. Jeremy Lewis's *Chatto Book of Office Life*, an anthology of writing about the office and one of the few books to treat the office as a literary theme, is subtitled *Love among the Filing Cabinets*[1] and emphasizes this common, though often underdeveloped, observation about the office: it is an arena of desire. This observation drives the more specific intentions of what follows in this book. And yet to approach an arena of desire from behind the blinkers of "what men get up to with women" would be to ignore a broader field of male sexuality. It is worth recognizing that up until the last two decades of the nineteenth century the office in American capitalism was an all-male environment and that the disciplinary culture of the office, therefore, developed largely as the organization of men by other men. The phenomenon of the glass ceiling, one of the primary discourses about women's employment in the United States since the Second World War, suggests that this organizational control remains in the hands of, and continues to pass among, men.

Eve Sedgwick has drawn critical attention to the kinds of relations men have formed with other men in such male-dominated locations. For her these relations are often structured by desire. But it is a desire where the experiences of even ostensibly heterosexual men do not fit into a field of male sexuality bounded by "heterosexuality." She suggests instead that male-male relationships take place in a potentially unbroken "continuum between homosocial and homosexual—a continuum whose visibility, for men, in our society, is radically disrupted."[2] One of the ways in which this continuum is disrupted is by the classificatory separation of heterosexuality and homosexuality, where heterosexuality becomes the template for acceptable male-male relations; that is, where affectionate contact between men, while it may take a variety of other forms, remains nonsexual.

In the following chapters I explore how the office, as an arena of desire, becomes a location where it is possible to observe the various forms this radical disruption takes as men manage and organize their relations with other men. And as these men—with the possible exception of the lawyer-narrator in "Bartleby, the Scrivener"—live apparently heterosexual lifestyles, it is the perpetual commotion at the heart of straight male sexuality as it has developed in America since the middle of the nineteenth century that I want to examine. The historical scope of this enterprise means that it is possible to chart the shifting dimensions of what Sedgwick has elsewhere called the male "crisis of definition."[3] One of the aims of this book, then, is to show that not only is capitalist value created in the offices of American commerce, but so are American men themselves.

For the present study, Sedgwick's alertness to the "visibility" of the continuum linking homosocial and homosexual is also important, since more often than not it is the hiding and obscuring of the continuum that is most evident in the texts I study here, however full of examples of intense homosocial relationships they may be. This raises the question of just where one should look to explore male sexuality. How does one discuss sexuality in a text, or in a social relationship for that matter, when there is no explicit thematization of sexual contact in that text or social relationship? Of course, what is *classified* as sexual contact is important here, and this is itself an issue about visibility. Despite sexuality and sexual contact not being thematized, they surely cannot be absent from a text completely. So where are they? Very often, as I will show, they are to be found in the epistemological organization of the visual regime of the office because, as well as being an arena of desire, the office is a sophisticated surveilling machine, particularly in its contemporary guise. Architecturally, open-plan workspaces, glass doors, glass-enclosed offices, and hard surfaces such as steel, chrome, and polished wood, all institute codes of visibility and reflection. The methods of monitoring employee performance, whether it be through direct supervision, career appraisal, or more recently and even more invasively through computer keystroke counting, the interception of electronic mail messages, and the availability of itemized phone bills, are testament to the way in which surveillance operates intensely in office environments.

What is surprising when one looks for the continuities linking the regimes of office culture in the mid nineteenth and the late twentieth century is precisely this emphasis upon methods of visual surveillance, however differently conceived and implemented. The office, then, is a visual regime, which becomes important at that moment in Western culture when the epistemological nature of society is changing, when, in Michel Foucault's terms, surveillance and disciplinary society as epitomized in Bentham's Panopticon are rearranging the organization of power relations.[4]

Indeed, the Benthamite penitentiary, introduced in Philadelphia in the

1790s, was taken up in America more seriously than anywhere in Britain or Europe[5] and was only the most obvious example of a Puritan inheritance that ensured surveillance technologies were readily incorporated into American society. The importance of their disciplining effects was enshrined in the very philosophical foundations of white American manhood[6] and came to operate even outside of an overtly Christian setting. Ralph Emerson could declare "nature" itself "is a discipline" and for him clearly one that functioned in the world of business and capitalism: "What tedious training, day after day, year after year, never ending, to form the common sense; . . . what disputing of prices, what reckoning of interest,— and all to form the Hand of the mind . . . The same good office is performed by Property and its filial systems of debt and credit."[7]

Following the rise of the mercantile and commercial cities along the eastern seaboard and the beginnings of industrial development there and in the West, the urban office from the 1830s and 40s onward was to be the very site where this reckoning of interest was executed and where the systems of debt and credit were controlled. From this time forward the office becomes an increasingly important location in America and as such is folded into a disciplinary culture that, through its panoptic architecture, will supervise the male bodies that work within its confines. The office is always, then, a site of surveillance.

Such surveillance will have different consequences depending on which male bodies undergo supervision and where these male bodies are placed in the continuum of male sexuality. The residual and often violent effects of this process of supervision are still with us. What is striking about the Clinton-Lewinsky affair is that the Republican drive to impeach Clinton relied to a large degree on proving the heterosexual consummation of the relationship in the face of Clinton's denial of "sexual relations with that woman." Likewise, much of the media coverage was obsessed with the sexual details of the affair, so much so that the endless reading of Clinton's body failed to position it in relation to a continuum of male sexuality and instead turned the affair into an entirely heterosexual occasion. The work of Sedgwick, however, suggests other ways in which the affair can be read. If one chooses to alter the focus and look other than directly at the heterosexual facts, then it is possible to suggest ways in which Clinton's time in "office" was marked by different kinds of scandals involving surveillance and male sexuality.

Clinton was a president who, it should be remembered, entered the Oval Office determined to implement legislation that would alter the status of homosexuality in the United States in important ways. His pledge to allow the open access of gay men and women to the military services created, however, only a deafening chorus of objections that eventually led to the compromise "Don't Ask, Don't Tell" policy. Implemented in 1994, the policy was meant to stop military personnel from inquiring about the sexual orientation of recruits and serving members of the armed forces, while leaving in place a prohibition on homosexual activity. Sexual orientation was meant to remain a private matter unless a serving member of the forces made an open declaration or unless information was received by commanding officers credibly suggesting that a service member was engaging in homosexual activity. No investigation could proceed without such information. Rather than easing the path for gay men and women to enter and serve in the armed forces, however, according to a report written for the Secretary of Defense in 1998, the "Don't Ask, Don't Tell" policy resulted only in an increasing number of military personnel being discharged for "homosexual conduct."[8]

The policy clearly traded in an unsustainable visual logic. If gay men remained closeted and preserved the visibility of the radical disruption in the continuum of male sexuality, then the military would not force them out of the closet and out of the services. What this policy failed to take into account, however, was that although the visibility of the continuum of male sexuality may remain radically disrupted in our culture, the process of surveillance means that male sexual behavior is constantly being monitored. Not formally, perhaps, during the application procedure for the armed forces, but continually in one's behavior.

In what follows, I rely on ideas set out by Lee Edelman to refine the relationship between surveillance and male sexuality. Edelman argues that since the eighteenth century, while the heterosexual male body is assumed to be natural and normal, the homosexual male body is constantly forced to offer up its own visibility to be read by others. Contradictorily, however, the homosexual male body must also defy this burden of visibility so that it may "pass" and thus be sought out and marked all the more vigorously. This continual vigilance, however, carries consequences for all male bodies since they must constantly position themselves in relation to the markers that signify the homosexual male body.[9] In the light of this idea it is clear, then, that the armed services could not stop looking for homosexuals; if anything, the "Don't Ask, Don't Tell" policy, by taking away the formal methods of un-closeting gays, only ensured greater vigilance and greater surveillance at an everyday level.

The most spectacular example of the ratcheting up of this regime of surveillance after the implementation of "Don't Ask, Don't Tell" can be found in the case of Timothy McVeigh. After seventeen years in the navy, McVeigh was charged with "sodomy and indecent acts" and recommended for honorable discharge for "Homosexual Conduct Admittance." The credible evidence for this course of action was an AOL Online member profile in which McVeigh had used the word "gay" to describe his marital status. The navy took this as a public admission of sexual orientation, reason enough to invoke an investigation, and evidence enough to justify discharge. Alerted to this entry on his member profile by the wife of one of McVeigh's colleagues to whom he had sent an e-mail, the naval investigators contacted AOL in order to verify that the profile was indeed McVeigh's. AOL's terms of service prohibited the release of this material, and yet they still provided the navy with information that named McVeigh as billing contact for the profile. McVeigh objected to the charges on various grounds: using only the name "Tim" in his AOL profile and not his surname meant, he argued, that he had not publicly identified himself as gay; using the word "gay" did not mean that he ever engaged in homosexual conduct as defined by the navy; and using the word "gay" was not the same as being gay or homosexual. None of which appeased a military committee whose chain of command stretched all the way back to the Oval Office and which was determined to utilize a methodology of the most intense investigative surveillance to discharge a longstanding and decorated officer in order to reinforce the radical disruption of the continuum between homosocial and homosexual.

Although McVeigh was eventually reinstated, the whole case contrasts starkly with the kinds of surveillance visited on Clinton. In that case, no end of scrutiny could turn either Clinton's proven "heterosexual conduct" or his failure to disclose the nature of this conduct to Congress into a dismissible offense. For McVeigh, intrusive surveillance that could turn up only the most intangible of evidence was enough to place him at the wrong point on the continuum of male sexuality and thus to ensure his immediate dismissal.

There are still further contradictions, however, between these two examples, ones that are rooted in the "office" both of president and of its spatial corollary in the White House. As well as his affair with Lewinsky, and as well as his compromise "Don't Ask, Don't Tell" policy which resulted in renewed discrimination against serving gay military personnel, Clinton instigated various military campaigns during his presidency that can be understood in the light of a sexual logic which more directly makes visible the unbrokenness of the continuum between the homosocial and the homosexual. Writing about Clinton's predecessor in the

White House, George Bush senior, and the Gulf War with Iraq, Jonathan Goldberg identifies a "militaristic *imaginaire*"[10] that places United States military action in uncomfortable proximity to a language of penetration. Part of the effort to mobilize a campaign against Iraq following the invasion of Kuwait relied, according to Goldberg, on a discourse of reversing the aggression that had been committed against Kuwait and, by extension, America. It meant inflicting on Iraq the aggression suffered by Kuwait, but at the same time demarcating between acts of aggression such that American aggression could be classified as legitimate while Iraqi aggression could be denounced as illegitimate: "Even as 'America' is invited to perform an act—Saddam's act—that act must be read and done otherwise."[11]

It must be done otherwise, Goldberg argues, because of the way that Saddam Hussein's acts are miscast—by the coincidental sound of his name and by the more sinister encoding of him in popular representations—as sodomy in the American cultural imagination. While returning the act of aggression implicates America in an act of sodomy—of regaining that active position that has been assumed by Iraq—the completion of the act must serve the purpose of distancing America from all accusations of sodomy: "If Saddam is blasted away, if the homosexual is destroyed, it would be impossible ever to suppose that proper male aggression could be misrecognized as sodomy."[12] Goldberg is alert to the important meaning that sodomy has in American culture. Indeed, the case of Timothy McVeigh is indicative of the way that United States citizens—even military personnel—have no rights of privacy when they are assumed to have engaged in consensual acts that legally are still described as sodomy. And the way in which the perpetrators of "sodomy and indecent acts" are so ruthlessly pursued and dismissed by the military seems to make sense in just the way that Goldberg identifies: removing homosexual men from service anticipates and disarms the suggestion that proper male aggression has anything to do with sodomy.

From the Oval Office Bill Clinton carried on the attacks against Iraq, as well as instigating similar missile attacks in Afghanistan and Sudan. Whatever the diplomatic or strategic rights and wrongs of these attacks, I would emphasize that they cannot be separated from the other sexual scandals that dominated Clinton's time in office. The very coincidence of the attacks on Afghanistan and Sudan on August 20, 1998, for instance, is indicative of the way that military action cannot be cordoned off from other aspects of male sexuality. Clinton defended the attacks on national television from the same office that his imminent impeachment hearing would identify as the location for the "inappropriate" sexual conduct with Lewinsky. Picking up on this coincidence, some Arab politicians and commentators dubbed the missile strikes "Operation Monica." By trying to raise his standing in the face of humiliation and to divert attention from his heterosexual conduct, in a confused strategy Clinton sanctioned the use of weapons of penetration against male counterparts overseas. Far from affirming himself as the tolerant president who came to office intent on improving the status of gay United States citizens, Clinton resorted to a policy that seemed only to ratify those structures of homophobia identified by Goldberg in the American "militaristic *imaginaire*." Going on the attack—literally—to regain the mantle of power that might be removed from him by impeachment, Clinton kicked ass overseas as a means of demonstrating that his heterosexuality could be put to "appropriate" purpose: the destruction of potential sodomizers.

I hope that these introductory comments help establish the ground for the arguments that follow. The Clinton-Lewinsky affair is in many ways a unique occurrence, but one that can be read as an example of the way in which—in tense and unpredictable ways—surveillance, the office, and male sexuality interact. Each of these themes would justify attention in its own right during the period covered by this book, but what interests me is the nature of their concatenation in an American setting and the way that the Clinton-Lewinsky episode only seems to allow access to a broader field of male sexuality when considered in conjunction with surveillance and the office.

The surveillance of the office is part of a wider social and cultural network of surveillance that crosses over the boundary that is artificially constructed by the designation of work and nonwork spaces. Without this wider dimension, what took place in the offices of the White House could have remained secret. Clinton's belief that he could protect himself from a wider network by lying and denial was embarrassed by the arsenal of surveillance techniques that were wheeled out to contradict him. And all this at the same time as he was presiding from the Oval Office over all sorts of surveillance strategies, the intention of which, as we can see in the case of Timothy McVeigh, was to violently position men at the unacceptable end of the continuum of male sexuality. Not only this, but implementing such a strategy also involved paranoically separating himself from that unacceptable end of the continuum by way of military campaigns that rescued for male heterosexuality the rights of penetration so that they were unrecognizable as sodomy and were themselves instigated quite calculatingly to distract attention from the Lewinsky scandal. The concatenation of these three elements of surveillance, the office, and male sexuality may not have been immediately apparent when the United States and the rest of the world looked into the Oval Office on the numerous occasions Clinton addressed his public, and yet it does not take too dramatic a shift of perspective to see how intimately they are entwined.

If this book is about the way that surveillance operates in culture, then, it is also about the surveillance of literary criticism and about where this criticism should look in order to articulate what Calvin Thomas has called "the exclusions and repressions"[13] that make heterosexuality possible. This book's perspective is organized by two principle considerations. First, that, since the American office was originally an all-male environment, the way it has developed through the nineteenth and twentieth centuries makes it a site particularly sensitive to the construction of male heterosexuality during this same period. Second, and consequently, that as notions of male sexuality in America are being rethought in the light of recent developments in queer theory, then literary representations of the office will be able to lay witness to many of the demands, constraints, and contradictions implicit in the formation of this sexuality.

In addition to the development and elaboration of this underlying argument, each chapter is positioned in relation to a more particular aspect of queer theory, cultural theory, or historical change so that what is achieved is not only a narrow concentration on the particularities of the office, but a broader analysis of the way in which what takes place in the office actually stands as an indicator of what is taking place in the wider culture. One theme that recurs throughout the book is the fragility of the boundary between the workplace and what lies outside it. This call for a broader analysis of the issues represented in these texts is also a call for studies of American literature in general to take much greater account of issues of sexuality in its analysis of texts. This point is emphasized here by using queer theory—sometimes supposed to be a narrow or specialist critical approach—to address the work of male heterosexual writers who are often represented as being concerned with broad, general, or universal themes. It also means that I have to clarify my decisions about which texts to concentrate on. I have avoided a survey approach and chosen instead to focus each chapter around a single text that represents a significant historical moment in the development of these changing patterns of surveillance and sexuality.

The book deals with the representation of these themes in three parts. In the first part I look at, in turn, Herman Melville's "Bartleby, the Scrivener" (1853), William Dean Howells's *The Rise of Silas Lapham* (1885), and *Babbitt* (1922) by Sinclair Lewis, in order to examine the boundaries of male friendship during this period. The first chapter establishes some of the core theoretical discourses that might provide a way of approaching the subject of male friendship in the context of the office at a time when the separation of sexuality into its modern binary classification was gathering pace. Lee Edelman's theory of homographesis is used to emphasize the link between the surveillance strategies apparent in the office and the logic of visualization and textualization that comes to dominate the representation of the homosexual male body. These initial chapters explore the ways in which each text is built around a close and desirous male friendship, but how this friendship is gradually closed down as the realization dawns in one of the characters that this desire may in fact be sexual. So while testifying to the potential fluidity of male desire during the late nineteenth and early twentieth centuries, these texts dramatize the solidification of that sexual classification that will become important during the next part of the twentieth century.

Part 2 examines the effects of major structural changes in the nature of office-based white-collar work upon straight male sexuality in the period between the end of the Second World War and the 1970s. Although supposedly demarcated sharply from homosexuality by way of a definition of sexuality that relied upon a combination of sexual object choice and "proper" biology and gender concurrence,[14] the feminization of office and clerical work and the increasing size of American corporations meant that straight male sexuality was never demarcated securely enough for its own satisfaction. In a heightened environment of surveillance, self-surveillance, suspicion, and accusation—because of the Cold War, a pervasive discourse of homosexual latency, and the fading of the connection between straight masculinity and an American business ethic that was enshrined in Babbittry—straight male sexuality in the office was potentially threatened by the legacy of that fluidity in male friendship evident in the earlier period.

Bringing the book to a close, part 3 will show how the sex and gender anxiety evident in straight male responses to the postwar world of office work is replaced by a different sense of how identity may be constructed in relation to work. These two chapters look at texts that fit uneasily within the categorization set up by epithets like "Blank Fiction" or "Blank Generation Fiction," so often used to describe American writing in the 1980s and 90s. The critical consolidation of these terms has emphasized certain common themes—"the extreme, the marginal and the violent . . . indifference and indolence"[15]—often with just cause. However, the corresponding emphasis in this critical writing on the pervasiveness and oppressiveness of a culture of consumption and commodification has, to my mind, resulted in the neglect of the importance of work and production and their contribution to identity formation during this period. The two chapters here try to redress this balance by exploring Nicholson Baker's *The Mezzanine* (1988) and *The Fermata* (1994) and Douglas Coupland's *Microserfs* (1995), novels that stand witness not only to the changing patterns of work in the last twenty-five years in American capitalism, but also to the way in which their male narrators experience these changes other than negatively. Indeed, the workplace for these narrators, whether it be the corporate office or the office located in the home (as in *Microserfs*), no longer carries connotations of loss and anxiety. Rather than rejecting the office like their predecessors did because it is unmasculine, these narrators are not threatened by the office because their straight male sexuality no longer seems dependent upon such masculinist discourses. Indeed, in the final chapter I argue that the very conjunction in the office of surveillance and the processes of inscription and description that inform Edelman's theory of homographesis may in fact be breaking down.

Part One

Managing Desire

Chapter One

"Dead letters . . . dead men?"

The Rhetoric of the Office in Melville's
"Bartleby, the Scrivener"

Although a good deal of recent critical attention to Melville's writing has
followed the lead of Robert K. Martin in addressing the issue of sexuality, the predominant themes in discussions of "Bartleby" remain changes
in the nature of the workplace in antebellum America and transformations in capitalism.[1] But if one of the enduring mysteries of the story is
the failure of the lawyer-narrator to sever his relationship with his young
scrivener once Bartleby embarks upon his policy of preferring not to, it
is a mystery that makes sense within both of these critical discourses.
On the one hand the longevity of the relationship dramatizes a tension
implicit in Michael Gilmore's suggestion that the lawyer-narrator strad-
dles the old and the new economic orders of the American marketplace.
Although he may employ his scriveners "as a species of productive property and little else,"[2] his attachment to his employees is overwhelmingly
paternalistic and protective. On the other hand, James Creech suggests
that *Pierre* (published just the year before "Bartleby") is a novel preoccupied with the closeting of homosexual identity within the values of an
American middle-class family, while Gregory Woods describes Melville
as the nearest thing in the prose world of the American Renaissance to
the Good Gay Poet Whitman. In this critical context the longevity of
the relationship suggests that the lawyer-narrator's desire to know Bar-

tleby, to protect him, to tolerate him, to be close to him, to have him for his own, and then to retell the story of their relationship, needs to be considered in relation to sexual desire.

The strength of the adhesive attachment between the two men, however, is never signalled explicitly in the text. Revelation seems closest only in two incidents towards the end of the story, the first when the lawyer defends his charitable treatment of Bartleby by recalling the "divine injunction . . . 'that ye love one another,'" the second immediately following Bartleby's death, when the lawyer-narrator discovers that his former scrivener once worked at the Dead Letter Office in Washington and readily admits that he can "hardly express the emotions which seize" him.[3] More important is the representational status that the relationship assumes in the lawyer-narrator's imagination when he follows this admission by asking himself a somewhat confusing question: "Dead letters! Does it not sound like dead men?" (45). While the literal answer to this question would be "no," it is possible to see the question as the final narrative moment in a story whose whole dramatic development focusses around the ways in which the emotional attachment between the lawyer-narrator and Bartleby is represented through the material processes of writing, reading, and death.

These processes are central to the representation of male sexuality, but for Melville these processes were not separable from economic considerations. This is evident most clearly in "The Paradise of Bachelors and the Tartarus of Maids" (1855) where the spermatic rhetoric of chapter 94 of *Moby-Dick*—"A Squeeze of the Hand"—is transplanted to an industrial paper mill. Looking into the pulp vats the seedsman-narrator sees they are "full of white, wet, woolly-looking stuff, not unlike the albuminous part of an egg, soft-boiled."[4] It is this stuff that will eventually solidify and be turned into the paper that will help him distribute his seed across the country; its mass production will enable the growth of the paper economy upon which the world of capitalist office work is built. Bartleby shares his "pallid" and "blank" outlook with the maids. When the seedsman-narrator writes the name of his young male guide Cupid onto a piece of paper and drops it into the spermy pulp then watches it travel untouched past the virginal maids through the machine to come out at the end of the process neatly incorporated into a foolscap sheet of paper, Melville is splicing together economics with gender and sexuality in a way that helps us to think how they underpin the reading and writing that are so much a part of "Bartleby."

This is why the economic citadel of the office is so important in

"Bartleby"; it is the place where the reading and writing are supposed to take place. Although the office has not been entirely overlooked in previous studies of this story, as a specific spatial site with the power to organize and structure personal and social relationships it has remained stubbornly underexplored, and it has not been considered at all in the literary field in relation to male sexuality.[5] Yet one only has to consider the lawyer-narrator's inexpressible emotion just mentioned, the importance of the screen behind which Bartleby sits in his "hermitage," or indeed Bartleby's refusal to explain himself in the workplace, to see that this office narrative is constructed from those pairings—public and private, surveillance and self-surveillance, disclosure and secrecy—that Eve Sedgwick has described as not only "crucial sites for the contestation of meaning" in Western culture since the latter part of the nineteenth century, but also as all being "indelibly marked with the historical specificity of homosocial/homosexual definition."[6]

A useful way of thinking about "Bartleby" as a product of the 1850s, then, is to think about it as a story that stands at the threshold of modern American anxiety about the crisis of male definition in capitalist culture. I want to treat "Bartleby" as a tense, desire-laden tale of an aging bachelor,[7] the lawyer-narrator, and a pale, innocent young man who is his scrivener. As will become apparent, notions of visuality play a key role in my thinking, and I want to pay particular attention to the lawyer, since in scopic terms the narrative is framed quite specifically through the visual logic of his recollection: "What my own astonished eyes saw of Bartleby, that is all I know of him" (13). Surveilling past events for the lawyer-narrator means trying to read Bartleby and his relationship with him all over again to search for the meaning of the relationship as it originally occurred.

The first thing I want to note about the office is that it remained outside the orbit of Foucault's attention in his studies of surveillance and the "carceral city." This is somewhat surprising, especially when one sets what he writes—that it was "the growth of a *capitalist economy* [which] gave rise to the specific modality of disciplinary power, whose general formulas . . . could be operated in the most diverse political regimes, *apparatuses or institutions*"[8] (my emphasis)—against the clear facts that the office and its various functions are tied so closely into capitalist development. Once it became necessary to control and finance industrialization, and once offices became the focal points for communication and the control of organizational complexity, it was no longer tenable to run large regional, national, and international concerns from the houses of merchants as it had been in the eighteenth century when administrative functions were often minimal. Only in the nineteenth century did cities begin to see the growth of specialized office quarters.[9] And yet although Foucault was more concerned with capitalist surveillance in factories and workshops than he was in offices, his analysis of the "imaginary geo-politics" of the city with its "multiple network of diverse elements—walls, space, institution, rules, discourse," allows the office to be considered as in many ways the paradigmatic focus of those new disciplines charac-terizing capitalist disciplinary society: supervision, assessment, visibility, the distribution of bodies in space, normalization, hierarchies of power.[10] The office, in its original manifestation, developed within the same logic and legacy of modernity which bequeathed a "vigilance of intersecting gazes"[11] to Western culture.

This development of the office was also part of one of the key features in the shift from a preindustrial economy to a capitalist industrial econ-omy in America: the separation of work from home. This separation, important across class divisions, was particularly important in terms of gender for middle-class businessmen and professionals, allowing each of the developing gender binaries to be allocated, via discourse, a zone in which they could legitimately operate: very generally, middle-class men in the workplace and "their" women in the home. Once men became as-sociated with the workplace, so male identity increasingly came to be configured through work.[12]

The lawyer-narrator represented in "Bartleby," then, despite his age, has by the mid nineteenth century evolved into a very sophisticated manager, one who is well attuned to the requirements of surveillance in organizing subordinate staff in an office and whose narrative is organized in a similar fashion. The opening five pages of the story make evident and crucial the location of bodies in space. The detail of the description of the walled-in office, which is at once poetic, meticulous, and domi-nated by a rhetoric of vision, continues that preoccupation with the mapping of space Melville exhibited in his sea narratives.[13] The lawyer-narrator conducts a roll call of his employees, one by one as if from a file he has on each of them. The surveilling proximity of his working re-lationship with them allows him to ascertain their most peculiar habits and idiosyncrasies, most of which revolve around routine, repetition, and regularity. In the end, the deficiencies of Turkey and Nippers—as the requirements of double-entry bookkeeping command—balance one another so that working harmony can be maintained.[14]

It is with the arrival of Bartleby, however, that the incoherence of this nominally well organized office space becomes apparent. First the lawyer is forced to explain how the office is actually split in two and separated by folding, ground-glass doors: "I should have stated before that ground glass folding-doors divided my premises into two parts, one of which was occupied by my scriveners, the other by myself. According to my humor I threw open these doors, or closed them" (19). Exactly why he feels he "should have stated before" that his office is separated by ground-glass doors is not clear, but at the very least it suggests the pressure to classify and organize in narrative as much as in business or—as I will show later—in men's relations with other men. Despite the lawyer-narrator trying to pass off the surveilling processes triggered by his opening and closing the doors by referencing his "humor," clearly the office is organized in completely different ways when the connecting doors are open or closed.

It is even worth asking why the lawyer-narrator needs doors between the two spaces to begin with. If, presumably, it occasions privacy for himself so that he can work in peace or entertain clients or colleagues, then it is shown later in the story— when all the employees sit down to verify documents in the lawyer-narrator's half of the office—how it is not always a private space for the lawyer-narrator. Indeed it alternates between being private and being public. Which it is at any given time depends on whether the doors are open or closed and who is there. But if the doors work to signify space—open and public or closed and private—it needs to be remembered that they are made from ground glass. While permitting light to pass through it, ground glass does not allow a direct, unobstructed gaze. This prevents the literal visibility of the workers to the lawyer-narrator, and so the regime of surveillance instituted by ground glass—and the similar kinds of glass that crop up in the fiction I deal with later—is not entirely equivalent to the forms of visibility instituted in the Panopticon. Workplaces are not prisons, after all, and the relationships between employers and employees are not equivalent to those of guards and inmates. The visual regimes of offices are thus dominated less by actual visibility than by *codes of visibility* wherein are delegated the relations of power that follow from a disciplinary culture of surveillance. The ground glass in "Bartleby" therefore institutes a code of visibility in the whole office, ensuring that the workers have hidden from their eyes the inspector who may be watching them while at the same time achieving the construction of privacy for the lawyer-narrator. Clear glass could not accomplish this.

The lawyer-narrator then makes two linked responses, both crucial to the development of the story. He first describes Bartleby as "motionless . . . pallidly neat, pitiably respectable, incurably forlorn"—adjectives and adverbs which register him in a role of passivity—but then also embarks upon a vital further demarcation of the office space. Despite the narrator's expressed idea that Bartleby's "sedate aspect . . . might operate beneficially upon the flighty temper of Turkey, and the fiery one of Nippers," Bartleby is actually given a desk behind a screen in the lawyer-narrator's part of the office. With Bartleby isolated from his sight but not from his voice, so, according to the lawyer-narrator, "privacy and society were conjoined" (19).

Several things are apparent here: the phonocentric conjugation of voice with society; the failure of the lawyer-narrator (tellingly) to adduce whose privacy it is he thinks he is preserving (it cannot be his own since while he can intrude behind the screen with his voice any time he chooses, Bartleby can also step out from behind the screen without knocking whenever he chooses); the admission that space cannot be marked by screens or doors but is more contingent than that and can be infinitely reassessed; and the lawyer-narrator's disavowing logic, which wants Bartleby to control his other employees while keeping him all to himself in his side of the office. Two classes of space produced so meticulously —in the office, in the lawyer-narrator's narrative—suddenly collapse into one another upon Bartleby's arrival while, once more disavowingly, the lawyer-narrator tries to demarcate them syntactically. By the admission that privacy and society, the private and the public, are proximate at the level of being internal to one another and through this increasing demarcation of his office, the lawyer-narrator is actually destabilizing the very coherence of the project he is professing. The consequences of this process will result in him having to keep on classifying and separating in this manner until he reaches a stage—which he does later in the narrative—where the incoherence of his strategy becomes clear to him and its link to male sexuality transparent. It is at this point that he will be forced to reorder both his office and his sexuality through the ultimate rejection and disavowal. This is the crisis which Bartleby provokes in the lawyer-narrator and which the lawyer-narrator is only able to piece together in his retrospective narrative, his reordering of events connected to Bartleby.[15] It is in the scopic frame of his narrative of Bartleby that he has to confront his own self and where he will recognize what thus far he has been passing over: that his identity as a man in the masculine and public world of work and patriarchy cannot permit the desire he has for Bartleby or other men to be vectored through sex. This places the story, then, squarely in that landscape where male-male relationships stand implicated in the continuum of male homosocial desire, which includes— and these terms are used anachronistically—homosexuality, homophobia, and a homosocial heterosexuality.[16]

In the light of this emphasis on the visual regime, Foucault's argument that the body becomes the site on which disciplinary power plays itself out[17] is insufficient as a way of explaining in more detail how the office and its surveillance strategies influence this realm of male sexuality. This argument needs to be supplemented by some more recent developments in thinking about male sexuality.

Lee Edelman has written how the imperative to produce homosexual difference as a determinate entity in the twentieth century and before has often relied on "reading" the body as a textual "signifier of sexual orientation."[18] As well as having been positioned in such a proscriptive relation to language—*peccatum illud horribile, inter christianos non nominandum*—homosexuality and homosexual men, along with their bodies, their clothes, gestures, language, certain buildings and public places of meeting, have always been positioned so that they are intimately related to questions of visibility and legibility. And especially so once it began to be assumed by the discourses of eighteenth- and nineteenth-century Western culture that a subject's relation to sexuality and desire was essential rather than contingent.[19] But at the same time as the homosexual man comes to be distinctively marked, becomes a text, Edelman goes on to argue that it must also be possible for those hallmarks that distinguish him to pass unremarked. Consequently

> heterosexuality has . . . been able to reinforce the status of its own authority as "natural" (i.e., unmarked, authentic, and non-representational) by defining the straight body against the "threat" of an "unnatural" homosexuality—a "threat" the more effectively mobilized by generating concern about homosexuality's unnerving . . . capacity to "pass," to remain invisible, in order to call into being a variety of

disciplinary "knowledges" through which homosexuality might be recognized, exposed, and ultimately rendered, more ominously, invisible once more.[20]

For Edelman this entry of homosexuality into the field of writing and textuality is the first thing his theory of homographesis denotes. But this writing of homosexuality is reliant upon a second order of visuality, where there is "the need to construe such an emblem of homosexual difference that will securely situate that difference within the register of visibility."[21] Such an emblem is effeminacy,[22] which increasingly comes to be interchangeable with homosexuality—especially as sexuality becomes more tightly linked with gender ideology.[23]

Under these conditions male sexuality becomes susceptible to two different and completely discontinuous readings—heterosexual and homosexual. While the necessity of a visual marker to separate them is compelling—since they must exist in the symbolic order of sexuality in the same way that gender difference does—the necessity of creating "homosexual difference" and "the homosexual" actually affects all male identities: one now has to read all male identities (and, of course, one's own male identity) to see whether they exhibit the hallmark of sexual difference. According to Edelman this

> textualizes male identity as such, subjecting it to the alienating requirement that it be "read," and threatening, in consequence, to strip "masculinity" of its privileged status as the self-authenticating paradigm of the natural or the self-evident itself. Now it must perform its self-evidence, must represent its own difference from the derivative and artificial "masculinity" of the gay man.[24]

The putting into writing of homosexual difference, then, also puts into writing the essentialized nature of identity, the result being—and this is the second thing that Edelman's theory of homographesis denotes—the deconstruction, or de-scription, of a metaphorical notion of identity, and the consequent deconstruction of the binary logic of sameness and difference upon which symbolic identity is based.

Edelman's position clearly suggests the centrality of a scopic constituent for the organization of male sexuality in modernity. Going further than Edelman, I want to make explicit that the links here with surveillance become increasingly irresistible. Visibility, according to Foucault, is "a type of location of bodies in space, of distribution of individuals in relation to one another, of hierarchical organization, of dispositions of centres and channels of power." Perfect for exercising power in the period of capitalist industrialization and population growth "because it can reduce the number of those who exercise it, while increasing the number of those on whom it is exercised," it is also perfect in the way that it induces "a state of conscious and permanent visibility" which ensures that individuals "are themselves the bearers" of a power situation.[25] This kind of operation might be summed up, to bring me back to the office, by way of a business cliché: the art of good management is delegation. Business organization and the Foucauldian system of power relations exist in the same tropological universe.

What I am arguing, therefore, is first that surveillance operates in the office in ways similar to the way it operates in those other institutions and apparatuses of capitalism and modernity identified by Foucault. Next, that surveillance, with all its associated effects and mechanisms for instituting and reproducing power relations, becomes the dominant mode for organizing power during that period in Western history when there takes place a discursive transformation in the way that the nature of subjectivity and identity are understood—when identity shifts from being contingent or metonymic, a series of acts which are not considered as excluding other acts, to being essential or metaphoric, when acts stand as representations of particular categories of persons. Surveillance operates in mutual alliance with this discursive transformation and performs a key role in preparing the epistemological groundwork for knowing identities and, in turn, knowable identities reinforce epistemological frameworks through continued surveillance and monitoring of these identities.

To further concentrate my argument again, I stress that Foucauldian surveillance is, in part, actually a sophisticated form of reading and that this reading is potently implicated in that maneuver whereby the male subject needs to be positioned in one of two increasingly discontinuous and hierarchically organized identities during the course of the nineteenth century—the homo and the hetero—where the boundary between these two needs to be policed constantly. And it is policed by the continuance of reading and surveillance,[26] by the entangled methods of regulation and deconstruction identified in Edelman's theory of homographesis.

In a similar vein, Jonathan Dollimore has identified how sexual contact between men as it has variously been signified through Western history—as sin, as vice, as unnatural, as crime—has carried with it a contradictory metaphysics of evil which has its roots in an Augustinian theology that places sexual perversion as a corruption of good that stands in subordinate but proximate relation to the dominant. This means that it is only possible to conceptualize evil through good. Dollimore identifies two kinds of relation which result:

> First: those proximities will permanently remind the dominant of its actual instability, all forms of domination being unstable to a varying degree, as well as produce a paranoid fear of impending subversion. So there will be both a justified fear as well as an excess of fear; second, that proximity will become the means enabling displacement and projection, while the justified/paranoid fears will be their motivation: proximity becomes a condition of displacement; which in turn marks the same/proximate as radically other.[27]

Here is why male-male sexual contact, while socially marginalized, has retained its central symbolic function in Western society. This metaphysical order is played out in the social and the cultural. The proximate is internal and yet has to be made "radically other" in an/other space. As the lawyer-narrator says, if Bartleby had admitted to having any friends or relatives, "I would instantly have written, and urged their taking the poor fellow away to some convenient retreat" (32).

Put simply, my argument is that the development of the visual regime of surveillance in the office and the development of the twin categories of homo and hetero in the nineteenth century, while they may simply coincide in temporal terms, are definitely not coincidental in the sense of only having an arbitrary relationship. The office, a surveilling regime constructed from those discursive pairings so crucial in the development of the epistemology of modern Western sexuality, facilitates a corresponding reading regime which works to reinscribe these discursive pairings. If it appears that this argument suggests that the office is organized solely in terms of sex, then I should make it clear that this is not what I am arguing. Clearly surveillance in capitalism serves other purposes, such as class control and the disciplining of labor. And yet these purposes are not separate from the work of surveillance and the construction of sexuality. While the office may be the site where many forms of capitalist surveillance take place, it is also not a site that excludes particular kinds of surveillance. If the binary of work and home is an incoherent one, then so must be the boundary which tries to secure for the workplace exclusive rights to a surveillance that is only about class and capitalism. Especially in a story like "Bartleby," which is so concerned with the emotional attachment between two men.

I think that Edelman's and Dollimore's work can join together at this point to help throw light on the development of the story in "Bartleby" as I have already described it, but more importantly they help in an analysis of what subsequently happens to the lawyer-narrator and the way that he manages the desire which only increases as Bartleby refuses to do what he asks of him.

Bartleby's initial refusal is a refusal to read, and while this means that Bartleby is not doing the job for which he is being paid, in a disciplinary regime of surveillance and self-surveillance the refusal to read—whether it be one's position in one's surroundings, the surveilling gaze, oneself— is an act that threatens more than just profits and efficiency. Likewise, in a regime where the reading of other men is becoming vital to the consolidation of identity within a gender, Bartleby's stance is particularly disturbing. This refusal to read is accompanied of course by his relative silence. "Relative" because Bartleby does speak, and he speaks things other than "I would prefer not to," a simple fact that has hardly registered in critical treatments of the story.[28] Gilles Deleuze insists upon this particular utterance as a formula "which every loving reader repeats in turn."[29] But just as "dead letters" sounds nothing like "dead men," so Bartleby's words sound nothing like a silence. His silence has always been conceived of as a "silence" because as a character Bartleby has refused self-explanation. He never does do the work of sharing himself or his secrets with the lawyer-narrator or with anybody else who might be considered a public.[30] Quite literally, Bartleby refuses to read himself in public; that is, he refuses to speak about himself in public: "he had declined telling who he was, or whence he came, or whether he had any relatives in the world" (28). Since Bartleby is unplaced as a man, the placing and the reading are all left to the lawyer-narrator. However, in the process of inscribing Bartleby in ways that place his strange mysteriousness and his unknowability in direct relation to those rhetorical structures that will later come to denote an effeminate homosexuality[31] (ways which the whole retrospective narrative of re-remembrance, re-constitution, and general hindsight of the narrative key into), the lawyer-narrator actually participates in the second stage of Edelman's notion of homographesis, the de-scription of any potentially metaphorical or fixed nature of male identity.

This reversal of the lawyer-narrator's surveilling gaze begins almost as soon as Bartleby refuses to read: "there was something about Bartleby that not only strangely *disarmed me*, but in a wonderful manner touched and *disconcerted me*" (21, my emphasis). Bartleby's refusal, instead of reflecting Bartleby back to the lawyer-narrator, actually makes the lawyer-narrator contemplate himself. The lawyer-narrator convinces himself disavowingly of Bartleby's usefulness to him. Not throwing him out becomes protecting him from a potentially less sympathetic employer: "To befriend Bartleby; to humor him in his strange wilfulness, will cost me little or nothing, while I lay up in my soul what will eventually prove a sweet morsel for my conscience" (23–24). Of course what it means also is that the lawyer-narrator can keep Bartleby close to him; Bartleby is successfully internalized not just by the spatial organization of the lawyer-narrator's side of the office but in the rhetorical maneuver that means that Bartleby is somehow literally inside the lawyer-narrator, an ingested "sweet morsel." So desperate is the lawyer-narrator to maintain Bartleby in his employ that he allows him all sorts of "strange peculiarities, privileges, and unheard of exemptions" which soon the lawyer-narrator becomes used to, so much so that "every added repulse . . . which I received only tended to lessen the probability of my repeating the inadvertence" (26).

This inversion or role reversal is continued during the lawyer-narrator's Sunday morning visit to his office. When he finds Bartleby "saying quietly that he was sorry that he was deeply engaged just then, and— preferred not admitting me at present" (26), the lawyer-narrator is the one who is forced into the position of having to "knock" to enter his own premises. Not only this. Bartleby, having made a home out of the office, has quite explicitly collapsed the home/work and public/private separation. He has domesticated the office. This also means feminizing it. The lawyer-narrator walks away, disconcerted by the way that Bartleby's "wonderful mildness . . . not only disarmed me, but unmanned me, as it were. For I consider that one, for the time, is a sort of unmanned when he tranquilly permits his hired clerk to dictate to him, and order him away from his own premises" (27). So, the lawyer-narrator is unmanned by not being able to control his employees and unmanned by having his office domesticated. But he is also unmanned, surely, by the rhetoric of penetration in Bartleby's refusal to admit him, to allow him to take that active position in the active/passive binary of sexual contact. Here one can see the classification of gender division beginning to affect relations between men. It is Bartleby's passiveness—a description reinforced over and over in the story—his "wonderful mildness," which is unmanning the lawyer-narrator. It bespeaks a manning which is susceptible to that second denotation of homographesis, the de-scription of a masculine male identity.

When the lawyer-narrator returns to the office and embarks upon the most thorough investigation of Bartleby in his absence, identifying each of his meager belongings, and through them his "miserable friendlessness and loneliness" (27), he recognizes the fraternal relationship which bonds him to Bartleby and which leads him "on to other and more special thoughts, concerning the eccentricities of Bartleby. Presentiments of strange discoveries hovered around me" (28). Considering the internalized state in which Bartleby exists for the lawyer-narrator, and considering the points I made in the previous paragraph about penetration, unmanning, and the instability of male identity, the nature of these "special thoughts" and "strange discoveries" would seem to be tied up intimately with this desire the lawyer-narrator is directing towards Bartleby.

What follows is the lawyer-narrator's intrusion into Bartleby's locked desk. This is a key moment in determining the lawyer-narrator's attitude towards Bartleby and one which has been prepared for quite thoroughly by the narrative. This moment needs to be read in the context of the lawyer-narrator having walked away from his office "incontinently"[32] when Bartleby refused him entry; in the context of Nippers's chronic indigestion, the references to nuts and spices, and the capitalist emphasis upon bodily regularity and control connected to the time clock of discipline; in the context of a phallic thematics of disarming; in the context of the lawyer-narrator having noted earlier that the "the interval between this [outside] wall and mine not a little resembled a huge square cistern" (14); in the context of a scopic regime of private and public and their importance in the male washroom—which is what the lawyer-narrator's office effectively becomes next to this cistern—when the urinal and the cubicle allow, respectively, the display of the phallus in public and the loosening of the sphincter in private.[33] In the light of all this, when the lawyer-narrator intrudes into the desk, the presence of an anal thematic becomes unmistakable.[34] In the desk, "Every thing was methodically arranged, the papers smoothly placed. The pigeon holes were deep, and removing the files of documents, I groped into their recesses.

Presently I felt something there, and dragged it out. It was an old bandanna handkerchief, heavy and knotted. I opened it, and saw it was a savings bank" (28).[35] For the lawyer-narrator it is this extraction of coins from Bartleby's desk/anus which leads to the clearest moment of surveillance of Bartleby, the moment when the lawyer-narrator recalls "all the quiet mysteries which I had noted in the man" (28). This passage of revelation is worth quoting at length:

> Revolving all these things, and coupling them with the recently discovered fact that he made my office his constant abiding place and home, and not forgetful of his morbid moodiness; revolving all these things, a prudential feeling began to steal over me. My first emotions had been those of pure melancholy and sincerest pity; but just in proportion as the forlornness of Bartleby grew and grew to my imagination, did that same melancholy merge into fear, that pity into repulsion. So true it is, and so terrible too, that up to a certain point the thought or sight of misery enlists our best affections; but, in certain special cases, beyond that point it does not. They err who would assert that invariably this is owing to the inherent selfishness of the human heart. It rather proceeds from a certain hopelessness of remedying excessive and organic ill. To a sensitive being, pity is not seldom pain. And when at last it is perceived that such pity cannot lead to effectual succor, common sense bids the soul be rid of it. What I saw that morning persuaded me that the scrivener was the victim of innate and incurable disorder. I might give alms to his body; but his body did not pain him; it was his soul that suffered, and his soul I could not reach. (29)

What is so tempting about this passage is that moment when the lawyer-narrator sees his "melancholy merge into fear" and his "pity into repulsion." In the light of Dollimore's ideas, what appears to be happening here is that the lawyer-narrator is fulfilling that maneuver his marking of difference in Bartleby has been moving towards. He is marking "the same/proximate as radically other." The melancholy and the pity which so connected him to Bartleby that Bartleby became internal to him now suddenly are transformed—how exactly does melancholy merge into fear, pity into repulsion?—into the fear and repulsion which will help him to paranoically separate himself completely from Bartleby. Following Dollimore and Edelman, the lawyer-narrator's very proximity to Bartleby is the reason for this fear and repulsion; it is the proximity caused by evil being internal to good and by de-scription being implicated in the process of inscription which relies so heavily on the never stable visual register. The impossibility of any separation haunts the lawyer-narrator: "I trembled to think that my contact with the scrivener had already and seriously affected me in a mental way. And what further and deeper aberration might it not yet produce? This apprehension had not been without efficacy in determining me to summary measures" (31).

The "summary measures" the lawyer-narrator decides upon are, of course, to fulfill his final separation from Bartleby. The lawyer-narrator, so culpable in first differentiating Bartleby by spatial surveillance, so culpable in opening up Bartleby to a surveilling gaze, so culpable in internalizing Bartleby in his own male identity, is now paying the spatial consequences, the consequences of a logic which tries to have as separate and external what is so proximate and internal. How can one separate oneself from that upon which one relies to be oneself? The lawyer-narrator is forced to do something once he realizes that Bartleby is "scandalizing my professional reputation . . . I resolved to gather all my faculties together, and for ever rid me of this intolerable incubus" (38). He moves his chambers, and Bartleby is eventually removed to the Tombs where he dies fairly soon after. And it is here that the lawyer-narrator asks his confusing question: "Dead letters! Does it not sound like dead men?"

If what I have written is true, then what has taken place in "Bartleby" is a form of projection and displacement. The lawyer-narrator is reviewing in his narrative not this strange character Bartleby, but himself. Bartleby is the location upon which the lawyer-narrator is written or unwritten. The lawyer-narrator and Bartleby, while constituted in the narrative as two separate characters, are actually a palimpsest of American male sexual identity in the middle of the nineteenth century. This means that the lawyer-narrator's question is not an attempt to understand Bartleby and therefore humanity, but an attempt to understand what it means to be a man in the public world of work of New York.

One of the features of the Dead Letter Office, and of the dead letters that would have reached it, was a breakdown in communication. The letters are deprived of their intended reader and are read instead by someone to whom they mean something different. The reader of the letters is the same—a reader—but different—not the intended reader—and the content of the letter consequently fails to "mean" because of context. When asking himself about the similarity of dead letters and dead men, the lawyer-narrator is referencing the reading of men by other men, and the likelihood that, as with the letters whose meaning is contextual, so it is with men in the environment of the office and of work. Relationships between men are now beginning to carry an increasingly important burden of reading and recognition, and conscious of this, men now need to display a meaning—masculine, active, solid—which will be read and understood in this context so that it will reach its intended receiver. Through his question the lawyer-narrator appears to be suggesting that Bartleby fails to do this. In the world of office work he has displayed all the wrong letters and has consequently been read out of context. Of course the lawyer-narrator knows exactly the context in which these letters should have been read: the context of male-male relations that permit sexual contact. And he knows because he recognizes that these letters are the ones internal and proximate to his own identity—"I never feel so private as when I know you [Bartleby] are here" (37)—but that this identity relies upon the disavowal of them and of male-male sexual contact if it is to survive safely in the public world in which he makes his living. The lawyer-narrator reads Bartleby and himself clearly enough, only then to consign the letters which make up Bartleby to the Dead Letter Office. He reads then disavows and claims not to understand.

The greatest paradox of all, though, lies in the fact that it is the lawyer-narrator himself who has been responsible for inscribing all these letters in Bartleby in the first place. He is the one responsible for visualizing and writing the narrative of Bartleby. In effect, the lawyer-narrator has written a letter to himself which he can consign to the Dead Letter Office once he has disavowed his desire for Bartleby so successfully that he can satisfy himself he does not understand the letter's content and that, therefore, the message does not really apply to him. This maneuver is reinforced by the enigmatic way in which the whole story of Bartleby is told by the lawyer-narrator. He tries to forget his reactions to Bartleby through the sublimation of his feelings of desire into the rhetoric which shapes the story: the damaging divisions between private and public, surveillance and self-surveillance, and secrecy and disclosure which underpin the link between such a phrase in the story as "hardly can I express the emotions which seized me" and others like "strangely disarmed," "special thoughts," "strange discoveries," and "our best affections."

That these divisions are understood by the lawyer-narrator himself to be damaging is witnessed by the way in which it is possible to read in Melville's story a meditation on the consequence of this whole process of surveillance, of the marking of difference, and of disavowal—namely death. Indeed, Robert K. Martin has observed that Melville was unable "to imagine what it might have been like for two men to love each other and survive."[36] Bartleby dies as a direct consequence of the lawyer-narrator's quest to be rid of that which is proximate but made radically other. It is the fracturing of male identity into radically discontinuous classes of sexuality which one can see beginning to take place in Bartleby, which will become more intense as the century goes on, and which Melville himself will dramatize so forcefully in *Billy Budd*. The results of this kind of epistemological organizing of identity are literally fatal. If dead letters sound like dead men, then dead men sound worryingly like dead letters; immediately identifiable but instantly made different and disavowed, it is the men who are made to bear the letters of their identity so visibly who end up suffering Bartleby's fate.

Chapter Two

"And that paint is a thing that will bear looking into"

The Business of Sexuality in
The Rise of Silas Lapham

As I have already shown in "Bartleby, the Scrivener," for Melville the office became a site within which his lawyer-narrator could not only fulfill those requirements of spatial delineation demanded by capitalist modernity—the binary construction of public and private space and the hierarchization of these two incoherent classes of space in order that power might circulate between them[1]—but the office also acted as a site for observation: explicitly of Bartleby, implicitly of the lawyer-narrator himself and the status of his attitudes towards masculinity and desire. As there was surveillance, so there was a mutual process of self-surveillance. There is also a case for suggesting that the office was operating in "Bartleby"—although only in a very primitive sense compared to what would happen in the twentieth century—as a laboratory in the way identified by Foucault.[2] For instance, in the lawyer-narrator's concerns over positioning Bartleby in a particular location in order to get the best out of Turkey and Nippers, there are intimations that part of the process of business and the office is trying out and developing new techniques and monitoring their consequent results under the pretense of improvements in efficiency.[3]

It is possible here to see the methods of surveillance in the workplace of disciplinary society coming to function in tandem with a logic of psychoanalysis which was itself part of that general "deployment of sexuality" supplanting the familial basis of the "deployment of alliance."[4] Work cannot be understood during industrialization outside of a discourse of changing family structures. Moving from the domestic economy of the preindustrial period to the nuclear family of urban capitalism and the suburban service economy, the family has, simultaneously, been an institution constantly on the point of collapse and constantly in the process of being protected, not least by the discipline of psychoanalysis as it assesses development from childhood to maturity through the relation of son and daughter to father and mother and tries to provide solutions to problems caused by some arrest or blockage in this development. As a laboratory of observation, then, the office—increasingly the altar of work in capitalist modernity—can be seen as one of those places where observation and monitoring become the means whereby one's individual motivations and one's psychic—that is to say almost by definition in Western culture one's sexual—formation might be evaluated.

Everyone who spends time in the office also spends time on the couch. Whereas the analyst in his own consulting room[5] takes notes and records conversations, in the office what is recorded is abstract information that nonetheless can come to draw—in the right hands—a detailed picture of each individual employee. Personnel files can record progression, development, moments of crisis; more covert files or files stored in the memories of managers may record information upon which judgments about one's future can be made. As well as this, there is the display of one's self in the workplace. It may not always take the form of a verbal confession, but might instead perhaps be a display of a disciplined body through the performance of the routinized repetition of certain requirements or indeed the nonperformance of these requirements or other requirements such that one may be placed—like Bartleby—as deviant in some regard.

At a certain level this connection of office and couch may seem tenuous. It is worth remembering here, however, that what I am arguing, after Foucault, is that disciplinary surveillance as an apparatus of power organizes the location of bodies in space so that modes of power are transferrable from one arena to another. For Foucault the prison is a site, or an example, of a broader process. I offer up a scene from William Dean Howells's *The Rise of Silas Lapham* which—even at this early stage of office development—might make the link between office and couch seem more concrete.[6]

This is the richly textured opening chapter of the novel, where Lapham is visited at his office by Bartley Hubbard,[7] a journalist from the local newspaper. Hubbard is interviewing Lapham for the "Solid Men of Boston" series. Like the lawyer-narrator in "Bartleby," Lapham immediately shows himself to be an efficient doorkeeper. Through his open office door he beckons Hubbard into his inner sanctum, finishes writing a letter, and then calls in one of his staff to make sure that the letter gets delivered. During this time Hubbard takes out his notebook and pencil and readies himself. "Well, sir . . . so you want my life, death and Christian sufferings, do you, young man?" Lapham asks him.[8] Before the interview begins in earnest though, Lapham "pushed the ground-glass door shut between his little den and the book-keepers, in their larger den outside" (4).

Here again it is worth noting that space is being demarcated incongruously. Lapham is about to tell a journalist his life story so that it can be published in a newspaper that everyone will be able to read. And yet he must still have his office door closed while the interview takes place in "private," almost as though the office provides some class of space that is equivalent to the confessional box or the consulting room. Not only this, but once more the strange juxtaposition of surveillance and self-surveillance is evident during the course of the interview. Public scrutiny of the "Solid Men of Boston," that is the surveillance of public opinion, relies upon the self-surveillance of Lapham, who is the interviewee, and upon his willingness to reveal himself—to reveal himself in the office, his workplace. The very reason Hubbard wants to interview him is because of what he does at work, what he has done and achieved from inside his office. The office is not just a convenient location for the interview; metonymically it offers a microcosm of the place of the businessman. Lapham reads himself in the office and is read by Hubbard, in order that he can be written and read outside of the office, literally, in the newspaper.

As a narrative device, what Howells achieves is the opening up of Lapham's past through a recorded conversation or description of events to an interlocutor: not a priest or an analyst, but a journalist. I would argue, however, that all three fulfill similar functions and that structurally the procedure, and the transfer of information, is startlingly similar. In and through the office what the reader sees is the juxtaposition of the revelation of Lapham's personal life and the entanglement of this with business, an entanglement which I want to develop in more detail later in its connection with Lapham's desires and with male-male relations. For now it is enough to point out that in this scene the office is the couch upon which Lapham, the patient and worker, offers his stories to the peripatetic note-taking analyst-journalist, Hubbard, who then writes up these stories for public consumption—just the way that analysts (and Freud of course was so important in this respect) write up their consultations and diagnoses.[9]

At yet another level it is impossible to ignore the position in all this of Howells's narrative, with its well-documented brand of American realism.[10] As D. A. Miller has pointed out in relation to the English realist novel, representation itself performs a policing job and "the genre of the novel *belongs* to the disciplinary field that it portrays." Omniscient narration, such as that one finds in *Silas Lapham*, is for Miller a panoptic vision which "constitutes its own immunity from being seen in turn. For it intrinsically deprives us of the outside position from which it might be 'placed' . . . to speak of a 'narrator' at all is to misunderstand a technique that, never identified with a *person*, institutes a faceless and multilateral regard . . . [and] the faceless gaze becomes an ideal of the power of regulation."[11] In addition, and directly in relation to *Silas Lapham*, Wai-Chee Dimock has suggested that the realist novel itself be considered an "economy," where "'Resource allocation' might turn out to be as much a necessity in the composition of a novel as it is in the composition of a society."[12]

I will show not only how the couch and the office, the family and work, are bound inextricably into the regime of capitalist disciplinary surveillance, but also how the narrative which represents them is itself connected to the same regime.

Although the theme of sexuality in the work of William Dean Howells has attracted critical attention before, much of the work done in this area remains dominated by a psychoanalytic approach that, while it pleads the case for the importance of the sexual domain, only manages to look "straight" past certain material male and female sexualities. Almost in ratification of Foucault's contention that "Choosing not to recognize [is] yet another vagary of the will to truth,"[13] the ways in which these sexualities are being produced, represented, and reproduced in the figurative realm of Howells's narratives remains unconsidered; Howells's major protagonists have been forced to lie back on the couch and offer themselves up to a kind of universalist analysis.[14]

This kind of approach has been the focus for arguments which have attempted to deconstruct psychoanalytic narrative discourse—both that of the professional analyst and the professional literary critic—to show how, at the most basic level, explanatory concepts such as the primal scene and the Oedipus complex[15] only serve to reify the centrality of heterosexuality, of the gender constructions male and female, and of the reproductive dyad mother and father. Furthermore, the rhetoric of psychoanalytic inquiry has itself been shown to be bound up within various logics that, while trying to figure and fix the sexual in relation to the heterosexual, can never rid themselves of the role of producing the epistemological frameworks by which those sexual behaviors and identities heterosexuality seeks to disavow, marginalize, or discredit, come to be known.[16]

And yet, despite these attacks, even such a committed critic of traditional psychoanalysis as Eve Sedgwick has conceded that psychoanalytic thought "remains virtually the only heuristic available to Western interpreters for unfolding sexual meanings."[17] What seems to be needed is a way of managing the double bind of a psychoanalytic approach, a way of managing the collaboration with what has been an oppressive hermeneutic regime, while at the same time trying to use that regime for the purpose of redirecting attention at the potentially unstable boundaries between the clear identities and fixed positions produced by a traditional psychoanalytic approach. In an important way, then, what is needed is the reclamation of the symbolic and imaginative domains of people's lives from traditional psychoanalysis. It is not to say that just because psychoanalysis is "damaged from its very origins"[18] that the realm of the psyche should be ignored. If anything quite the contrary: because psychoanalysis is flawed, it must not be left to determine the production of discourses about sexuality.

This preamble is by way of an introduction to my thinking about *The Rise of Silas Lapham* in relation to the office, business, and male sexuality and about the previous psychoanalytic attention that has been paid to the novel by Elizabeth Stevens Prioleau. She has taken the bold step of identifying a combination of phallic, anal, and spermatic economies operating within the text, most particularly through the symbolism of the paint—the source of Silas Lapham's fortune—that his father discovered "in a hole made by a tree blowing down" (7). For Prioleau the whole novel is structured in terms of phallic condition:

The dinner party [where Lapham's family dines with the Coreys] marks a turning point in Silas's affairs. The phallic swelling, pounding, seizing, and spending cease and reverse. He begins a descent back into the hole from which the paint sprang—the disorganized irrational subconscious—and predominant imagery changes to deflation, flaccidity, slippage, and contradiction.[19]

She goes on to suggest that "Silas's . . . sublimation of enjoyment into moneymaking, is a classic case of anality."[20] Finally, in the light of the spermatic economy doctrine of the nineteenth century—where "sperm and money were synonymous; wealth accru[ing] through mature, stringent repression; bankruptcy, through immature, undisciplined indulgence"—Silas's house-building enterprise becomes an example of overextension and sexual incontinence.[21] This spermatic economy, combined with a thematic of anality—a thematic of tightening and squeezing— leads Prioleau to declare that for Howells "the sexual theme had unexpectedly taken over his business novel."[22] The entanglement or incongruity of love (sexual) plot and business plot in the novel has been a problem for critics of the book since its publication,[23] and yet what Prioleau is making clear is that sex and business are intimately bound together at the level of the rhetoric of the novel. Unfortunately, Prioleau can only then go on to write that what Howells gives us is "an affirmation of sexuality that harmonizes the sexes and echoes the great erotic solutions of history."[24]

My misgivings about this kind of conclusion should be clear enough from the comments I made earlier, but I do not want to abandon Prioleau's valuable reading of *Silas Lapham* entirely. It is rather the logic of Prioleau's reasoning that I challenge. What is more important is the way the binding of the themes of sex and business cannot be considered outside of men's relations with other men, material relations which are integral to the novel in a way that informs and indeed constitutes the basis of the foregrounding of the various phallic, anal, and spermic thematics Prioleau identifies. What I want to do, in a way which "risk[s] the encounter with psychoanalysis,"[25] is to take the issue of sexuality in the novel in a direction other than harmonized heterosexuality.

The historical dimension of the novel is important here. Wai-Chee Dimock has written about the grounds and boundaries of capitalism in relation to *Silas Lapham*.[26] Drawing on and rereading the controversial work of the historian Thomas Haskell, Dimock has argued that capitalism— a system that brings members of a population into closer obligatory contact with one another—simultaneously develops not only institutional but cognitive provisions which prevent these obligations from becoming liabilities.[27] Reverend Sewell's "economy of pain" (249) is just such a cognitive response, and Dimock even reads the realist novel—which, of course, Howells was responsible for developing and advocating in the United States—as part of this cognitive response.

Although she never mentions how this cognitive response to capitalism may relate to sexuality,[28] there are clearly consequences in the realm of the relations men form with other men, especially in the light of the continuum of male homosocial desire as hypothesized by Sedgwick.[29] The historical shift into capitalism is likely to demand a restructuring of this continuum, and if capitalism is marked by a keener sensitivity to questions of connectedness and obligation, then the increasing importance of the categorization of male-male relationships into homo and hetero in the nineteenth century[30] provides a backdrop against which it is possible to organize one's conception of the status of a relationship, most particularly what is acceptable in the relationship and what is not when certain behaviors, actions, and attributes become marked in relation to a class of sexuality. These features of male-male relations—their changing nature, the changing regulation of them, the changing structure of monitoring one's behavior in relation to other men—are particularly crucial in business when it is in the business world where men approach other men. I have shown already that it is when he feels his professional and public reputation to be at stake that the lawyer-narrator finally determines to rid himself of Bartleby.

Recognition of this kind of historical and economic shift makes the paint that is the source of Lapham's fortune, and the hole from which it appeared, intelligible in a way completely at odds with Prioleau's interpretation. Going back to the first figurative representation of this scene again—"a hole made by a tree blowing down"—it is possible to see the interesting conjunction of Lapham's father, a symbolic phallus and a symbolic anus. Prioleau is reticent about interpreting the hole as anus—preferring to see it as Lapham's "irrational subconscious"—and yet her emphasis upon anality in the rest of her argument makes the link much more tenable than she herself allows. While Prioleau never directly says what she means by anality, in Freudian terms the repression of desires and pleasures connected with the anus are what helps turn feces into gold, and, as Sedgwick has pointed out in relation to another novel that is all about money and anality—Charles Dickens's *Our Mutual Friend*—these desires and pleasures are erotic desires and pleasures that should not be considered in isolation from questions of love between men, economic status, adult genital desire and repression connected to the anus, and the particular historical condition of gender relations.[31]

There is a moment in Howells's text which draws attention to just these issues, and it takes place during that same scene that I argued earlier serves the purpose of opening up of Lapham's past: the interview with Hubbard. It is the description of how Lapham's father originally found the paint "sticking to the roots [of the tree] that had pulled up a big cake of dirt with 'em" (7). Prioleau, despite her emphasis upon a spermatic economy, refuses to treat the paint as sperm in this instance because she is too eager to see it as a "procreative essence"—and everybody knows that whatever else the phallus, the anus, and male sperm can do together, they cannot procreate. And yet this description is a rich motif for the anxieties surrounding anal penetration, ejaculation, and withdrawal.

Taking this figurative representation of the paint and the hole as my starting point, I want to constitute one relationship in *Silas Lapham* as a love story which has never been identified as a love story before: the relationship between Silas and Tom Corey. By doing this I hope to generate a reading of sexuality that does not look "straight" past the material relations men were forming with one another in the social and economic world of late nineteenth-century America.

One way to approach the relationship between Silas and Tom Corey psychoanalytically would be to configure them as father and son. Tom might be the reincarnation of Silas and Persis Lapham's son who died when he was still a child (16). This would provide an opportunity to discuss the more general nature of the homosocial bonds formed between fathers and sons in American culture and the induction of boys and adolescent men into the realm of adult manhood—and clearly these bonds and induction processes are important and problematic at the same time. However, this configuration would also at the most basic level retain the primacy of some familial relationship in structuring men's relations with other men. But familial relations are not exclusively determining of men's affective development. Tom Corey has a father in the novel, and one of the more interesting aspects of the story is the way that Lapham, as someone outside the family, outside of a father-son relationship, is so important in influencing Tom's career and emotional life. Setting up Lapham and Tom as father and son would result in the erasure of the important facts that Lapham is *not* Tom's father, that he is influential because he is *not* Tom's father, and that he is influential because he is *different* from Tom's father.[32] By discussing patern*ali*ty as opposed to paternity, the relationship between Lapham and Tom is also shifted into the sphere of the economic that is so entangled with the sexual.

What is striking about Lapham and Tom Corey is precisely their difference from one another. The age difference is self-evident. In addition, of course, there is the social gulf which so famously—even as it was breaking down—structured Boston society at the end of the nineteenth century—the gulf, that is, between the emerging middle class[33] on the one hand and a merchant aristocracy on the other. This division structures the relations between the Lapham family and the Corey family in Howells's novel. Lapham is the farm boy born "pretty well up under the Canada line" but who "was bound to be an American of *some* sort, from the word Go!" (4). The American sort he becomes is the wealthy, self-made businessman who moves to Boston because of the demands of expansion and organization in the rapidly growing post–Civil War industrial economy when his paint business takes off. With this social background there goes a concept of masculinity and manliness which Lapham both represents and supports. His physical size—the "square, bold chin . . . solid bulk" and the "pair of massive shoulders" (4) of the journalist Bartley Hubbard's description—is emphasized right from the start. A Civil War veteran, with a constant reminder of Gettysburg buried in his leg (16–17) and with his nonstandard accent, Lapham is the kind of man who thinks "the landscape was made for man, and not man for the landscape" (15) and who likes his women to be women from the same mold: "not silly little girls grown up to *look* like women" (14) but women who can share a joke and who are capable of looking after their husbands' businesses while they are away fighting (17). Lapham describes his marriage to Persis, at least in its early stages, as an almost muscular partnership: "I used to tell her it wa'n't the seventy-five per cent. of purr-ox-eyed of iron in the *ore* that made that paint go; it was the seventy-five per cent. of purr-ox-eyed of iron in *her*" (15). Persis would seem to be the perfect subject for a "Solid Women of Boston" series, if such a series could have been conceived of in the aristocratic eastern city of the time.

And if these muscular qualities apply to women, then for Lapham they should certainly apply to men. Wondering why Bromfield Corey supports his son Tom so beneficently, Lapham argues that he likes "to see a man act like a man. I don't like to see him taken care of like a young lady" (59). Lapham is well acquainted with the Corey family history "and, in his simple, brutal way, he had long hated their name as a symbol of splendor." Bromfield Corey was to Lapham "everything that was offensively aristocratic" (93), not least because instead of going into his father's business Bromfield travelled in Europe and became a painter. Lapham's animosity towards Bromfield Corey is, of course, entirely mutual. At the dinner party which forms the centerpiece of the novel, Corey remarks "that nothing but the surveillance of the local policeman prevents me from applying dynamite to those long rows of close-shuttered, handsome, brutally insensible houses" (200) owned by Boston's new rich: men like Lapham.

Yet despite these differences Silas and Tom Corey manage to form a remarkable closeness and "friendship," the sort of friendship which Lapham manifestly fails to propagate with other men who exist across the social and status divide in Boston. There are two key links here by which this friendship is formed and fostered: Lapham's business and Lapham's daughters. Both, I want to argue, are the means by which Lapham and Corey can become and remain close to one another, but it is also important that Tom's reasons for wanting to get involved with Lapham's paint business be explored first.

It is Mrs. Lapham who understands men's, and Silas's, relationship to business: "his paint was something more than business to him; it was a sentiment, almost a passion. He could not share its management and its profit with another without a measure of self-sacrifice far beyond that which he must make with something less personal to him" (51). And it is this attachment of Lapham to his "passion" which Tom Corey recognizes as well, especially after spending time away from Boston with "the cowboys of Texas" (67). This changed his attitude towards men like Lapham. While *Silas Lapham* is a novel in which the failure of Silas to integrate into the upper echelons of Boston society has always been emphasized, as can be seen in the case of Tom, it is just as clearly about movement in the opposite direction. Tom admires Lapham for his attachment to his "passion." "Perhaps his successful strokes of business were the romance of his life," he suggests to his father (67). And from there it is the shortest of steps to Tom saying that he wants to go into business with Lapham, to share his "passion" and "romance."

Clearly financial and career considerations are important here, but it is the nature of Lapham's business, the nature of his character, "simple-hearted and rather wholesome" as Tom describes it (68), which attracts him to Lapham. There is just as clearly a discourse about masculinity operating in Tom's arguments. It is the cowboys of Texas that Tom recognizes in Lapham, a muscular masculinity that he associates with business and the attachment of men to business. Far from being drawn to Lapham's daughters—Penelope and Irene—Tom is attracted to Lapham himself, and this is evident in the way the romantic plot between Tom and Penelope develops.

As a plot it works in a conventionally romantic way. A chance meeting between Tom and Mrs. Lapham and Irene while they are on holiday is the first point of contact, one which does not involve Penelope. The next point of contact is also by chance (65). Tom just happens to be walking down the street where the new lots of houses—including the Laphams's—are being built. From these chance encounters the narrative—after misreadings and intrigue—eventually marries off Tom and Penelope. But heterosexual romance plots need to be considered in the context of wider social relationships. Why does Tom make the effort to wander around a new housing development on his first day back in Boston after his return from Texas? Why, when the Back Bay area, the water side of Beacon Street, was known in Boston as "the Diphtheria District" (382)? Perhaps the effects of Texas can be seen here. Tom is a young man determined to make his future not in the old world of his father but in the new world of business, the fruits of which can be seen in the new houses. Tom is placed metonymically by the narrative in relation to this environment, and it is surely no coincidence that it is here where he meets Lapham for the first time—in that part of the city which witnesses what Tom's father tells him when he arrives home later, that "money . . . is the romance, the poetry of our age" (65).

So: money as "romance," business as "romance," and paint as "passion." In relation to the kind of rhetorical construction of money and business in *Silas Lapham*, heterosexual romance quickly begins to lose the sort of transcendental qualities Elizabeth Stevens Prioleau wants to give it when talking about the "harmony of the sexes." What I am suggesting is that there is no romantic intent on Tom's part towards Penelope until well after he has met Silas and decided he wants to share Lapham's "passion" and "romance" and that his affection for Penelope cannot be considered in isolation from his desire to join Lapham's business. Tom certainly never does have any romantic affection for Irene, the better beauty of the two sisters. The narrative tells the reader twice that in their first meetings Tom pays as much attention to Mrs. Lapham as he does to Irene (26 and 29) and that the reason for this is because of Mrs. Lapham's skill as a nurse to Mrs. Corey when she became ill. When Tom sees the family by chance in their new house, it is the intensity of the relationship formed with Silas that is striking. It is Silas who gives Tom a guided tour of the house, in the process of which, as well as bragging, he "swelled out" (55). This phallic symbolism clearly has nothing to do with the "harmony of the sexes" since it is all for Tom Corey's benefit; it is a phallic symbolism which stands at the heart of the relationship between Silas and Tom. Lapham is swelling metaphorically with the pride which comes as a result of having made money from his "romance" and "passion" and wanting to show that it makes him as good as anybody that Tom Corey might know. Yet again, sexuality—this time in the form of a phallic thematic—and business are intimate partners. From this tour of Lapham's house, Tom goes home and suggests to his father that he should share Lapham's "passion" and "romance." Tom does not want to be "taken care of like a lady" either. Lapham, meanwhile, lies in bed that night telling his wife that "I could make a man of that fellow, if I had him in the business with me. There's stuff in him" (60). The same "stuff" perhaps which—the symbol of biological maleness, the guarantee of manly succession in a patriarchal society (as long as it is "spent" properly of course)—Lapham's father found "sticking to the roots that had pulled up a big cake of dirt with 'em" (7) when the tree blew down and the paint first appeared. Perhaps it is Lapham's hope that by "having" Tom in the business with him he can "squeeze" this "stuff" out of him.[34]

What I have described so far is the way in which the discourses of business, gender, and geography can be seen to be coalescing in *Silas Lapham*. Simply, it is possible to see the traditional binaries of American culture stacking up as a kind of palimpsest of connection:

new money	old money
physical	rational
body	mind
active	passive
masculine	feminine
west	east
frontier	city

These oppositions clearly begin to affect the discursive constitution of male sexuality in the second half of the nineteenth century. But what makes *Silas Lapham* intriguing from the viewpoint of thinking about male sexuality is precisely the movement between these oppositions that takes place through Silas and Tom. In effect, each is trying to move from one column to the other, although exactly how much varies depending on the category. Silas does not want to move towards the feminine (although he actually does at one point in the novel, and I will come back to this because it clearly shapes his relationship with Tom), but he does want to become part of the city, part of the east where the established money resides. Where Silas and Tom actually meet is somewhere in between. The fact that these oppositions can be traversed suggests that in terms of male sexuality the hetero and homo distinctions, which might form the next row in the table above, cannot be as secure in the text as they would be if this movement between categories were not taking place. In general literary terms, the tension of discursive or rhetorical category divisions like those set out above must in some way influence those other category divisions which, discursively or rhetorically, are supposed—or *made*—to go hand in hand with them.[35] In *Silas Lapham* there is a tension between business and Boston society that represents the tension between the developing categories of hetero and homo.

I want to concentrate on the way that this tension figures in the narrative, first by thinking about Silas's office and his past, and then by considering this in relation to the development of the plot of the novel. I want to show that in the construction of Lapham's muscular homosocial masculinity, the traces remain of what it excludes and of what a psychoanalytic approach might help to re-include. Key to my thinking here will be one particular scene in the novel: the confrontation between Silas and Tom in Silas's office which takes place the day after Lapham embarrassed himself at the Coreys' dinner party by breaking down and causing Tom to become disgusted with him—immediately after which Tom asks for Penelope's hand in marriage. It is the traces that remain, but which are excluded, that Tom discovers in this office scene. As I hope to show, these traces have also—significantly—been signposted long before in the character and past of Lapham himself.

It is in the opening chapter, during the office interview with Bartley Hubbard for the "Solid Men of Boston" series, that Lapham fails to speak the name of his first and only male partner in business, William Rogers. When this point in his history comes up, "Lapham dropped the bold blue eyes with which he had been till now staring into Bartley's face, and the reporter knew that here was a place for asterisks in his interview, if interviews were faithful" (17). Only three pages before this, Lapham has pulled his gaze away from Bartley in a similar fashion. In the course of the "long stare" he had been directing at Bartley, "Lapham . . . had been seeing himself a young man again, in the first days of his married life" (14). There is a telling discrepancy between these two incidents: in the latter, Lapham's gaze is filled with memories of himself and Persis, memories which the narrative reveals; while in the former, Lapham's gaze is unexplained, left silent, left to be covered by "asterisks" in Bartley's article. If by looking at Bartley, it is possible for Lapham to read himself as a young married man, what else is it that by looking at Bartley he *also* reads about himself as a young man? Whatever it is, "Bartley divined, through the freemasonry of all who have sore places in their memories, that this was a point which he must not touch again" (17). This "point" seems to be completely overdetermined in relation to the discursive production of male sexuality that was developing in the second half of the nineteenth century. It is a point that conjoins silence, close male-male relations (through the rhetoric of freemasonry), the psyche (through memories), and the body—or at least that one sore place upon it. The consideration of one further piece of evidence might help in making even more sense of this textual moment and of the reason Bartley is in Lapham's office to begin with.

It is the paint that turned a hole in the ground into a "*gold*-mine" (10). It is here that the incident with Rogers, named but unnamed, is labelled in the language of business. More than any familial primal scene, the paint and the hole from which it emerges is the primal scene for Lapham: the source of his wealth, the source of his status (or lack of it) in Boston society, and the focal point around which his relationship with Rogers revolved and continues to revolve. The anal and the spermatic economies of hole and paint suggest that however much critics from the end of the nineteenth century to the present day have constituted *Silas Lapham* as a novel about one man's morality, what grounds this morality is the symbolic regime of male sexuality. Rogers wants to get his hands on Lapham's paint, the thing which is so precious to Lapham that, as Persis notes, "he could not share its management and its profit with another" (51); where "management" and "profit" can again be seen to be linked to the anal and the spermatic. The control of the sphincter, the "management" of bodily regularity are—in psychoanalytic terms at least—the very things which result in the "profit" that one can then "spend." But there is in *Silas Lapham* a wonderfully contradictory and confused relation between anal and spermatic economies. If Prioleau is right, and the spermatic economy is one closely connected to the production of money and its disposal, then what exists in *Silas Lapham* is a system unlike that of *Our Mutual Friend* where the repression of anal desires results in the turning of feces into gold. Instead, repression of anal desires somehow produces not dust heaps but paint, the manly "stuff" which to be truly manly has to be conserved, and if "spent" at all then "spent" for the purposes of the heterosexual family—Lapham's house. So *Silas Lapham* actually manages to displace anal anxiety into a productive spermatic masculinity.

In the light of this, the moment when Lapham refuses to speak Rogers's name—when he dips his eyes from Bartley in the office, and Bartley understands that this is a moment for asterisks—is a moment in which the whole knotted logic of an emerging male sexuality can be seen to be operating.[36] While in Lapham's muscularly heterosexual relations with Persis the discourses of romance and marriage provide an avenue for discussion with Bartley, in Lapham's muscularly homosocial relations with Rogers the discourses are split into two: business and silence, the latter signalling what the former manifests by other means. Romance and desire between men in the homosocial world of Silas Lapham is sublimated into the rhetoric of business, that area which men define as a man's domain.[37]

This is where the capitalist rhetoric of "approaching," obligation, responsibility, and liability identified by Dimock can be seen to be operating; it is in this business domain that Lapham's relationship with Tom Corey is forged. And it is from here that these obligations and responsibilities are then vectored down the avenues of family and marriage.

This rhetoric of approaching can quite evidently be seen in Lapham's interview with Bartley and then in his relationship with Tom Corey. The office is one of those sites[38] where men can legitimately meet, physically, with other men. Lapham positions his "leather-cushioned swivel chair" in front of Bartley "so near that their knees almost touched" (3); he later stands before Bartley and "put up his huge foot close to Bartley's thigh; neither of them minded that" (15). And Lapham does not hesitate to take Bartley's "thumb and forefinger and put them on a bunch in his leg, just above the knee" (16). It is always worth asking how moments such as these resist or invite their being read in relation to sexual desire; what might suggest that they are or are not some kind of sexual foreplay. In this scene with Bartley, I would suggest that physical closeness is a form of social foreplay where sexual contact is not even on the bottom of the agenda. Lapham displays a muscular homosociality as a way of trying to forge a link with Bartley. Bartley despises him for it; such actions allow him to class Lapham as primitive and unsophisticated. In his newspaper article, he displays his superiority to Lapham by including "gibes" he knows "Lapham's unliterary habit of mind" will not recognize (5). When Bartley's wife asks him not to make fun of Lapham, Bartley agrees. "Nothing that *he*'ll ever find out" at any rate (24). Bartley as the analyst-journalist has read Lapham's office performance all too well, and he has no time for the self-made, primitive *nouveau*.

Tom Corey has slightly different feelings for Lapham and men like Lapham. For Tom and for Lapham a relationship develops which is far more complex, one where those binaries of cultural formation intersect. Close as Lapham and Bartley become in the office—the closeness of the priest and confessor, the analyst and the patient—their social differences and desires prevent them having to put a limit on the obligations of friendship. Having approached one another in the office they may now separate. But obligations, responsibilities, and liabilities play a key part in Lapham's relationship with Tom. What becomes evident is that these obligations are vectored down the avenues of business, the family, and marriage.

What I suggest, in addition, is that Lapham's relationship with Rogers sheds light on Lapham's relationship with Tom. Together they form a triangular circuit of desire between men. Rogers, "a tallish, thin man, with a dust-colored face, and a dead, clerical air, which somehow suggested at once feebleness and tenacity" (46)—a description of disgust and of Bartleby-esque similarity—is a former partner in Lapham's "passion," whom Lapham divorced for fear that if he "hadn't got him out he'd 'a' ruined me sooner or later" (48). Ruin is the accusation Persis lays at Lapham's feet for his treatment of Rogers. Lapham's desire to be rid of Rogers—and the story of the separation never is fully replayed but left constantly under "asterisks" in the novel—over their dealings in the business of paint, that symbolic territory which I have shown to be linked to the anal and spermatic economies of male sexuality, seems to be a desire that was not a purely financial one. As in Bartleby, the desire to be rid of another man—an employee, a partner—is governed by other considerations. But Lapham's willingness to take on Tom, and his enthusiasm for the task of making a man out of Tom in the realm of business, suggests that these other considerations might be ones of a muscular homosociality that the feeble Rogers threatens, especially when he keeps returning and threatening to "blight everything" (47). Especially when he keeps returning for money.

The word bribery does not appear in *Silas Lapham* but, as with "Bartleby, the Scrivener," there is a rhetoric which suggests some such relationship. The obligation that Lapham feels towards Rogers, even as he declares his "conscience is easy as far as he's concerned, and it always was" (47), threatens to cross that boundary where obligation becomes liability. That is the potential in a system where knowledge about someone's private life has come to denote "sexual knowledge, and secrets sexual secrets" and where "one particular sexuality . . . was distinctively constituted as secrecy."[39] Bribery operates at the juncture of obligation and liability. Lapham's disavowing response to Persis's concern about his crowding out of Rogers is a response which the rest of the novel gradually exposes.

But as it does so, of course, Lapham is in the midst of his relationship with Tom. When Tom visits Lapham's office to ask for a job and declares that he believes in his paint, Lapham "lifted his head and looked at the young man, deeply moved" and "warmed and softened to the young man in *every way*" (my emphasis, 77–78). Such a welcoming response from Lapham would surely be disproportionate to Tom's comment were it not for the fact that the language of business is a coded language in which men can talk to one another about their most intimate feelings. To declare that you believe in another man's "passion" is to declare something about that man. It is here that the relationship between Lapham and Tom Corey begins to move into the realm of affection. After telling him that he is short of time at the beginning of the interview, Lapham now makes time for Tom. "Don't hurry . . . Sit still! I want to tell you about this paint . . . I want to tell you *all* about it" (78). Of course, in the light of my comments about paint and anal and spermatic economies it becomes difficult to read even short sentences like this outside of a sexual thematic.[40] What follows is Lapham missing his boat home to remain in the office and tell Tom all about his paint. He shows Tom a photograph of the mine and tells Tom the story in "unsparing detail," and then he invites him home for the evening.

It is during this evening visit that Irene and Penelope and Mrs. Lapham begin to discern the possibility that Tom is interested romantically in Irene. Acutely, but wrongly as it turns out, Penelope suggests that "this talk about business is nothing but a blind" (88). She thinks Tom is there because of Irene. He is not. Neither is he there because of

Penelope. He's at the house because of Lapham. And with a "guiltless laugh" Tom goes home the next day to tell his mother that he has "made an engagement with Mr. Lapham" and stayed up pretty much the whole night talking about business (100–1). Tom offers not the slightest intimation that any of his excitement at being accepted by Lapham is connected to the opportunities it will give him to be close to either of Lapham's daughters. It is through Tom's mother that Howells broaches this possibility. She probes Tom, who barely admits to noticing either Irene or Penelope. "Is Mrs. Lapham well? And her daughter?" she asks. "Yes, *I think so*," is all Tom can find to say (my emphasis, 101). "I suppose it's the plain sister who's reading 'Middlemarch'" she carries on. "Plain? Is she plain?" asks Tom, "as if searching his consciousness" (101). In addition, consider this passage which follows immediately:

> "Tom!" cried his mother, "why do you think Mr. Lapham has taken you into business so readily? I've always heard that it was so hard for young men to get in."
>
> "And do you think I found it easy with him? We had about twelve hours' solid talk."
>
> "And you don't suppose it was any sort of—personal consideration?"
>
> "Why, I don't know exactly what you mean, mother. I suppose he likes me."
>
> Mrs. Corey could not say just what she meant. She answered, ineffectually enough:
>
> "Yes. You wouldn't like it to be a favor, would you?"
>
> "I think he's a man who may be trusted to look after his own interest. But I don't mind his beginning by liking me. It'll be my own fault if I don't make myself essential to him." (103)

One could interpret this as Mrs. Corey trying to get her son to consider the possibility that Lapham is luring him into his business in order to marry one of his daughters off to him. Of course, as far as heterosexual romance is concerned, Tom's casual, disinterested responses and his refusal to get his mother's point might be seen as little disavowals to keep her off the scent, so antagonistic would she be to such an outcome. My argument is that only in retrospect can these moments be interpreted in this way; only with the (be)hindsight which would structure all moments and relationships as being connected to a heterosexual outcome. But if one refuses this logic, then these moments add up to nothing of the sort. They are the remarks of an intelligent young man who, while he can remember the details of his hours of conversation with Lapham, can barely remember how Irene is or what Penelope looks like and cannot understand what his mother is driving at. Indeed, he is too excited about becoming "essential" to Lapham to recognize any of these things. And this excitement is fulfilled on his first day. "He was in love with his work . . . He believed he had found his place in the world, after a good deal of looking, and he had the relief, the repose, of fitting into it" (105–6).

Lapham is equally unaware of any potential love interest that his employing Tom might initiate. Lapham sees Tom as a mark of the respectability of his business. Taking on someone with Tom's established Boston background helps Lapham navigate the transition of those cultural binaries mentioned earlier. It is Lapham's wife who plays a role similar to Tom's mother. Both, seemingly, have marriage at the front of their thoughts. Persis refuses to let Lapham bring Tom to Nantasket.

> "If he wants to see Irene, he can find out ways of doing it himself," she tells him.
>
> "Who wants him to see Irene?" retorted the Colonel angrily.
>
> "I do," said Mrs. Lapham. "And I want him to see her without any of your connivance, Silas . . . I understand what *you* want. You want to get this fellow, who is neither partner nor clerk, down here to talk business with him. Well, now, you just talk business with him at the office." (112–13)

Far from wanting him for his daughters, Lapham wants Tom for himself. He takes him for rides in his buggy, and for Tom these are times when, though he "could hardly have helped feeling the social difference between Lapham and himself, in his presence he silenced his traditions, and showed him all the respect that he could have extracted from any of his clerks" (113). Again, the dynamic that produces desire between Lapham and Tom is their social difference and the negotiation that takes place where social status and economic status cross.

And yet it is this same difference that can never be erased, regardless of the desire Lapham displays by wanting Tom close to him in the business and by extension in his home or the desire Tom displays for Lapham by wanting to be close to him through his business career. Just how far the belief that Silas and Tom share in one another can be sustained, though, is shown when the social difference between the two men is brought into stark contrast, and this is also the moment when the heterosexual love plot—Tom's love for Penelope—takes off. The juxtaposition of these two events is crucial to my theory about the romantic attachment of Silas and Tom.

Social difference erupts during the course of the dinner party which Lapham and his family are invited to. Penelope is the key absentee here. Although connected to Lapham by being his daughter, the narrative places her so that she is not connected so closely that she becomes part of Lapham's performance at the dinner party. The performance itself is a drunken one, where Lapham holds forth on his army life and on everything else, and he leaves the party believing that by talking so copiously he has triumphed. It is only the next day that "the glories of the night before showed poorer. Here and there a painful doubt obtruded itself and marred them with its awkward shadow" (214). Next day at the office he finally calls Corey in to see him and to ask him what the other guests had said about him.

Once more, the office setting is crucial here. The association of self-surveillance with the office as set up in the first chapter of the novel is here continued as Lapham reviews his behavior. Corey tries to pass—"'There was nothing—really nothing'" (216)—but Lapham persists and links his behavior with Corey's position in his business. Having shown himself not to be a gentleman, that thing he prizes above all else, Lapham says, "I will give you up if you want to go before anything worse happens . . . I know I'm not fit to associate with gentlemen in anything but a business way." Tom's reaction is itself bizarre. "'I can't listen to you any longer. What you say is shocking to me—shocking in a way you can't think . . . I have my reasons for refusing to hear you—my reasons why I *can't* hear you . . . Oh, there's nothing to take back,'" he says, "with a repressed shudder for the abasement which he had seen" (217–18).

What follows is a scene of revelation for Tom that has striking resemblances to that moment of revelation in "Bartleby" when the lawyer-narrator perceives what it is about his scrivener that has been at the heart of his desire for him and resolves to get rid of Bartleby. The office in *Silas Lapham* is operating as a site for the reading of Silas by Tom. What perhaps marks the difference between this novel and "Bartleby" is the way that Tom's thoughts are so structured by concerns of class and social status; this is hardly surprising, however, since the desire he feels for Silas is structured by these very same concerns and by the attributes which are associated with them—the body, the frontier, the active, and so on.

[Tom] thought of him the night before in the company of those ladies and gentlemen, and he quivered in resentment of his vulgar,
braggart, uncouth nature. . . . Amidst the stings and flashes of his
wounded pride, all the social traditions, all the habits of feeling, which
he had silenced more and more by force of will during the past
months, asserted their natural sway, and he rioted in his contempt of
the offensive boor, *who was even more offensive in his shame than in his trespass.* . . . He shut his desk and hurried out into the early night . . . to try
and find his way out of the chaos, which now seemed ruin, and now
the materials out of which fine actions and a happy life might be
shaped. (my emphasis, 218–19)

So Tom is repelled by those qualities in Lapham that are different from
those qualities in himself, the same qualities which attracted him to
Lapham in the first place after his trip to Texas. But in many ways what
triggers this moment when attraction turns into repulsion is Lapham's
behavior, the way that he becomes "more offensive in his shame than in
his trespass." What Tom sees in Lapham is exactly what Lapham has excluded from his character in order that he can appear the self-made,
primitive, frontier businessman, "the drunken blackguard" (217)—the
soft, weak, and feminized qualities that resurface in his self-surveilling
pity and shame and sentimentality.

Without fully entering the debate surrounding sentimental, romantic
fiction and its relation to realism and naturalism, it needs to be pointed
out here that there is a discourse about the proper role of the novel taking place in *Silas Lapham*, and in Howells's work in general, a discourse
which is clearly decided in favor of the nonsentimental. I contend that
this kind of aesthetic terminology should not be disconnected from social sexual relations. The "regime of heterosexual male self-pity," so
Sedgwick has written, "has the projective potency of an open secret."
More particularly, "from the 1880s through the First World War . . . the
exemplary instance of the sentimental ceases to be a woman per se, but
instead becomes the body of a man who . . . physically dramatizes, *em-
bodies* for an audience that both desires and cathartically identifies with
him, a struggle of masculine identity with emotions or physical stigmata
stereotyped as feminine."[41] While Lapham might not actually produce
the stigmata—of tears—he certainly appears to be on the verge of doing
so. It is precisely this self-pity and its relation to the binary of masculine-
feminine that is exposed to Tom at this point in the narrative. What
is also exposed is the open secret of sexuality that links masculine

and feminine to the establishment of the boundaries of hetero and homo.

What Tom also confronts by seeing this in Lapham is the status of his own desire, his desire for Lapham through his "passion"—the paint, the economic as well as symbolic currency of masculinity and male sexuality. Tom is shocked, disgusted, and conscious of the "ruin" which might follow were this desire to play itself out bodily, because of course he sees how his own desire leans towards the feminine and the homosexual. It is from this position that he must forge a "happy life."

But after this initial shock and disgust, Tom actually attempts to commit himself to Lapham. After three hours of walking, he ends up on Lapham's doorstep. The following passage is worth quoting at length, and it is worth noticing—in the context of the chapter which succeeds it when Tom declares his love to Penelope—just how absent Penelope is from his thoughts:

> He had often taken it very seriously, and sometimes he said that he must forego the hope on which his heart was set. There had been many times in the past months when he had said he *must go no farther*, and as often as he had taken this stand *he had yielded* it, upon this or that excuse, which he was aware of trumping up. It was part of the complication that he should be unconscious of the injury he might be doing to some one besides his family and himself; *this was the defect of his diffidence*; and it had come to him in a pang for the first time when his mother said that she would not have the Laphams think she wished to make more of the acquaintance than he did; and then it had come too late. Since that he had suffered quite as much from the fear that it might not be as that it might be so; and now, in the mood, *romantic and exalted, in which he found himself concerning Lapham*, he was as far as might be from vain confidence. He ended the question in his own mind by *affirming to himself* that he was there [at Lapham's house], *first of all, to see Lapham* and give him *an ultimate proof* of his own perfect faith and unabated respect, and to offer him *what reparation this involved* for that want of sympathy—of humanity—which he had shown. (my emphasis, 220)

Once again, he is not visiting the Lapham house to see either of the two daughters but to see Lapham, and the phrases I emphasized in this passage suggest—however obliquely and euphemistically—that he has determined to express his desire. When Lapham does not open the door, Tom is genuinely surprised and disappointed. The only member of the family in the house is Penelope. After talking for a while, Tom utters his commitment of desire to her: "I—I didn't expect—I hoped to have seen your father—but I must speak now, whatever—I love you!" (227).

What are we to make of this about-face in Tom's behavior? John Seelye has asked this question in relation to Howells's realism: "Would a sensitive young man, most particularly of Corey's social background, make such a dramatic turnabout, from reviling Lapham for his boorish insensitivity, to rushing to his home in order to make known his feelings for Penelope?"[42] According to Seelye, the marriage of Tom and Penelope is fundamental to "the working out of the novel within the framework of Howells's sub-textual argument about literary realism." Penelope's decision to marry Tom and not suffer in a romantic fashion allows the novel to assert realistic over romantic fictional values. Tom's about-face is the "hole" in the text which opens the way to an examination of the novel's "infrastructure."

Seelye's argument stands as insufficient, because it takes for granted a heterosexually-oriented outcome, refusing once again to configure holes in *Silas Lapham* in relation to any homosexual thematic. From the retrospective position of seeing the heterosexual romantic outcome as somehow expected, or obvious, or natural, Tom's declaration of love suddenly makes sense—in Seelye's reading—of all that has happened previously in the novel; every incident can be reexamined and found to have been leading up to this moment when Tom declares his love for Penelope. It is clear that Tom desired Penelope from the beginning; only the skill of the narrative prevented the reader from seeing what was obvious all along. Here we have the realistic novel as open secret in its very formal construction. But take away the positional logic of a heterosexual outcome, replace it instead with a logic which admits desire between men, and Tom's utterance is far less clear-cut. Yes, it is plausible that Tom has come to see Lapham to ask him for Penelope's hand in marriage or to tell him that he loves his daughter. But, in the context of what has happened at the office earlier, it is just as plausible that Tom has come to the house determined to make amends for his earlier treatment of Lapham by telling Lapham it is him he loves. The very tenor of the sentence suggests this: "*I hoped to have seen your father—but I must speak now, whatever—I love you!*"[43]

Until this moment when he declares his love for Penelope, there is nothing in the text which in any way positions Tom's desire in relation to her. It is only in retrospect that incidents can be read to produce this positioning of desire. This retrospective reading is one which not only assumes but actually produces *as it assumes* the naturalness and predictability of the heterosexual romance. What is lost—or turned into an open secret—in this process is the struggle by which heterosexual romance has to erase all knowledge of same-sex desires from its field of vision. What in Seelye's "realistic" account is a plot device to open up the text so it can deal with questions of realism, in my account becomes a moment which encapsulates the displacement of what is classed as unacceptable desire. Loving and marrying Penelope (and Penelope instead of Irene, because Irene is too sentimental and too closely linked to Lapham's sentimental outburst at the dinner party, from which Penelope was absent) allows Tom to remain close to Lapham—in business, through family—while preserving his dissociation from that which might otherwise "ruin" him: homosexual desire. There is no way, then, that one can see the marriage of Tom and Penelope outside of the patriarchal system of the transfer of women. Lapham, Tom, and Penelope form an intensely powerful erotic triangle, one that involves issues not only of desire and sexuality, but also of social class, aesthetics, and American identity.

As Seelye notes, this incident in the office between Lapham and Tom, and Tom's subsequent declaration of love to Penelope, constitute what amounts to the climax of the novel.[44] What happens subsequently is nothing less than a justification of the kind of realistic enterprise which, while denigrating sentimental or romantic fiction, is rearranging the epistemological aesthetics of late nineteenth-century American culture in ways which directly concern the discursive production of sexual categorization. Reverend Sewell's rhetoric of the "economy of pain" (249) and Lapham's adherence to the logic of it, together with the fact that Lapham is made a victim of one moment of sentimental self-pity, suggests something of Howells's conceptualization of such "weakness." Lapham's supposed moral rise in the final part of the novel is based upon the recognition of weakness in himself.

Here his dealings with Rogers again become important. "I guess Rogers saw that he had a soft thing in me, and he's worked it for all it was worth" (269), Lapham argues. Rogers is increasingly demonized as the novel draws to a conclusion. Lapham accuses him of being a liar and a thief—worthless and yet at the same time not so worthless that he is capable of bringing about Lapham's financial ruin. There is the ghost here—in addition to the things I mentioned about Rogers earlier—of that evil perversity Dollimore identifies in Western culture, that evil perversity parasitical on good, that places Rogers in relation to a corrupting sexual perversity. Rogers, by selling Lapham shares which turn out to have no value, is being placed in association with abstract money; money that is superficial and inauthentic and which infects Lapham, the "Solid Man" of Boston. Lapham's moral rise consists of resisting the taint of Rogers by refusing to go along with Rogers's corrupt plans to sell the next-to-useless interest in the railways they have to unsuspecting foreign buyers.

Ultimately, Lapham becomes a gentleman in the eyes of others by the pragmatic way in which he copes with adversity: "All those who were concerned in his affairs said he behaved well, and even more than well, when it came to the worst" (365). Of course, he has ruined Rogers in the process, and he feels the pain of this: "This was his reward for standing firm for right and justice to his own destruction: to feel like a thief and a murderer" (344). But in the end it is no matter because, first, Rogers deserves everything he gets—by being so homosexually located (wanting to get his hands on Lapham's paint mine, his "hole" and his "stuff"), and second, because Lapham has achieved something more important than wealth: the articulation of a code of suffering—pragmatic, masculine, righteous—that will help to structure the social oppression of homosexual men and women, by making them the main targets of its scapegoating projections.[45]

Chapter Three

"A dream more romantic than scarlet pagodas by a silver sea"

The Businessman and the Fairy Child
in Sinclair Lewis's *Babbitt*

Henry Childs Merwin had some very clear advice for his fellow American men in 1897. In his article "On Being Civilized Too Much" for the *Atlantic Monthly*, he exhorted them to "Leave the close air of the office . . . and go out into the streets and the highway." They should, he wrote, "Consult the teamster, the farmer, . . . or the drover," because "From his loins, and not from those of the dilettante, will spring the man of the future."[1] Merwin was, of course, completely wrong. While the legacy and the myth of agrarian and frontier virtues clearly marks American masculinist culture throughout the twentieth century, the rise of an urban, corporate, service economy from the end of the nineteenth century ensured that a good proportion of the men of the future were formed and shaped in just that location Merwin suggested they flee: the office.

I want to look at a novel here—Sinclair Lewis's *Babbitt* (1922)— whose author chose not to leave the office and instead addressed the consequences of a post-frontier culture on masculinity and ultimately on male sexuality. Lewis, perhaps more than any other male writer of this period, was alert to how the changing landscape of gender was affecting America's urban workplaces. Merwin might have depicted the world of urban professional, middle-class work as less and less capable of ratifying a man's manly status, but he was fairly short on the details of just how workplace practices could produce such potentially disastrous consequences for American manhood. Lewis, on the other hand, was no stranger to the office or its sex and gender matrices. He worked in the advertising industry; met his first wife, Grace Livingstone Hegger, in a New York office-building elevator; and joined the debate about female office workers in his second novel *The Job* (1917).[2] As Anthony Di Renzo suggests, Lewis remains an important figure because, in his early business stories, he was the first American writer to address the office as the "hot-house for the despairs and delusions of the American Dream."[3] Lewis shows in two of these stories—"Honestly—If Possible" and "A Story with a Happy Ending"—that consolation for these despairs and delusions might be found in romance between male office workers and secretaries. But as the harshness of his satirical attacks on business grew fiercer in *Babbitt*, such consolation becomes increasingly distant.

My attention to the office as a discrete environment also serves the purpose here of drawing attention to a fault line in the historical conceptualization of America in the period between the latter part of the nineteenth century and the publication of this novel. However unwittingly, cultural historians have followed Merwin's advice and fled the office in their discussions of this period in favor of arguments about the nature of American business and capitalism that are all too often generalized and abstract. In T. J. Jackson Lears's terms, for example, Merwin's injunction can be seen as part of an antimodernist crusade against the conditions of late nineteenth-century America, conditions that in large part, Lears argues, resulted from "the shift from the disorganized entrepreneurial capitalism of the earlier nineteenth century to the organized corporate capitalism" that relied upon "a hierarchical bureaucracy of salaried executives."[4] Similarly, for Gail Bederman, the remaking of middle-class male identity at the turn of the century that saw "masculine" virtues replace "manly" ones was driven by the rise of large-scale enterprises at the expense of small-scale capitalism, the expansion of low-level clerical work, and a succession of economic depressions.[5] But while Lears and Bederman both offer compelling analyses of this period and leave no doubt as to the changes that took place, their accounts of shifts in business and economic organization go no further than these broad remarks. What Jonathan Freedman has described as "the complex tangle of experiences that is life in an advanced capitalist economy"[6] is left unexplored.

This attenuated historical focus is the result of a long-standing discourse that has automatically constructed business as something which for American men has always had something to do both with being American and with being a man, without sufficiently explaining how these relationships operate in practice. It is a discourse utilized by writers like Lewis himself. For Babbitt it is the way the American man does business that separates him from "the decayed nations of Europe." As he says:

> One thing that distinguishes us from our good brothers, the hustlers over there, is that they're willing to take a lot off the snobs and journalists and politicians, while the modern American business man knows how to talk right up for himself, knows how to make it good and plenty clear that he intends to run the works. . . . He's not dumb, like the old-fashioned merchant. He's got a vocabulary and a punch.[7]

This classic piece of Babbittry equates a certain way of doing business with an American spirit, as well as equating it with a certain kind of modernity—not "old-fashioned"—a certain kind of masculinity—a "punch"—and with a certain kind of honesty, mastery, and "straight" way of talking. But while historical accounts of this period draw upon comments like these in order to naturalize the association of business with America and with manliness, what they lack—and what by contrast Lewis manifestly provides—is an account of the way men experienced the more generalized alienating phenomena of business or capitalism *at work* and how this experience *at work*—that place which for Babbitt was "fireproof as a rock and as efficient as a typewriter; fourteen stories of yellow pressed brick, with clean, upright, unornamented lines" (39)—consequently helped organize their conceptions of gender and sexuality. Rather than standing structural economic and gender changes side by side and hoping that a link emerges, what is of interest here are "the kinds of emotions, cathexes, rages, desires, fears, complacencies, exaltations, and depressions elicited by capitalist culture" and how these experiences "inflect . . . the constitution of desire."[8] The workplace, then, is an interface, a site where Lewis, by representing men directly meeting and interacting with the newly gendered demands of business and capitalism, fills in the gaps left by historical accounts of economic change.

It is necessary, then, to make a distinction between the American office and American business and to return to those novelists who chose not to flee the office. For while the growth of large corporations clearly ensured the expansion of American capitalism at the end of the nineteenth century and the beginning of the twentieth century, it was the office more particularly that started to become trouble for American men at just this time. What follows is an account of the way that the "overcivilization" debate with which Merwin was engaging intersects with the notion of the office as a site of potential danger for American men once it becomes, with the help of efficient typewriters operated by women, increasingly mixed in gender and a potentially feminized environment. I will argue more specifically that this problem of gender in the office ultimately becomes a problem of sexuality in *Babbitt*. In Lewis's novel, George Babbitt experiences a crisis of masculinity in the course of his desire for another man, Paul Riesling, while this crisis is precipitated by the acute regime of surveillance into which Lewis places Babbitt.

In one way it is only a minor observation to note that Lewis's narrative first introduces the reader to George F. Babbitt not just on any day of his working life, but on that day when it first becomes apparent to him that what will preoccupy him for the foreseeable future—in relation to his family, his work, and his home—is a sense of anxiety and alienation. Clearly *Babbitt* and many other novels draw the impetus for their narrative from just such moments of disjuncture. However, since it requires that the narrative fulfill the task of examining the causes and consequences of this crisis point, this device can also be seen to initiate almost immediately a visual logic in the text that is then carried on in more detail elsewhere by the narrative. It is the same visual logic of surveillance that I discussed in the preceding chapters. And it is just such a visual logic that informs the language and codes that Lewis's panoptic third-person narrator uses to throw light on and reflect the city of Zenith on the novel's opening page: "shining new houses," "illuminated," "crimson lights," "polished steel leaped into the glare," "celluloid eye shades," "sheets of glass," and "glittering shops" (11). Much as Howells opens up Lapham to his readers through the office interview at the beginning of his novel, so Lewis opens up Babbitt with this visual apparatus.

This network of surveillance which the narrative immediately establishes becomes even more elaborate when one considers Babbitt's work. The realtor must not only be a "seer of the future development of the community" blessed with "Vision" (49), Lewis writes, he must also be a surveiller who "knows his city, inch by inch, and all its faults and virtues" (50). And then there is Babbitt's private office, "a coop with semi-partition of oak and frosted glass" (40), from which he surveils both the outer office where his employees work and the city of Zenith. Just as in "Bartleby" and *The Rise of Silas Lapham*, this frosted or ground glass marks the separation of superior and subordinate staff, performing the institution of a general code of visibility within the office, while marking the status of the office's occupants: Babbitt can reveal himself from behind the frosted glass whenever he chooses, without any warning; his employees cannot disturb him without the warning of a knock. But once he does pass the boundary that the frosted glass provides, Babbitt is certainly aware that his outer office is one of the places where he too comes under a penetrating and disturbing scrutiny. Before leaving for home, after a run-in with Stanley Graff, it is noted that:

> a chill wind of hatred blew from the outer office . . . [Babbitt] was distressed by losing that approval of his employees to which an executive is always slave . . . He was as afraid of his still-faced clerks—of the eyes focussed on him, Miss McGoun staring with head lifted from her typing, Miss Brannigan looking over her ledger, Mat Penniman craning around at his desk in the dark alcove, Stanley Graff sullenly expressionless—as a parvenu before the bleak propriety of his butler. He hated to expose his back to their laughter . . . (77)

It is scrutiny like this, of course, which Babbitt exerts upon his employees as well, but one of the consequences of this environment is that it forces Babbitt to engage what I have argued so far is the unavoidable partner of a regime of surveillance: an ongoing self-surveillance or monitoring of one's own thoughts and actions. While he might previously have taken for granted this self-surveillance, the crisis point of alienation and anxiety where the novel opens forces him, and the reader, to confront the whole process. This may well account for his frustration with his office. "Normally he admired the office, with a pleased surprise that he should have created this sure lovely thing . . . but to-day . . . It was a vault, a steel chapel where loafing and laughter were raw sin." This is a day when Babbitt wants to "beat it off to the woods" (41), that place, presumably, where the claustrophobia of the workplace regime of surveillance and self-surveillance does not operate.

The consequences of this situation for male sexuality begin to become apparent when one considers how surveillance and self-surveillance operate just as vigorously for Babbitt in the gendered, all-male world of the Good Fellows. When Babbitt wakes on the morning on which the reader first encounters him, it is with memories of the night he has just spent playing cards in the "bold man-world" at Vergil Gunch's. When he dresses for work, he puts on the spectacles that make him "the modern business man; one who gave orders to clerks," followed by "the rest of his uniform as a Solid Citizen," observing the "elk's tooth—proclamation of his membership in the Brotherly and Protective Order of the Elks," and finally pinning to his lapel the Boosters' Club Button, "his V.C., his Legion of Honour ribbon, his Phi Beta Kappa key" (18–19). This everyday, but elaborate, preparation for display in the public world of work and business and the Athletic Club is testament to the importance of representing oneself to others as a man in this "bold man-world," as a member of the world of muscular masculinity and frontier manhood which is part and parcel of the world from which Babbitt is drawn. The surveillance of the office is plainly now extending beyond the office here. But, as secure as this kind of self-presentation would appear to be, even Babbitt recognizes that it might, by one false piece of display, be entirely undermined. In one brief moment of social classification the narrative reveals this possibility: "people who carried cigarette-cases [Babbitt] regarded as effeminate" (19). This observation, however, cannot be considered in isolation from one of the minor themes that dominates Babbitt's life during this period: his quest to give up smoking. And it leads back to the office, because Babbitt, just a "week ago . . . had invented a system of leaving his cigar-case and cigarette-box in an unused drawer at the bottom of the correspondence-file, in the outer office" (47). Placing his cigars and cigarettes in such an awkward and public place, he believes, will prevent him from constantly reaching for them. It is a system that fails utterly. So even though Babbitt considers the cigarette case to be an emblem of effeminacy, he cannot divorce himself from such an emblem.

It is through the generalized narrative structure of surveillance and self-surveillance and through the insertion within this structure of local incidents like the cigarette case that a novel like *Babbitt* seems to make itself available to a critical reading that incorporates rather than neglects —as much *Babbitt* criticism has done, in favor of a discussion of Boosterism, the world of commerce, and Babbitt's rebellion against that world—the subject of male sexuality. Even though the relationship between Babbitt and Paul Riesling takes up a relatively small proportion of the narrative, Babbitt's anxiety and alienation throughout the novel can be seen to revolve around his relationship with Paul. Not only this, but it also becomes clear later in the novel that for Babbitt their relationship is defined primarily by his dreams of the fairy child, the slim, white, and eager girl of whom Babbitt is dreaming when the novel opens (12) and whose gender slips at other points in the narrative so that "fairy girl" becomes "fairy child." To date, the closest reading of the fairy child in *Babbitt* has suggested that this imaginary character acts as a way for Babbitt to express his desire to escape from his wife and his friends and the world to which he belongs; thus, in psychoanalytic terms, it symbolizes Babbitt's repression.[9] Whether or not this argument holds water, it does little to throw light on the specificity of the symbolic representation of this repression: a fairy. Such an image could, in fact, signify in a completely different direction in the culture of early twentieth-century urban American culture.

Nearly forty years after Basil Ransom famously remarked in Henry James's *The Bostonians* that "The whole generation is womanized; the masculine tone is passing out of the world,"[10] Sinclair Lewis was writing about an American culture in which the challenge against the perceived threat of womanization,[11] the threat of the nation "going astray,"[12] had been taken up—often by way of a Social Darwinist exaltation of primitive male passion that set out to reinvigorate adult manhood with the boyish virtues that had apparently been devalued by the womanized manhood it was seeking to reform.[13] In the last part of the nineteenth century, this reinvigoration was promoted through the cult of primitivism that was part and parcel of the rituals played out in the increasingly popular fraternal lodges and secret societies restricted to adult men.[14] At the beginning of the twentieth century it was these men who tried to thwart the threat of womanization and overcivilization by transferring the task of socializing boys from women to themselves.[15] These were the years that saw the start of the Knights of King Arthur, the Sons of Daniel Boone, and the Boy Scouts of America in 1912.[16] And it was the world of urban professional, middle-class work that was seen as less and less capable of ratifying a man's manly status.

It was also during just this period of attempted reinvigoration that the relationship between male effeminacy and homosexuality, at least in large American cities, came to be such a focus of attention—through the discourses of inversion, of the woman's soul in a man's body, and of the woman within.[17] Whether or not one agrees with the Foucauldian concept of the invention of homosexuality, the increasingly tight entanglement between the language of gender and the language of sexuality raises the profile of the effeminate homosexual to an unprecedented level. If, as Edelman has argued, male identity is constantly having to filter itself through the discursive mesh of hetero and homo formations from the latter part of the nineteenth century, then the self-surveilling alertness of men like Babbitt can be seen to be focussed in just this direction. It becomes part of their everyday observation—as with the remark about cigarette cases—but also part of their terms of conversational engagement. Paul Riesling is placed very closely—more closely than any other male character in the novel—to just these discursive structures of effeminate homosexuality, and it is the desire Babbitt directs towards him that is the source of his anxiety and alienation towards the "bold man-world" of Boosterism.

George Chauncey has shown how gender inversion in New York— a city with which Lewis was very familiar—was condensed quite explicitly at this time in the persona of the "fairy," who in both working-class and middle-class culture "stood at the centre of the cultural system by which male-male sexual relations were interpreted." Indeed, he goes on to argue that "the fairy influenced the culture and self-understanding of *all* sexually active men" and thus "offers a key to the cultural archaeology of male sexual practices and mentalities in this era and to the configuration of sex, gender, and sexuality in the early twentieth century."[18] For Chauncey it was the stereotypical figure of the fairy that often acted as a role model in two senses: for those men who wanted to find some means of articulating their same-sex desires in public, taking on the persona of the fairy allowed them access to an urban same-sex subculture; for those men more concerned with protecting themselves against womanization, the fairy stood as the *sine qua non* of everything that was wrong with society and the benchmark for gender surveillance.

It is during one misogynistic and antieffeminate discussion that Babbitt meets Paul for the first time in the novel, a moment when Babbitt is literally, and untypically, speechless. Sidney Finkelstein is making fun of him, telling a joke about how Mrs. Babbitt buys his shirt collars for him and how this is a sure sign of a man who only wears a size thirteen —a man, that is, who is not only small and weak, but emasculated because he is small and weak. Paul enters the Athletic Club and on seeing him Babbitt is not only distracted and unable to defend himself against Finkelstein's charge, but also eager to lever himself away from the environment which produces such male banter:

"I—I—" Babbitt sought for amiable insults in answer . . . [he] cried, "See you later boys," and hastened across the lobby. He was, just then, neither the sulky child of the sleeping-porch, the domestic tyrant of the breakfast table, the crafty money-manager of the Lyte-Purdy conference, nor the blaring Good Fellow, the Josher and Regular Guy, of the Athletic Club. He was an older brother to Paul Riesling, swift to defend him, admiring him with a proud and credulous love passing the love of women. (63–64)

Babbitt follows Paul to the men's room and instead of spending lunch as he normally would with the rest of the members, and despite understanding that in the Athletic Club "privacy was very bad form," he "wanted Paul to himself" and so they sit and eat at a small table. This attachment Babbitt feels for Paul is of long standing. His roommate at university, Paul had been Babbitt's "refuge till [he] was spelled by Zilla Colbeck," leaving Babbitt's evenings "barren" (92) and his only future a loveless marriage to Myra. It is difficult not to identify the relationship between Babbitt and Paul as a relationship of desire, especially on Babbitt's part. His desire to be with Paul, to follow him—even into the washroom, to imagine their youthful time together so fondly, and most obviously of course, to escape with Paul to the woods of Maine.

All the time, however, this desire Babbitt directs towards Paul is a desire that is being directed towards a man who is no Booster. With "his dark slimness, his precisely parted hair, his nose-glasses, his hesitant speech, his moodiness, his love of music," he exists for Babbitt "to be petted and protected" (48). The nicknames Babbitt has for him— Paulski, Paulibus—are not so much brotherly as lovingly affectionate while simultaneously pointing to otherness by making him over as East European or Latinate. Nowhere is Paul's effeminacy made more evident than on the train journey that the two men take to Maine as they head away from the city on their escapist trip together. As a conversation ensues in the railway carriage amongst men Babbitt considers "The Best Fellows You'll Ever Meet—Real Good Mixers" (139), Paul is the only one not to join in. When he does finally interject some time later, he commits what Babbitt describes as "an offence against the holy law of the Clan of Good Fellows. He became highbrow" (144). This consists of Paul remarking on the picturesque way the light is shining on a junkyard on the edge of a city they are passing through. While the other men stare at Paul, Babbitt jumps somewhat uneasily and somewhat clumsily to his friend's defense in an effort to appease them and hasten the moment by. For someone as aware as Babbitt to the signal that carrying a cigarette case can give out, then becoming highbrow situates his companion—and therefore himself—all too closely to those feminized signals which might give away a man's sexual desires to a group of scrupulously observant men. And yet what else could Babbitt expect from a man whom he has proudly told the world of Good Fellows could have been a great violinist, painter, or writer? (48). The difference between the two situations, however, can be seen to be vast. Being boosted by a respected man like Babbitt for your productive genius, even though it is artistic genius, is a moment of bonding; letting slip an aesthetic aside about a junkyard to a carriageful of strange men when he has previously ignored them to the extent that they consider him "a snob, an eccentric, a person of no spirit," places Paul as a member of that world so lambasted by Basil Ransom. Paul's judgment on the beauty of the junkyard is at the very least a "false delicacy"; more likely, in the eyes of the men who are his audience and who stare back at him, he has marked himself as a very particular kind of man.

As well as a moment like this, there are other ways in which the narrative positions Paul Riesling in proximity to discourses of effeminacy and homosexuality. It is, after all, not Babbitt who has the emasculating wife, but Paul who has to put up with Zilla's insults about his passivity and his lazy and cowardly nature (135). And it is Paul who is made to carry the weight of the unstable identity that Edelman asserts is part of all male identity but which is projected onto the homosexual in a defensive maneuver that works to reassure heterosexuality that it is internally stable and coherent. It is Paul—like on the train—who is made to display his weaknesses, to give himself away. Not only does he conduct his sexual affairs so indiscreetly that Babbitt discovers them, he is marked as deviant by his shooting of Zilla and his subsequent imprisonment.[19]

But it is in Babbitt's response to these episodes that Lewis's narrative articulates the entangled nature of male desire. The moment when he discovers Paul having dinner with Mrs. Arnold seems to make a lot more sense in terms of this desire when one considers the way in which Babbitt experiences his relationship with Paul beforehand. On the trip to Maine together "they slipped into the naïve intimacy of college days" (150), "stretched voluptuously, with lifted arms and backs," and "sighed together" (149). Babbitt wishes that Paul had a daughter so that she could be married to his son Tom (192). And several times Babbitt remarks on the special nature of his relationship with Paul. It is with Paul that "he relaxed" and "fled from maturity" (200), and it is with Paul that he has his only relationship that is not "Mechanical" and which can bear "the test of quietness" (227). The evening he sees Paul and Mrs. Arnold "a thing happened which wrecked his pride" (240). Babbitt plays the role of the jealous lover not only in his efforts to disparage her appearance— he describes her as "a flabbily pretty, weakly flirtatious woman of forty-two or three, in an atrocious flowery hat. Her rouging was thorough but unskilful" (241)—but also in his attempts to prevent the two of them sleeping together. He first offers to meet Paul later at his hotel, then tells him that he is going to be there; then when he does get to the hotel, he lies his way into Paul's room by telling the clerk that he is Paul's brother-in-law. Yet all this without knowing why he's doing it: "On his way up in the lift Babbitt wondered why he was here. Why shouldn't Paul be dining with a respectable woman? Why had he lied to the clerk . . . ? He had acted like a child. He must be careful not to say foolish dramatic things to Paul." But from somewhere Babbitt alights on the reason for his actions. "Suicide. He'd been dreading that, without knowing it. Paul would be just the person to do something like that. He must be out of his head . . . Zilla . . . she'd probably succeeded at last and driven Paul crazy" (243). Once again, in a move which articulates Edelman's central argument, rather than trying to express his feelings for Paul or recognizing his desire for Paul—feelings and desire which might be uncomfortable and which might force him to pay attention to his own male identity— Babbitt convinces himself it is Paul who is "crazy" and who might commit suicide and must be stopped by a rhetoric of morality and family values. But with Babbitt's jealousy there comes forgiveness and, further, a desire to be complicit in Paul's deceit. Not only does Babbitt cover Paul's tracks by sending Zilla a postcard testifying to seeing him in Akron when he was in Chicago, he parades his privileged knowledge of Paul's affairs in front of Zilla by visiting her on his return and persuading her not to be so hard and severe on Paul. In terms mapped out by Sedgwick, Paul's affair becomes a homosocial secret that ties Babbitt and Paul together via the effects it can exert over the woman who is argued—wrongly of course—to be the cause of Paul's affair and his need for more supportive female company in the first place.

But if Lewis's narrative is alive to these kinds of homosocial operations in the realm of male desire, then it is alive also to the ways in which these operations cannot be ensured. Paul does, after all, end up shooting Zilla. And perhaps not incidentally with the emblematically homosocial gun that he and Babbitt used to shoot rabbits together. What is fundamental to my argument is the way in which Paul's imprisonment is the catalyst to Babbitt's disillusionment with the world in which he lives. It is not until Paul is taken away from him and he is forced "to realize that he faced a world which, without Paul, was meaningless" (259), that the world view which fixed Babbitt so securely becomes distorted, so distorted that he questions the very importance not only of the world of commerce but of the reproductive family relationships which support capitalist patriarchy:

> He plodded into the house, deliberately went to the refrigerator and rifled it. When Mrs Babbitt was at home, this was one of the major household crimes. He stood before the covered laundry tubs, eating a chicken leg and half a saucer of raspberry jelly, and grumbling over a clammy cold boiled potato. He was thinking. It was coming to him that perhaps all life as he knew it and vigorously practised it was futile; that heaven as portrayed by the Reverend Dr. John Jennison Drew was neither probable nor very interesting; that he hadn't much pleasure out of making money; that it was of doubtful worth to rear children merely that they might rear children who would rear children. What was it all about? What did he want? (263)

It is at this point that Babbitt makes a startling admission that makes the link between Paul Riesling and the fairy child explicit.

Before explaining this moment, it is worth mentioning just how the fairy child has been depicted up to this point in the narrative. Babbitt's dreams about her young, feminine form are romantic and sexual in nature—"she was so slim, so white, so eager!" But the fact that she is cordoned off from the real world by being placed in Babbitt's dreamworld is instructive about the disjuncture of romance and realism in American literary history and about the ramifications this disjuncture has in terms of gender, effeminacy, and male sexuality. It is almost as if by being kept in this dreamworld Lewis's narrative avoids the accusation of being romantic, and Babbitt himself avoids the accusation of being *a* romantic, or—in the gender/sexuality grid encompassing this accusation—he avoids being called a "fairy."[20] Yet it is through the link with Paul Riesling that the fairy child breaks through from the dreamworld into Babbitt's life, since Paul has been so relentlessly positioned as a "fairy." After asking himself what it is that he wants, Babbitt fulfills this transition: "But he did know that he wanted the presence of Paul Riesling; *and from that he stumbled into the admission that he wanted the fairy girl—in the flesh . . .* he had made a terrifying, thrilling break with everything that was decent and normal" (263, my emphasis). All of this, of course, is not to deny the threat of extramarital heterosexuality to some sense of morality and decency in Babbitt's worldview. But it is the figuration by which the narrative proceeds that makes Babbitt's desire for Paul so central to what follows in his affair with Tanis Judique.

We might usefully ask how exactly Babbitt stumbles from the recognition that he wants the presence of Paul in his life to (a) the admission that he wants the fleshly pleasure of the fairy girl, (b) the pass he makes at Miss McGoun, and (c) the fulfillment of that fleshly pleasure through a woman in the person of Tanis? This is a complicated knot of desire. But what seems apparent is that in the realm of Babbitt's sexuality there is no straightforward alignment of sexual object choice with gender. In the light of this, it would be hard to make the case that Babbitt embarks upon his affair with Tanis to shore up his masculine heterosexuality. His affair with Tanis is a result of his wanting Paul in his life and wanting the fairy child, whom he associates both with Paul and with women like Miss McGoun and Louetta Swanson, whom he also tries to seduce (267–68).

This apparent displacement makes more sense, however, when it operates in a culture where "normal and decent" sexual desire cannot include sexual desire for another man, but when such desire cannot be banished entirely from even the most outwardly heterosexual identity. In such conditions it must be displaced instead into more acceptable relationships, thus fulfilling that process whereby, according to Lee Edelman, "homosexuality might be recognized, exposed, and ultimately rendered, more ominously, invisible once more."[21] It is in just this manner that Babbitt's desire for Paul is articulated. Tanis gives Babbitt the "presence of Paul in his life" in the guise of a heterosexual affair. Immediately before meeting Tanis for the first time, Babbitt has visited Paul in prison, remarking that if "in this place of death Paul was already dead" then "something in his own self seemed to have died" (269). Then when he listens to Tanis talk, Babbitt decides that he likes her voice because— surely remembering his violin-playing friend—there was "music in it and a hint of culture" (270). It is her "refinement, savvy, *class*" (305) that represent a reincarnation of Paul, because these are exactly the markers of character that Paul has been aligned with in the narrative. It is these markers that attract Babbitt to Tanis and the "highbrow" Bohemian Bunch with whom she mixes. In this company Babbitt is expected to be "boyish and gay." He meets "overdressed and slightly effeminate young men" (319) and, despite his initial discomfort, tries "to be one them" and even begins to "rejoice" when "the most nearly intelligent of the nimble youths, begin to like him" (320). What I am suggesting here, then, is that once Babbitt considers Paul to be "already dead," he tries to compensate for his loss by replacing Paul with the cultural references by which Babbitt recognizes him.

With Babbitt, of course, there is always the added dimension to this process that the reader cannot believe a word he says. Babbitt and his fellow Boosters are masters of hypocritical language. While they all vent their anger against the Union Club, not a single member of the Athletic Club has ever refused an invitation to join (59). Babbitt's showboating public speeches are made up of a tissue of newspaper editorials, advertisements, and other men's speeches. He uses a language in which the status of the information can never be trusted. This has to be taken into account just as much when thinking about sexuality as when thinking about business or politics. Babbitt might express his relationship with Paul in brotherly terms, but then Babbitt is also a man not afraid to "whoop the ante," as he puts it (52), when it comes to writing adverts for properties he is trying to sell.

It is also important to note that while he is engaged in his affair with Tanis—that affair which is somehow a way of having Paul's presence in his life through his association of Paul with the fleshly desire for the fairy child—the full weight of the regime of gendered group surveillance is brought to bear on Babbitt. This affects him in minor ways, such as being teased by members of the Athletic Club when they learn— through the network of surveilling knowledge that operates in this community—that Babbitt has left his office to go to the movies one afternoon. But when he defends the strikers to them during the city labor dispute, he "was vaguely frightened" (302). When he gets back in his car after stopping to listen to a crowd of protesters, he notices that Vergil Gunch's "hostile eyes seemed to follow him all the way" (303). Then one afternoon "three men shouldered their way into Babbitt's office with the air of a vigilante committee in frontier days" to try and talk him into joining the Good Citizens' League. This is a key moment for Babbitt, and the fact that the confrontation takes place in his office is significant.

The aim of the three men is to test Babbitt. The surveilling regime of the office is the perfect environment in which to get Babbitt to examine himself and the way he's been leading his life since Paul's imprisonment, to examine the territory that has been opened up by his linking of Paul, the fairy child, and his affair with Tanis—that complicated knot of de-

sire that I have tried to reach through the juxtaposition of Babbitt's office life, a seemingly casual remark about a cigarette case, his ownership
but attempted disavowal of such an object, and the depiction of his desirous relation with the "fairy" Paul. While Babbitt initially refuses to
join the Good Citizens' League, the visit from the three men—in whose
"whelming presence Babbitt felt small and insignificant"—is enough to
effect paranoia in him: "He was afraid to go to lunch at the Athletic
Club, and afraid not to go. He believed he was spied on; that when he
left the table they whispered about him" (357). As a result of this and
during Myra's illness, Babbitt begins to see "the ancient and overwhelming realities, the standard and traditional realities, of sickness and men-
acing death, the long night and the thousand steadfast implications of
married life" (363).

So, having questioned the value of the family and of reproductive relationships in the aftermath of Paul's imprisonment, and having used
this skepticism to embark upon the fulfillment of his desire for Paul
through the figure of the fairy child and the affair with Tanis, Babbitt—
under the influence of a vigorous surveilling regime—is now returned
to the family and to the culture upon which "the standard and traditional
realities" of family life rely by finally agreeing to become a member of
the Good Citizens' League. The fact that the heterosexual family is so
central to this whole trajectory inevitably brings into the equation all
those types of sexual relationships which, in comparison, are classified
as deviant. Not only Paul and Zilla's childless, gender-inverted marriage;
not only Babbitt and Tanis's extramarital affair; but most centrally of all,
given the pivotal nature of the relationship between Babbitt and Paul to
the shape of the narrative, men's relationships with other men and the
strain they impart on the legitimacy of heterosexual marriage once the
basis of such a relationship shifts from one of promoting one another's
interests to loving one another sexually. After opening up this possibility momentarily, Lewis's narrative quickly covers it up again.

There are times in *Babbitt*, then, when Babbitt himself appears to be
part of two different men's worlds. There is the "bold man-world" of
Vergil Gunch's cards evenings and the Athletic Club and that other
man's world where he and Paul are free to stretch voluptuously and sigh
together. With Paul in prison, that "place of death" as Babbitt calls it
(269), being subjected to the ultimate disciplinary regime, it is the former
that asserts itself all too violently and in whose vigilant gaze queer men
and women still reside.

It seems to me that "Bartleby," *The Rise of Silas Lapham*, and *Babbitt* exemplify very tense and instructive moments when the boundaries between queer and straight identities are in the process of being established or collapsed. The desire between men in these texts fails to be expressed sexually, primarily because of the dangers posed by the fulfillment of this desire. As literary artifacts, then, these texts shadow the binary classification of sexuality in America as it begins to take shape. George Chauncey suggests that gay life was more tolerated, more visible to outsiders, and less rigidly separated in the last part of the nineteenth century and first third of the twentieth century than it was in the second third of the twentieth century.[22] It is the closing down of this tolerance that concerns me in the next part of this book, particularly as it relates to and is expressed through the straight male office worker.

Part Two

Postwar Unsettlement

Chapter Four

"The spirit of work weaves a magic wand"

From Babbittry to Gray Flannel via Tropical Incorporation

The office world of *The Man in the Gray Flannel Suit* is a long way removed from the mid nineteenth-century office world of "Bartleby." Instead of a small, all-male environment in the all-male public work world of business, it is now a vast mixed-gender environment. But in another way *The Man in the Gray Flannel Suit* witnesses what I have been suggesting in the previous three chapters: that the office is in part organized around sexuality and that it is a site where the scripting and de-scripting of male identity and sexuality is an ongoing process. What is important in *The Man in the Gray Flannel Suit* is precisely the way in which the consolidation of the sexual binary of heterosexual-homosexual has become so hierarchized in the office. What one finds in the office of Wilson's novel, as well as the familiar way in which male desire is written and unwritten, is the unwillingness of straight male sexuality to content itself with resolving these dilemmas on a personal level. Instead, there is a perception that the straight nation is threatened at a systemic level by a supposedly subordinated homosexuality.

As a prelude to my reading of *The Man in the Gray Flannel Suit* in the next chapter, this chapter is an exploration of some of the major developments in office and corporate culture that were taking place in America; not just developments in the years between the publication of *Babbitt* and the publication of *The Man in the Gray Flannel Suit*, but also changes that began to occur from that period at the end of the nineteenth century onward when the nature of American office work, office workers, and corporate identity began to change decisively. It is this legacy that provides one part of the conceptual and rhetorical background against which the narrative of Tom Rath—as archetypal Organization Man— is played out. For my purposes, the two main changes in this period were the feminization of office work and the growth in sheer physical size of the large American corporations. What interests me here is the ways that these changes are spliced together in *The Man in the Gray Flannel Suit* with another crucial part of the background that informs the novel: the by-now familiar Cold War rhetoric of "Un-American activities." Wilson, like a good number of other fiction and nonfiction writers of the 1950s,[1] was involved in a process that not only sought to question the value and the effects of the business organization and Organization Man culture, but also did so within a rhetoric that positioned the business organization itself as Un-American.

The Cold War logic that transposed the external threat from communism into a threat from within knew where to look to find signs of treachery. It was suspicious of the organization-inspired homogenization and collectivization of American life in general, developments which at worst might be seen as a kind of pseudo-Sovietism. But this suspicion needed to be tempered because, of course, it might itself betray an Un-American suspicion about the very nature of capitalism, the thing upon which Cold War America relied for its wealth and superpower status. As a result this suspicion had to be focussed, and it was focussed upon the very men—and the motives of those men—who were in charge of organizations.[2] Anticommunism in Cold War America was never very far from homophobia, a point I will develop later. And so the organization run by a man, or group of men, whose masculinity was anything less than manifestly wholesome was therefore a site where the tensions were readily apparent of a Cold War imagination that could not bring itself to criticize capitalism *per se* but instead displaced discontent onto men like Ralph Hopkins, head of the United Broadcasting Corporation in *The Man in the Gray Flannel Suit*.

In 1870 just two percent of American clerical workers were women. By 1930 this figure had risen to fifty percent.[3] Margaret Hedstrom argues that there are two competing versions of just why women came to take up office positions in such large numbers. On the one hand, this initial burst in the employment of women is seen to be a result of the introduction of new types of jobs—mainly typing and stenography—that were marked as female right from the very beginning because of their mechanical nature. Women were only able to enter the clerical workforce once the jobs had become "rationalized, deskilled and degraded" and certainly in these initial stages had no prospect of serving an apprenticeship like the former male clerks did which would enable them to occupy some higher position in the office hierarchy, such as bookkeeper, chief clerk, or manager. In this vision of the employment of women, then, "office work assumed the characteristics attributed to other jobs that are sex-typed as women's work: relatively low pay, little responsibility, and limited opportunity for advancement."[4]

What this version of events allows no room for, however, is the tremendous social debate about women's office work which circulated in American culture around the turn of the century. Women's employment in offices clearly was not just another step in the processes of labor cost-saving and rationalization. As Hedstrom points out, office jobs for women paid relatively well compared with factory work and were considered to be of a higher status than factory jobs. So much so that office work became respectable for the daughters of middle-class families and a sign of upward mobility for women from working-class families. What is important here is that "women entered the masculine world of business and shared their workplaces with men," resulting in opponents of this shift not only questioning the stamina of women to work at all, but also predicting that women would begin to assume the "mannish traits" that were associated with business.[5]

This change had ramifications not just for office spaces but for city spaces as well. Kate Boyer has described how the rise of the female office worker led women to enter those parts of urban culture previously dominated by men, not only offices but banks and restaurants and office sectors of towns and cities, producing as a result "distinctly 'modern' forms of urban femininity" and anxiety about "what it meant to be a woman in this new, modern city landscape."[6] Much of this anxiety revolved around the scrutiny of female bodies which were made to participate in a discourse of virtue and responsibility.

What is relevant here is what is happening to the gender-separated spheres of mid nineteenth-century culture. Ann Douglas has tried to argue that middle-class women during this period somehow became entrenched in a cultural sentimentalism that went hand in hand with this kind of gender-separation, to the extent that sentimentalism "provides a way to protest a power to which one has already in part capitulated" and is a cultural aesthetic that "provided the inevitable rationalization of the economic order,"[7] an aesthetic which, Douglas goes on to argue, the Social Darwinist and muscular masculinity crusade in the 1890s used in turn by articulating its arguments through mass culture forms. But so keen is Douglas to locate her discussion in the realm of the aesthetic that she fails to take account of the transformations "on the ground" which saw, in offices in particular, wholesale changes in the working relationships between men and women which were "feminizing"[8] American culture in a completely different way. It had less to do with sentimentalism than with a questioning of the construction of gender.

Alexandre Dumas remarked that if women "put one foot inside an office, they would lose every vestige of femininity."[9] For me, perhaps a more interesting question to ask is what happens to men when women put not just one foot but their whole bodies, their whole gender, their whole sexuality into the office? Public opinion and discussion about female office workers surely betrays not just a concern for the role and status of women but, coexistent as any gender constructions are, a concern about the role and status of men. Dumas's remark, the worry in the late nineteenth and early twentieth century about women adopting "mannish traits" through work, and the rise of the muscular masculinity movement—whatever the scientific and biological evidence they purported to base their positions on—all display a recognition that one's gender was not only liable to change, but that it might do so as a result of the social position and space one occupied. If what I have argued already about offices is true—that the surveilling and surveilled environment causes trouble for male identity because of the way in which it constantly forces a monitoring of this identity—then the entrance of women into offices adds yet another problematic consideration, certainly for straight male identity. Just what was the acceptable nature of male-female relations in the office to be? If, before, the office had been an all-male space where even the most problematized male identity might find some solace from the status that this fact bestowed, what now happened once this all-male preserve was overturned?

It is just these concerns that I will examine, although the focus of this approach inevitably means a neglect of the lives of female office workers.[10] I want to make the case that although there were strategies of retrenchment that tried to deflect the impact of a female presence, this presence forever tainted the ability of men to be completely straight in the office. From this period on, straight masculinity was increasingly under threat in the office, and in part this was related to the second major development in twentieth-century corporate culture: the growth of the large corporation.

One form of retrenchment was the way in which the influx of women into office jobs actually helped strengthen the positions of men in the workplace hierarchy. While women were occupied in the most menial and least career-oriented jobs—often working only until they married —men could move into the ever-expanding number of lower- and middle-management jobs that were being created in the business world.[11] And during the depression of the 1930s office managers faced social pressure to keep jobs open to men but not to women.[12] In other ways, of course, the office could now be considered to be heterosexualized by the presence of women, and nowhere is this process enshrined more clearly than in the development of the relationship between boss and secretary, a relationship that plays an important role in both *Silas Lapham* and *Babbitt*.

For Lapham, Miss Dewey stands both at the center of his obligations to other men (she is the daughter of the man who saved his life) and at the center of the secrets he keeps from his wife. But it is her beauty— or rather the fact that she is "pretty"—that seems to draw her most attention during the course of the novel. Bartley Hubbard describes her as "an uncommonly pretty girl." In response to which Lapham says only: "She does her work,"[13] which is clearly not the reason for her employment. Tom Corey and Walker sit discussing her one lunchtime. Not only is she described as "pretty" on four occasions, but Walker remarks how it's "*pretty* hard on the girl" and Corey counters by judging that "She seems to be kept *pretty* busy."[14] In this overdetermination of Miss Dewey's appearance one can see the way women are not only immediately sexualized when they enter the office—to the extent that rumors about their sexual conduct could be enough to get them dismissed[15] (and this is just the way in which Miss Dewey circulates in Lapham's office in Walker's account of her)—but also concomitantly commodified as in some way a spectacle to be consumed and circulated amongst men. The surveillance of the office operated just as strongly on women as on men, and in many ways it instituted a new and different form of office surveillance: the surveillance of female bodies by men.

At this point it might be possible to enter the debate about the cultural and erotic objectification of women and the consequences of this process, but instead I want to deal with the question not so much of what is happening to women in this situation but of what is happening to men.[16] At a very basic level this extra plane of surveilling activity which proceeds from the introduction of women to offices ratchets up the overall importance of visual surveillance in this environment. This is, after all, precisely the period in which Frederick Taylor developed his time and motion practices (although *The Principles of Scientific Management* was not published until 1911, Taylor started his studies in the 1880s). It was a period of rationalization in the economic sphere, not just at the instigation of monopoly capitalists but of Progressive reformers as well who wanted to provide some means for controlling the economic and social system.[17] At a basic level, too, it is likely that men responded to this heightening of the surveillance effect by displacing the anxieties that they experienced—and were experiencing now even more forcefully—in the surveilling regime of the office onto their relationships with women in the office, making women the conduits for the circulation of ostensibly homosocial intentions and deriving some ratification of their identity as a result. Again these are ways in which the introduction of women to the office was met by straight male retrenchment.

And yet it is precisely the ineffectual nature of this retrenchment that is most noteworthy. If anything the introduction of women to the office only increased male anxiety. Babbitt's stenographer, Miss McGoun, is no innocent ready to answer her boss's every call; she is one of the office staff, along with Miss Brannigan, who leaves Babbitt "afraid of his still-faced clerks." She makes him nervous: "in his effort to leave the office casually merry he stammered and was raucously friendly and oozed wretchedly out of the door."[18] Later in the novel, when Babbitt has decided to seek compensation for the loss of Paul in the flesh of the fairy child, he first thinks of Miss McGoun. But when he approaches her, "searching for a topic which would warm her office personality into friendliness," he fails miserably and is left to defend himself, and his masculinity, in the face of this rebuff: "Course! Knew there was nothing doing!"[19] This kind of nervousness and disavowal in the face of refusal witnesses a vexed masculinity in the office when confronted by women. And it is here that one can start to see how this shift in office culture has become linked to a wider anxiety in turn-of-the-century America about just what being a man meant.[20]

As Clare Eby has demonstrated, one way to read *Babbitt* is as a companion piece to the works of Thorstein Veblen.[21] Veblen linked business and masculinity very tightly. Eby argues that Lewis constructs *Babbitt* in the manner of Veblen's gender-distinguished separation of "industry" —the effort that goes into making something—and "exploit"—the conversion of energy previously directed elsewhere for one's own benefit. In modern business women were left to perform the "industry" in all manner of repetitive and tedious jobs, while "exploits" were marked as male privileges and men were left to do battle to further their own positions, through a predatory business ethic which came to define manliness itself. But Veblen also argued that manliness and acceptable masculinity depended not so much upon individual deeds as upon group collaboration *among* men, collaboration which stretched from the sports field, through the Athletic Club, into business, politics, and ultimately warfare. This is Babbitt's world. In the previous chapter I discussed ways to see inside of this world and articulate the contradictions implicit within it that influence male desire. Additionally, however, *Babbitt* also introduces a rhetoric of "standardization" into this whole issue of manliness and masculinity. Eby argues that it is precisely Babbitt's self-identified "rebellion against the pull of standardization [that] provides the key which unlocks the satire and his critique of manliness" because he is "too myopic to see that his revolt against standardization enlists him in a battle against manliness."[22] As Veblen and Lewis were aware, manliness and "normal" masculinity actually *relied* upon standardization and upon the conformity that becomes evident in the language of "Babbittry," the clichés and stock phrases. Eby concludes that "men . . . who recognize themselves only by their group identification, *cannot* be autonomous."[23]

Here, then, is the double bind of American masculinity in the early twentieth century, the legacy of which will characterize *The Man in the Gray Flannel Suit*. Having become dependent upon group solidarity for definition as men, yet deprived of the individual status—by standardization, rationalization, the cultural logic of the Fordist assembly line, and the Taylorist management ethic—that was enshrined in the nation's constitution as their heritage, men would now, in the workplace, in the office, have to spend more and more of their time amongst those women who were themselves a product of the "New Woman" movement of the 1890s. The closing of the frontier in the 1880s separated most men irrevocably from a symbolic heritage that was replaced by

mass cultural representations of that heritage. Reduced to the role of vicarious consumers, a role which had been traditionally assigned to women
in the nineteenth century, it is hardly surprising that this double bind
began to be articulated as a "loss." The arrival of women's suffrage in
1920 could only symbolize the further erosion of masculine privilege.

In many ways the straight male experience of office life at the beginning of the twentieth century represents a link in the chain of shifting
cultural organization. Babbitt is fighting a losing battle when he tries to
suggest that in Zenith "the realms of offices and of kitchens had no al-
liances."[24] As women moved out of the domestic environment and into
work and men were forced to make the transition between those historical periods categorized by Elizabeth and Joseph Pleck,[25] the separation
of work and home became even less coherent than it was in the nineteenth century, and American manhood embarked upon a long period
(perhaps as yet unfinished in some sections of the male population—
see chapters 6 and 7) which was characterized by self-pity, regret, suspicion, and an intense problematization of the categories of man, manliness, and masculinity; a period in which the legacy of a pre-urban, pre-
civilized, pre-feminized world lingered in the cultural imagination. Many
American men actually experienced this phenomenon through office
work and through an increasingly omnipresent white-collar discourse in
American culture which was a response to shifting patterns of business
organization. All of this leads to the second major theme that I want to
sketch out as background to *The Man in the Gray Flannel Suit*.

The period between the late nineteenth century and the Second World
War was also crucial for the consolidation of the large corporation in
the American economy. Compared to other capitalist economies, the
shift in scale was dramatic. Almost from their very beginnings, American companies embraced new managerial techniques and organizational
structures to facilitate their own and the market's expansion.[26] This phenomenon was particularly marked in the railway and communications
industries[27] which were themselves the means by which a vast capitalist
system spread across the continent and the means by which many small
towns lost independence and autonomy and came to rely on those distant cities that not only bought what they produced but also supplied
what they needed to participate in the consumer market. So swift, indeed, were these economic changes that Douglas Tallack has argued that
they produced in American modernism "a less oppositional, but sometimes more engaged, relationship" with material changes than existed in
European modernism and that "even in the era of high aesthetic mod-

ernism . . . capitalism and its technology were creating the depthlessness and relational quality which have since been identified as defining characteristics of the post-modern."[28]

It is important to stress as well that however much people experienced the changes in the material culture of capitalism that resulted from this transition as consumers, they also experienced these changes as producers. Ironically, however, as the distance between citizens and consumers in the market economy of mass culture began to shrink in terms of time and distance, the distance between the office worker and the process of production (if there was one at all) grew steadily. In many ways, then, the act of vicarious consumption was matched in the culture of "modernity" by the rise of new workers who spent their day engaged in vicarious production, merely facilitating or oiling the production process that took place out of their sight. Such was the growth in clerical and ancillary employment that by 1957, for the first time in America, the number of nonmanual workers surpassed the number of manual workers.[29]

This kind of territory is, of course, open to examination in the light of Frankfurt School theorists such as Theodor Adorno, Max Horkheimer, and Herbert Marcuse.[30] If capitalist modernity in general saw the decline of artisan and craft skills, the alienation of labor in the rationalized, disciplined, and bureaucratized work world, and the rise of a culture industry that helped reinforce the basis of capitalism outside of the workplace with its selection of standardized and mass produced artifacts, then how applicable might this idea be to America in the face of such wholesale and rapid corporatization? In fact the very nature of the rapid transition in America might actually make this kind of approach less inviting. What would be occluded is an account of the particular historical relationship between corporatization and standardization in mid twentieth-century America and the past from which it has grown. There is a sense in which business in America has something to do with *being* American, whereas in Britain or France or Germany this national dimension remains, at the very most, unarticulated. While Silas Lapham struggles to confirm business as an acceptable American occupation in Boston, Tom Corey's commitment to it shows which way the tide is turning. George Babbitt represents the culmination of the process.

Yet even though Babbitt's speech, and his whole personality, have passed into the businessman folklore of American capitalism, by the middle of the century he became an impossible template for most American men to follow since fewer and fewer of them were in a position to exhibit the attributes discussed in the previous chapter which Babbitt credited to them: masculinity, honesty, mastery, and a straight way of talking. Even executives in some position of power within these new corporations would lose personal experiential contact with the kind of "sane and efficient" business life Babbitt promotes as American. In 1900 it was estimated that two-thirds of executives had run their own enterprise. In 1950 the figure had dropped to one in ten.[31] More and more men would be working not as businessmen but as employees in offices and in the type of buildings where Babbitt's real estate office is located—the place from which Babbitt ultimately wants to escape to go off to the woods with Paul Riesling. The world of business, dominated by Scientific Management techniques, would become loaded with a freight of contradictions: it was the place where one was supposed to prove oneself to be an American and a man, yet the place which was mechanized and feminized and where one did what one was told by a hierarchy that for many men was literally out of sight. After he starts working at United Broadcasting, one of Tom Rath's colleagues tells him he's been working there four years and has "never laid eyes on Hopkins . . . I have no idea in the world what kind of man he is" and for all the power Hopkins has inside the company, the colleague says, outside of it "he's nothing."[32]

In many ways a backlash against the organization of business began to appear. And so tight was this relationship between business and male national identity in America at an ideological level that the changes that took place in the first half of the twentieth century produced a rich and valuable testimony to the process culminating in a whole raft of books in the 1950s of which the most famous are William H. Whyte's *The Organization Man*, David Riesman's *The Lonely Crowd*, and C. Wright Mills's *White Collar*. Products of the same mass market which had created the changes to which they address themselves, these books are testimony to the way in which self-surveillance changes in line with economic and social formation—they witness self-surveillance at a cultural and social level —and to the extent to which this backlash gripped the popular imagination in the postwar period.

Not that this backlash was absent in the fictional domain. In 1939 in *Tropic of Capricorn* Henry Miller begins the envisioning of the office as a self-conscious space that surpasses anything in "Bartleby," *Silas Lapham*, or *Babbitt*. In these texts, while the office operates as an important site for the circulation of discourses about desire and identity, it rarely becomes an object to be analyzed in itself. This is because all the offices in these texts belong to businesses that are relatively small and thus still personal. Miller, however, positions the office in relation to just the things that I have been discussing—masculinity and male identity in the face of corporatization. For Miller America is a cesspool and "Over this cesspool the spirit of work weaves a magic wand; palaces and factories spring up side by side, and munitions plants and chemical works and steel mills and sanatoriums and prisons and insane asylums,"[33] yet he still chooses to locate his protagonist, the narrator, in the office world. And as the office becomes a self-conscious object of analysis, so do its surveillance strategies, the ones that I have argued in previous chapters were there right from the very beginning. The job of the narrator of *Tropic of Capricorn* is "to float from office to office and observe the way affairs were conducted by all and sundry. I was to make a little report from time to time as to how things were going" (18), all at the behest of those "unseen powers" that emanate from the faceless Cosmodemonic Telegraph Company. Installed as a surveiller, this narrator for the first time witnesses how the office has truly become an experimental laboratory in American culture for the study of its employees, a movement that began to be represented in "Bartleby" and *The Rise of Silas Lapham* and that became more important after the Second World War when certain characteristics were desirable in an employee while others— communism and homosexuality in particular—needed to be identified and rejected.

Yet as interesting as this objectification of office culture and its analysis is in *Tropic of Capricorn*, Miller's analysis is bounded by his unmistakable brand of individualist and manly rhetoric. While he seems to be aware of the potentially damaging effects of this kind of intense and destructive surveillance regime, at the same time he seems completely unaware that the rhetoric with which he seeks to counter it might actually be part and parcel of the very same regime. Miller uses the office to embark upon an intense self-surveillance whose ultimate goal is the ratification of the belief that when "I take my place in the crowd which mills about the platform that I am the most unique individual down there" (201) and of the philosophical proposition that "If the self were not imperishable, the 'I' I write about would have been destroyed long ago" (12). This is Miller's attempt to counteract an American life which, for him, had come to resemble "a grand chancre on a worn-out cock," America presumably being the cock itself, even though "you couldn't see anything resembling a cock anymore. Maybe in the past this thing had life, did produce something, did at least give a moment's pleasure, a moment's thrill. But looking at it from where I sat it looked rottener than the wormiest cheese" (19). This image of corporatized America as a worn-out (penetrative) cock transformed into a holey (penetrated) cheese—impotent perhaps because not producing what cocks are meant to produce—says a lot about Miller's conception of how American masculinity is reliant upon the economic system.

Along with this phallic concern there is, as in *Silas Lapham*, a corresponding attention to anality and scatology. Not only is America a worn-out cock and a cesspool, but the narrator's office "was like an open sewer, and it stank like one," even though "There wasn't time to take a crap" (19–20). No time to crap but crap everywhere. Yet even in his relentless pursuit of sex with women in the office, it is to men like Roy Hamilton and Grover Watrous that the narrator turns to find "the very essence of things" (133). This dystopian figuration of American culture as it passes through a process of modernization, while analogous to other European perspectives on modernity, is surely different (with the exception perhaps of D. H. Lawrence) in the emphasis it places on individualist and masculinist virtues and is much closer to the principles enshrined in Babbitt's speeches than perhaps Miller himself was aware. While Lewis's satire sets up a dialogue between the advocates and opponents of the ideas expressed by Babbitt about patriotism, business, and masculinity —and represents these tensions through the relationship of Babbitt and Paul—Miller's rush to privilege the "I" of his narrator and the "eye" of his surveillance of American life seems to lock him into a kind of self-pity that relies not only upon a sense of loss and victimization, but upon a reinvigorated, patched up, and productive, penetrating cock as the solution to this condition.

Miller's is fighting talk, in a way that places it in a terrain elegantly explored by Richard Slotkin.[34] The central premise of Slotkin's work on the myth of the frontier in American history is that the original ideological motive for the myth—the justification for the establishment of colonies—has since been used to account for other passages in American history—economic growth, military expansion, and modernization. Within this myth is a narrative in which "separation" and "regression" are precursors to a subsequent upturn of fortunes. Additionally, conflict was "a central and peculiar feature of the process," most notably in the "savage war" which characterized westward expansion.[35] What is happening in *Tropic of Capricorn* is the strange way in which the processes of separation and regression are, as it were, secularized and removed from the geographical frontier once the frontier was closed and instead are transplanted into the corporatized mass culture that, according to Slotkin in his delineation of a "populist" ideology, represents "a loss of the democratic social organization, the equitable distribution of wealth and political power of the agrarian past."[36] This notion of loss of masculinity in *Tropic of Capricorn* is experienced squarely in the territory of corporatized culture.

For what Miller is doing in part in his novel is redefining the enemy of populist American values. The danger as Miller's narrator sees it comes not from without—on the other side of the frontier, outside the nation—but from within; it is the Cosmodemonic Telegraph Company and its like which have turned American life into a "grand chancre" and which Miller escaped from by moving to Europe in 1930. It is not the western frontier that represents the location for separation and regression, it is the frontier of the Organization and its dehumanizing structures and value systems. It is but a short step from this to the words of William H. Whyte, who, in the final chapter of his analysis of postwar corporate change, urged men that they "must *fight* the Organization . . . the peace of mind offered by organization remains a surrender."[37] Hopefully this point will begin to make clear the issues that I want to pursue in my discussion of *The Man in the Gray Flannel Suit*.

In many ways the Second World War supplies the conduit through which Miller's idiosyncratic and aesthetic condemnation of the Organization links with the popular appeal of Whyte's "Organization Man" thesis. The feminization of office and clerical work, which had slowed during the depression years, gained pace again as labor shortages during the war brought more women into areas such as bookkeeping which had remained dominated by men. Federal government employed an extra 800,000 women during the war.[38] Between 1940 and 1970 women's share of clerical jobs grew from one-half to three-quarters, and as the supply of young single women was exhausted many of these were now married women who delayed leaving work until they were pregnant instead of leaving when they married.[39]

At the same time the political situation in America was shifting. Thomas Schaub, charting the background to the production of Lionel Trilling's *The Liberal Imagination*, has written about the way in which the "old liberalism" of the 1930s gave way to a "new liberalism" of the 1950s that, less equivocal in its condemnation of totalitarianism, replaced a commitment to progress and liberation with greater emphasis on human motive. This shift mirrored the shift in formal politics which saw the decline of New Deal Democrats and the rise of a conservative Republicanism that was suspicious of social reforms it considered potentially subversive. Against the background of the perceived threat of communism, liberals recognized that if they wanted political power they must reposition themselves as far away from communism as possible and as a result became themselves more conservative.[40]

In response to the realities of mass society, there were also awkward questions that needed to be answered about the United States. Having just come through a war against one totalitarian regime, and now having to square up to another as the world map was quickly redrawn, the mass culture of American society was in danger of looking suspiciously like the manipulated mass culture of Nazi Germany and the Soviet Union.[41] Understandably, there was a need to differentiate and defend American society and culture. Douglas Tallack has identified some of the arguments that American intellectuals used in this defense, and he suggests that the work of writers like Daniel Bell, David Riesman, Reinhold Niebuhr, Lionel Trilling, and Richard Hofstadter coalesces around "the concept of political (rather than primarily ethnic or cultural) *pluralism*," the central doctrine of which was that in America "power has been dispersed, from a ruling class or party into a plurality of veto groups" who "represent religion, neighbourhood, occupations" and a host of other sectional interests which give people some sense of the reality of their lives and their position in the political culture.[42] The reality of American culture, it was argued by Daniel Bell, was more complex than could be accounted for by a simplistic theory that equated mass society with totalitarianism.[43] Bell also denied that the consolidation of power in America was top heavy.

And yet this push to produce some defense of American culture, by consolidating an idea of a pluralist consensus, should set alarm bells ringing. The commitment of a response can often be a measure of the threat that it perceives itself to be under. If American society and culture was as strong as is suggested in this consensus narrative, then there would have been no need for the other narratives—of subversion, threat, suspicion—which circulated during this period. The defense of American pluralism outlined by Tallack needs to be seen also as a way of disarming the threat that was felt so acutely at the national and international political level. And it was disarmed, particularly in popular social criticism and in literary study, by shifting the focus away from the historical and political onto an ahistorical naturalization of societal conflict at the level of human nature. This is where Schaub identifies the shift to human motive, or psychology: "within the binary assumptions of cold war thought, global confrontation and psychoanalysis tended to blur into a psychopolitics that affirmed anxiety and conflict as realistic and inevitable consequences of sustaining freedom."[44] Once again, in line with Slotkin's argument, conflict becomes important.

And conflict becomes tangled with the issue of freedom in the post-war world at a fundamental level: Soviet communism represented a threat to American capitalism and freedom and therefore it needed to be defeated through conflict—in Korea, in Vietnam, in Cuba, in Central America. And yet, as I have already pointed out, there was a narrative being played out in postwar American culture which felt the necessity to separate American culture from totalitarian Nazi and Soviet culture, a necessity testifying to a fear that there really was some similarity. This process of separation and disavowal, although contradictory, since it re-lies upon a logic that seeks to recognize bipolar difference in the face of correspondence, remains nonetheless an important process in the cul-tural figuration of conflict, because what it facilitates is the ability to have the bipolar opposite *within one's own culture*. In Cold War terms this means being able to identify that which is in opposition to oneself *within oneself*. This process of separation and disavowal is precisely—following Edelman and Dollimore—how I have considered male sexuality in the previous chapters. What one sees as this process operates at an institu-tional level is the formation of the House Un-American Activities Com-mittee in 1938 and its spectacular rise up the chart of public notoriety in the 1940s and early 1950s. It is the logic that enabled Joseph McCarthy, symptomatically, to ask: "How can we account for our present situation *unless* we believe that men high in this government are concerting to de-liver us to disaster? This *must* be the product of a great conspiracy."[45]

So, at the heart of American government, that democratic political institution which precisely *separates* the United States from the Soviet Union, a threat is perceived. The other defining factor which separates the United States from the Soviet Union is, of course, economic: de-mocracy against totalitarianism and capitalism against communism. As I mentioned earlier, the association of business and patriotism has a firm heritage in American culture, and yet so has democracy—and this still comes under the scrutiny of a rhetoric of Un-American Activities. It is precisely the affiliation between business and the American nation which causes business to become suspect. Henry Miller was already alert to this before the Second World War and clearly other writers—

Theodore Dreiser, Upton Sinclair, F. Scott Fitzgerald, John Dos Passos, to name only a few of literally dozens—have contributed to a critique of the effects of capitalism and industrialization in American culture. What was different about Miller was the way in which he consolidated the notion of the corporate Organization *per se*—in the guise of the Cosmodemonic Telegraph Company—as a potential threat, just in the same way that McCarthy consolidated the political institution as a potential threat. The problem, of course, with these types of Organizations was that they exhibited too many similarities with Communist and Nazi forms of organizations ever to be truly safe—similarities of scale, the position of the individual within them, the control over them being exercised by so few people. Anonymity in a huge Organization might produce alienation, but it might also allow people to be invisible and secretive, hence the need for the vigilance of men like McCarthy.

In the climate of postwar America it is a short journey from the sort of suspicion that Miller articulated about the Organization to the binding of this suspicion into a more general suspicion and distrust of Organization culture as Un-American. And it is worthwhile at this point to consider just how the Organization was considered in the most famous book of popular sociological criticism in the 1950s, bearing in mind at the same time the way in which feminization and the links to a rhetoric of sexuality begin to become palpable.

When William H. Whyte declares that "collectivization . . . has affected almost every field of work,"[46] it is hard to recognize quickly that he is actually talking about America and not the Soviet Union. But this is just the argument that he makes. And what concerns Whyte is the battle between the individual and authority. And against the charge that he might be overemphasizing individualism at the expense of some sort of community association, Whyte argues that society has become so dominated by the Organization that concentrating on individual resistance will not produce what he calls "an excess of individualism" (17).

The Organization for Whyte represents a threat to the Protestant Work Ethic upon which American capitalism was founded, but it is the repetition of an anti-Soviet rhetoric in his discussion of the Organization which is so telling. Organization men are "imprisoned in brotherhood" (16), while the corporation, "it has become clear, is expansionist" (23). In addition, Whyte provides a useful survey of the techniques used to satisfy the "Organization's demands for conformity" (160), the most important of which he considers to be personality testing. He estimates that in 1952 one-third of American corporations used personality tests, and not just to screen new employees but to monitor existing ones. He also notes the rise of psychological consulting firms, some of which sound as though they have come straight out of George Orwell's or Aldous Huxley's notebooks—Psychological Corporation, Polytechnic Personnel Testing Laboratory. Almost in desperation he declares that "There's no limit to what some people would like to see done" (164).

At heart, through a lens of anti-Sovietism, Whyte sees the replacement of the Protestant Work Ethic with the Social Ethic which he believes is creating "a tyranny of the majority" (364) that has an immediate impact on American men: "More and more, the executive acts according to the role that he is cast for—the calm eye that never strays from the other's gaze, the easy controlled laughter, the whole demeanour that tells onlookers that here certainly is a man without neurosis and inner rumblings" (148). Here Whyte is tapping into that strain of male anxiety about masculinity which was so much a part of postwar American culture. Forced to accept the control of the Organization and to smile while he's doing it, the American Organization Man does indeed become neurotic. The Organization for Whyte is anti-masculine: "No matter what name the process is called—permissive management, multiple management, the art of administration—the committee way simply can't be equated with the 'rugged' individualism that is supposed to be the business of business" (22). This oratory sounds familiar because it could almost be Babbitt declaring that the businessman "doesn't have to call in some highbrow hired-man when it's necessary for him to answer the crooked critics of the sane and efficient life."[47] That the organization is anti-masculine is a point Henry Miller makes too. While superficially America "looks like a bold, masculine world; actually it's a whorehouse run by women" (39).

To counteract this development of the committee way, Whyte has his advice to fight the Organization. But he also posits a way in which the spirit of Babbitt might be transferred to this postwar situation in another way:

> the true executive is the one who remains most suspicious of the Organization. If there is one thing that characterizes him, it is a fierce desire to control his own destiny and, deep down, he resents yielding that control to The Organization, no matter how velvety its grip. He does not want to be done right by; he wants to dominate, not be dominated. (143)

What Whyte succeeds in doing in his book is to present the Organization both as a Sovietizing and as a de-masculinizing force and therefore as Un-American on both counts. The blindness to women in the Organization which, in the light of what I have written about the feminization of the office is all the more surprising, becomes hardly surprising at all if one accepts that the last thing Whyte wants to think about is women. What he wants to think about is American men, and what he wants to map is the threat to America which to him can only mean the threat to the "rugged individualism" of American men.

David Savran has argued that this gender distinction is crucial to an understanding of American Cold War culture because of the way it not only "splits the world in half along a different axis," allowing even Nixon and Khrushchev to find something in common to which they could raise a toast, but also because of the way that "the antagonism between capitalism and communism is displaced and reconfigured as an opposition between men and women."[48] And yet neither the work nor the domestic environments that were available to fifties American Organization Man lived up to the ideological inheritance that constituted manhood and masculinity in America; instead of the suburban, corporate lifestyle there remained "a more heroic and maverick ideal that, during the 1940s and 1950s, always ghosted 'the organization man' and determined the shape of his dreams."[49]

Lee Edelman and Alan Sinfield have both extended the importance of this gender distinction into the realms of male sexuality by articulating the ways in which the association of homosexuality with effeminacy, which had become so important during the late nineteenth and early twentieth century, is consolidated in the Cold War environment. Taking the case of Walter Jenkins, Lyndon Johnson's chief of staff, who was arrested in 1964 and charged with performing "indecent acts" with a Hungarian-born man in a public toilet, Edelman—following his theory of homographesis—demonstrates how the demonization of homosexuality after the war relied upon the promotion of an idea of gay sexuality as an "alien presence" that was unnatural precisely because it was Un-American and resulted "from the entanglement with Foreign Countries —and foreign nationals—during the war."[50] Thus homosexuality was treachery almost by definition. In addition, alongside the psychoanalytic strain which blamed homosexuality on weak mothers, Edelman identifies a "Cold War discourse of 'momism' that implicated mothers in narratives of subversion through the weakening of masculine resolve against the insidious threat of Communism."[51]

For Sinfield, the psychological attempts to justify the nuclear family and condemn homosexuality as dysfunctional, made it "only a small step to the thought that anyone who didn't fit in was implicitly queer."[52] This dysfunctionality was of major concern because the nation needed to be as fit and sound as it possibly could be to defend itself against the threat of communism. Freudian psychoanalysis and notions of latency worked to interrogate the script of each man's masculinity and produce a situation whereby homosexuality was Un-American because it denuded the values of the manly man.

More particularly, perhaps, the impact of the Second World War heightened the importance of latency in American culture in another way. Alan Bérubé has noted how the Second World War witnessed the first full-scale attempt to screen armed forces recruits for signs of homosexuality, and yet how at the same time war mobilization provided the space for many gay and lesbian men and women to meet one another and for many others to discover their homosexual identity for the first time.[53] The gay and lesbian recruits who slipped through the net of surveillance were then protected to some extent when they put on their uniforms, one could argue, because those markers of homosexuality emphasized by Edelman suddenly become less visible when everyone is made to look the same.[54] Such a situation raised anxiety about how one could identify the homosexual. In the postwar world of the male office worker this anxiety is perpetuated when the army uniform is swapped for a uniform of gray flannel. Especially when the Kinsey Report had suggested the prevalence of male homosexuality. Such was the anxiety in official quarters about the links between homosexuality and Un-American activities that the focus of McCarthy's attention quickly came to include the identification of homosexual men as well as Communists. In the light of these kinds of arguments, Whyte's consideration of the treachery of the Organization and the articulation of a resistance to it mean that his engagement is with proper kinds of manhood and the way that they are locked in with the economic structure. The Organization that no longer has anything to do with "rugged individualism" threatens to weaken the masculinity and the straight sexuality of men who work for it.

The two major changes that I have identified in American corporate culture—the feminization of office and clerical work and the growth in the size of corporations themselves—produced effects that were unpredictable and uncontrollable. It is testimony to the sheer inadequacy of the discourses of masculinity in the face of the knotted logic of male identity that these changes left many men feeling displaced, disoriented, and confused about just what it took to be the man that was represented to them in the discourses of masculinity. Yet men who allied themselves to the perpetuation of such discourses were able to recuperate the twisted logic of these discourses to such an extent that men's lives were literally at stake because of them. One cannot lose sight of the fact that it was an issue at the level of the corporate world because of the myth of the particular American past against which feminization and corporate growth were set.

Cold War culture, burdened with the tasks of trying to make sense of these changes and of fitting them into a discourse which all the time had to articulate a sense of threat rather than embracing the Organization—corporatization had after all been responsible for making the American economy the wealthiest in the world—remained locked within a contradictory logic. Two revered ideological values could no longer be made to cohere: masculinity and business. Masculinity was under threat *at the workplace* because of the gender-unified nature of the *site* of work. It was also under threat from a Freudian psychologization of sexuality that articulated homosexuality as dysfunction and yet raised the possibility (through latency) that this was a condition that might affect all men. And as homosexuality by this time was securely grounded in the gender grid that equated it with effeminacy and feminization, men who worked at the office would be confronting the very environment of feminization each day. While the demarcation of jobs and glass ceilings helped to secure the superior *status* of men at work, even this status was undermined because of the way in which these executive positions no longer carried with them the trappings of the independent, pioneering spirit that held back Silas Lapham in the social world of Boston and yet, at the same time, was forging the success of American capitalism. Lapham is the hero of Howells's novel, not of Boston society. In many ways he remains the hero of Cold War culture, despite the unattainability of his achievements in corporatized, collectivized society.

C. Wright Mills described this society "as a great sales room, an enormous file, an incorporated brain, a new universe of management and manipulation,"[55] while for David Riesman it was now marked by a shift from inner-direction to other-direction that became "the principle mode of insuring conformity in the American middle class."[56] The threat to the individual is their paramount concern. And it is precisely because the

Organization carried so many of the markers of communist organization that it became so demonized, even more so because the business that went on inside it could no longer be considered to be masculine. Sovietized and feminized, the Organization had become treacherous and queer. This is the background against which *The Man in the Gray Flannel Suit* must be considered.

Chapter Five

"Opaque glass bricks"

Sloan Wilson's Gray Flannel Man
in the Queer Organization

Starting with the office in "Bartleby," codes of visibility incorporated into the architecture of office spaces have played an important part in the construction of my argument. The ground-glass doors separating the two sides of the lawyer-narrator's office, as well as Bartleby's screen, the ground-glass door which separates Silas Lapham's den from his book-keepers' den,[1] and the "semi-partition of oak and frosted glass"[2] that isolates Babbitt's private office, might all initiate a wider discussion of the relationship between visibility and male sexuality. Sensitive to cultural and technological shifts, architecture can not only express the particular historical shape that these codes of visibility take, but also lead inexorably back to Foucault's contention that disciplinary power can operate through the most diverse apparatuses. I want to begin thinking in more detail about *The Man in Gray Flannel Suit* from just such a historically coded moment of visibility.

One lunchtime, Tom Rath, in his quest to earn more money than he can at the Schanenhauser Foundation, follows a tip-off from a friend and visits the offices of the United Broadcasting Corporation to inquire about vacancies. Earlier that morning he has put on his best gray flannel suit and on the way to the office has stopped off to buy a clean white handkerchief and to have his shoes shined. After being fielded by "a breathtakingly beautiful girl with money-colored hair,"[3] Tom waits underneath the picture "of a big-bosomed blonde" (8), one of United Broadcasting's leading stars, for his initial interview with a man called Everett, who is the same age as Tom and is also wearing a gray flannel suit: "The uniform of the day, Tom thought. Somebody must have put out an order" (8). Once inside Everett's office, the first thing Tom notices is that it is "a cubicle with walls of opaque glass bricks, only about three times as big as a priest's confessional."[4] I want to concentrate on the opaque glass bricks that apparently form the office walls, most particularly because this description of the glass bricks as *opaque* is patently wrong.

Glass bricks were first developed at the end of the nineteenth century in Europe and became popular during the late 1920s with the rise of the Art Deco movement. The use of these bricks spread especially quickly in the United States during the 1940s and 50s, as part of modern, futuristic architectural design.[5] Crucially, however, glass bricks have always been made from translucent glass. In contrast, opaque glass is used primarily in the production of small-scale and decorative glassware, since the cost of producing it on any larger scale would be prohibitive.

While Wilson's misdescription could easily be passed off as a simple error, the repetition of the misdescription on two further occasions suggests that it may actually be part of an emerging pattern at this early point in the novel—a pattern that is important because of the way that *The Man in the Gray Flannel Suit* takes its lead from Miller's *Tropic of Capricorn* and establishes a *vision* of the Organization from one who is part of it but somehow subservient and underneath it. "Bartleby," *Silas Lapham*, and *Babbitt* are all texts in which the narrators or major protagonists wield power in their work environments, part of the attraction of the narratives being the way in which the basis of this power is both explicated and problematized. But the virtue of Wilson's novel is that it witnesses the economic process whereby power in bureaucratized American capitalism, although perpetually present in one's work environment, has receded beyond grasp—conceptual grasp as much as physical, or more so—to a vanishing point where one has little immediate contact with it in any traditional sense. Here then we have a narrative that wants to be seen as being written from the bottom up. This sense of vertical hierarchy is clearly important in a corporate environment where actually meeting power physically means getting in an elevator and travelling upward. And elevators are prominent and thematically important in *The Man in the Gray Flannel Suit*. At the same time, for a straight family man like Tom

Rath to consider himself at the bottom, or as the bottom, has implications in the epistemology of sexual logic. When one considers that William Whyte's incantation that "the true executive . . . wants to dominate, not be dominated"[6] would be ringing in the air just a year after *The Man in the Gray Flannel Suit* was published, these implications become clear. Being the bottom means being the one who gets fucked.

This situation in itself, by articulating oppression in the terminology of anal penetration, suggests something about the homophobic nature of straight male anxiety in the corporatized world. But Wilson's opaque glass bricks suggest to me a much more sophisticated commentary on the constitution of Cold War sexuality. The second instance of misdescription occurs shortly after the first. Having been given "a long printed form" by Everett that takes almost an hour to complete—and that includes a question asking the applicant to list the names of countries visited—Tom is invited back to United Broadcasting for a second interview, this time with the more important Gordon Walker. He finds Walker "closeted in an inner office which was separated from the rest of the room by a partition of opaque glass brick" (9). The pattern this repetition contributes towards is one that structures the Organization as impenetrable. To describe the bricks correctly as translucent would suggest that the Organization is—if not entirely transparent—then something which might have some light thrown on it. The substitution of opaque for translucent creates an entity that is altogether more mysterious, unknowable, and concealed; one where the characters that lie behind it—Everett, Walker, and ultimately Ralph Hopkins—remain unexamined and out of sight.

There are plenty of rumors about Hopkins, but none of them come from anyone who really knows him. The process of making Hopkins a national personality is the job for which Tom gets hired. But he finds himself in an organization which passes information in mysterious and invisible ways. After waiting twenty minutes to see Walker, Tom is struck by how, without any "audible or visible cue," one of the two secretaries tells him that Walker is ready to see him (9). Neither is there any visible sign of work being done. The two secretaries sit reading black notebooks, their telephones and interoffice communication boxes silent; Walker sits behind a desk that has on it only a blotter and a pen (9). This is a world which is not only unfamiliar and secretive, but which literally hides itself for Wilson behind its architecture of opacity—and its homologously opaque work practices—and in so doing alienates the straight family man like Tom.

And yet what Wilson's narrative does is to give the lie to this rhetoric of opacity. It suggests that the higher echelons of the corporate world are impenetrable and unknowable and yet simultaneously creates and envisions them. And this is no neutral envisioning; it constitutes an ideological intervention. Tom gradually works his way up through the opaque offices of Everett and Walker, and of Bill Ogden, and through their gray flannel suits, before finally landing on the fifty-sixth floor and the office of Ralph Hopkins with its breathtaking view of New York City (40). The narrative sets as its task the gradual penetration and exposure of the Organization in a way which cannot be separated from those other Cold War discourses of exposure that had as their targets communism and homosexuality, since ultimately exposing the Organization means not only criticizing and questioning it (since clearly this is no bad thing in itself) but criticizing it by using a rhetoric that juxtaposes it with communism and homosexuality. Clearly, in terms of my general argument, I am more interested in how the Organization is placed in relation to homosexuality, but Tom's suggestion that somebody has put out an order decreeing that gray flannel be the uniform of corporate life more than hints at some form of regimentation in American mass society. In this way it echoes those dystopian visions of social commentators like Whyte, Riesman, and Mills who looked at the 1950s as an era in which the individual ceded authority to the committee or the group. This is the pressure which Tom feels and the result is that his life is one of perpetual anxiety in the face of this opaque but envisioned pressure.

What remains interesting is the way in which the exposure of the Organization takes place alongside and is deeply interwoven with the exposure of the constituent parts of Tom's male anxiety. In many ways, it is possible to see the narrative of *The Man in the Gray Flannel Suit* as a battle not just between the Organization and the little guy, but between the nature of what lies beneath the supposed opaque façade of the Organization and the real opaque façade of Tom's gray flannel suit. The two are constructed against one another, and Tom is clearly the hero. While Everett gets him to complete a form that takes nearly an hour, Walker requests that Tom write his autobiography: "Explain yourself to me," he instructs Tom. "Tell me what kind of person you are" (11). Tom is made to sit in a small, bare office, and in a chair "which had been designed for a stenographer and was far too small for him" (11) but fails to find anything that he can type about himself that might help him to get the job. Instead he provides a curt paragraph giving his date of birth, his education details, his career to date, and then concludes—in terms reminiscent of Bartleby—by typing that "I do not wish to attempt an autobiography as part of an application for a job" (14). This act of defiance constitutes Tom as a character who will stand firm against the supposedly penetrating but impenetrable bureaucracy of Organization personnel management techniques. Yet it only makes sense when one considers that it is an act of defiance at being made to surveil himself in an artificial and feminized environment: the stenographer's chair is too small for him, of course, because stenography is a female job; and instead of writing his autobiography by hand, he is made to *type* it. This ordeal in itself acts as a motif for the way in which the office potentially feminizes men and for the male response that may result. But while the information he provides for Walker is cursory, in the passage of the forty-five minutes he spends thinking about what he should write, Tom reveals to the reader the complex landscapes through which his anxiety about Organization life is played out.

At the beginning of the novel Tom himself suggests there are four primary landscapes, and although he eventually comes to see "How connected everything is!" (240), initially he maintains the hope that they are unrelated:

> There was the crazy, ghost-ridden world of his grandmother and his dead parents. There was the isolated, best-not-remembered world in which he had been a paratrooper. There was the matter-of-fact, opaque-glass-brick-partitioned world of places like the United Broadcasting Company and the Schanenhauser Foundation. And there was the entirely separate world populated by [Tom's wife and children] Betsy and Janey and Barbara and Pete, the only one [of the worlds] worth a damn. There must be some way in which the four worlds were related, he thought, but it was easier to think of them as entirely divorced from one another. (22)

I will condense the first and the last worlds into one under the heading of the nuclear and extended family to leave just three. The more specific claim that I make is that the corporate world of office work is actually the site through which Tom's war and family experiences are filtered in order that they can be made sense of, that office work for Tom is both the place where wartime experience is transferred into heterosexual family life and also the place where the ideological imperatives of war and family might be undone without a demolition of those opaque glass brick partitions behind which the Organization—so Wilson's narrative suggests—seeks to hide and protect itself. This is a demolition that Wilson's narrative is keen to undertake and that will rescue Tom's masculinity at the expense of the demonization of Hopkins and of Organization culture.

As Elaine Tyler May has shown, the American family of the 1950s needs to be understood in terms of both political and domestic ideology.[7] In her study she tries to conjoin the diplomatic history of the Cold War with the sociology of affluence, suburban expansion, and the baby boom in order to show how the "legendary family of the 1950s . . . was not, as common wisdom tells us, the last gasp of 'traditional' family life with roots deep in the past," but was in fact "the first wholehearted effort to create a home that would fulfill virtually all its members' personal needs through an energized and expressive personal life."[8] This is why Tom can describe his family world as "the only one worth a damn." The diplomatic and the domestic for May are linked by the principle of containment. The home became the place where potentially disruptive social forces might be kept under control. Much of the narrative of *The Man in the Gray Flannel Suit* works to foster this same principle. In the subplots about the death of Tom's grandmother, his inheritance of her estate, Betsy's ambitions for her husband and their children, and their ultimate transformation into important members of their community, there is obviously an aspiration to consolidate the role and the importance of the heterosexual family and the heterosexual family home. But, in line with May's observations, the difference between aspiration and reality is painfully clear in Wilson's novel.

At one level the reality of domestic frustration is written onto the very fabric of the Raths' house. The living room wall is decorated with "a huge crack . . . in the shape of a question mark" as a result of Tom's anger when Betsy bought a glass vase he thought they did not need (1). Although Tom refuses the symbolism of this crack, the fact that Wilson chooses to open the novel with this description suggests something of the way in which the family home is central to the novel's other concerns and the way in which it is a place that cannot be taken for granted in postwar American culture: it is an institution that needs to be constantly recuperated and reproduced.[9] And just as May questions the extent to which the white suburban family of the 1950s has its legacy in the past, *The Man in the Gray Flannel Suit* suggests that Tom is actually trying not to repeat the failures of his own family, especially of his father, Stephen Rath.

Before Tom begins his job for Hopkins, the narrative provides a vague account of the sad demise of Stephen. Sent home from France just before the armistice "for unexplained reasons" (19), he worked in New York for a large investment firm. The "dim echoes of rumor which survived" (20) to reach Tom suggested that he had either quit this job or been sacked about two years before he killed himself in a car crash. And while Tom is convinced there must have been "quite a chain of events leading up to" his suicide (20), his grandmother never reveals it to him. All he remembers is that as a young boy he overheard his mother talking to a minister about how "Poor Steve was raised on lies . . ." (21), only for this conversation to end abruptly when they notice he has entered the room. An old friend of his father's, Sims—the local lawyer who balks at having to administer justice on strangers but who will help Tom to secure his inheritance—tells Tom that his father had a nervous breakdown during the war and that it was the consequences of this that meant he was unable to hold down his job or look after the family estate, four-fifths of which he frittered away on poor investments. On a desk in his office, Sims keeps a picture of Stephen Rath "smiling boyishly" at the camera (51). This is a photograph that Tom has never seen before.

The manner of the dissolution of Stephen's life and the secrecy surrounding it, together with Sims's devotion to keeping a thirty-year-old photograph of an old friend *in his office* where he can look at it all day long, suggest that it might be possible to provide a reading of their relationship which positions it at the very boundary of homosocial and homosexual desire. While there may be no evidence of any sexual scandal, Stephen's crisis becomes a scandalous secret in a culture where doubts about masculinity slip into accusations of effeminacy and homosexuality, the latter being something that one is made to keep secret. If this is so, then the recognition (and disavowal) of the relationship between Stephen and Sims by Tom—in the context of Cold War discourses about homosexuality as mental illness or mental weakness, latency, and containment—could be seen to structure his commitment to Betsy and his children and their future while marginalizing and undermining men like Hopkins and the Organization. I explained in chapter 2 that I have no intention of privileging father-son relationships. What I want to emphasize instead are the more general parallels between Tom and his father. Both have fought in wars, both carry the legacy of the war with them—Stephen through his mental problems, Tom through his obviously heterosexual affair with Maria and his son by her—and both face the problem of reintegrating into a postwar society. Stephen's nervous breakdown, his postwar profligacy, and his inability to work or to maintain his family, all bear the hallmarks of a crisis of masculinity: the inability to fight and to be successful in business. In many ways these are the qualities which Tom tries to secure despite the obstacles that are in his way.

Tom worries about these obstacles. He worries about the administrative and financial burdens of life. Whereas his father and his grandmother in turn had little notion of budgeting, Tom's social position ensures that he needs to make the most of what money he earns to try to haul himself up the ranks so that he earns more. At the same time, even when he gets his job with Hopkins and more money, he is "depressed and pessimistic" (59). He is worried that the job might not last; he is worried about having to work with Ogden and about his grandmother's house and the servant Edward who lays claim to it. "Dreams of glory," he says, "I've spent my whole life getting over them" (63). This anxiety increases as the narrative progresses and Tom's lack of self-confidence becomes evident. It seems to reach a peak not coincidentally when he and his family are in the process of moving from their suburban house into Tom's old family home:

> I'm doing all right on my job. Hopkins likes me. We're really being smart to sell this place and move to Grandmother's house. We're going to make a damn good thing of it! He couldn't convince himself.
> . . . Suddenly he had a picture of himself hanging around his grandmother's house, precisely as his father had, with nothing to do. He glanced down and found he was gripping his right thigh so hard that his knuckles were white. He hadn't done that for some time. Why the hell should I get scared in peacetime? he thought. (118–19)

Snapping himself from this scared and melancholic state, Tom gets back to his family, the source of his security, by offering to help with the packing and telling his daughter a story.

Indeed it is Betsy's constant reassurances and shoring up of his morale, and the conviction that his family is the only thing worth a damn, that keeps Tom going. Betsy it is who is the "conscientious household manager" (1), who develops the real estate plans for the land that comes with Tom's grandmother's house, and who "with remarkable self-possession" (246) finishes off the debate to decide whether a new school should be built in South Bay, a decision which will determine the success of the real estate venture. *The Man in the Gray Flannel Suit* draws this familial world as one with which Tom can cope, the one without which he would be lost. It is what lies outside it that so threatens and worries him and with which he can only cope if the home and family remains solid. The two things that stand outside of it most vividly for him are the other two worlds he disparages: his war experiences and his experience of work. More particularly, though, they are precisely what threaten the security of his home and family life.

Waiting in Italy to be sent to the Pacific after the war in Europe is over, Tom spends eight weeks with a young woman, Maria, whom he meets in a bar that she had entered "with painfully obvious intention" (78). She becomes pregnant and Tom leaves. Like his other war experiences, this is something which Tom does not reveal to Betsy. He does not reveal to her that he killed seventeen men, that he accidentally killed his best friend with a hand grenade, nor that he was so desperate to keep warm at one point that he killed a young German soldier by stabbing him repeatedly in the neck, ramming the knife home "with all his strength until he had almost severed the head from the body" (74), just to get hold of his leather jacket. He deems these experiences too difficult to confront in the company of Betsy. At the very end of the novel, when Tom has eventually been forced into revealing the existence of his son and of his relationship with Maria, and when the cursory details of his life during the war are exposed as well, Tom still refuses to talk to Betsy in any detail. She prompts him to discuss it, but Tom says, "No. It's not that I want to and can't—it's just that I'd rather think about the future. About getting a new car and driving up to Vermont with you tomorrow" (272).

There is little doubt that the wartime life of a paratrooper in Europe must have produced sufficient fear that no one would want to recall it, and I do not mean to deny the horror and the impact that these experiences produced. Yet what I find compelling is the disingenuous manner in which these experiences are turned into narrative in *The Man in the Gray Flannel Suit*. Tom Rath, while not willing to discuss his life in the one world that means anything to him, spends his whole time discussing it elsewhere. At every opportunity he returns to the war, even though he points out early in the novel that "Only masochists can get along without editing their own memories" (13). When Walker asks him to write his autobiography, the number of men he killed is one of the first things to come into his mind; when he is walking to the office one morning, he notices a man wearing a leather jacket and this leads him to retell at length the story of killing the young German guard (70–77); and he reserves some of his harshest criticisms of Organization men like Hopkins by comparing him to "some poor inoffensive colonel who never had to jump sitting behind a desk, drinking coffee maybe, and wisecracking with a sergeant about when they were going to get their leave"

(39). By Tom's standards of toughness these men are hardly "men" at all. Not only this, but the incantations which Tom used during the war to get him through difficult moments before a drop or on the ground—"It doesn't really matter," "Here goes nothing," "It will be interesting to see what happens"—he also repeats to himself when things are difficult at work—before a meeting, before he has to negotiate some agreement. So in a sense then, Tom, while he does not want to recall the war in his relationship with Betsy, also continually wants it with him as a resource he can draw upon to explain and justify his pessimism and depression and to bolster his sense of masculinity in the corporate world.

The deployment of this strategy is reminiscent of Eve Sedgwick's contention about Captain Vere in *Billy Budd*. There she argues that we know "Vere suffers in secret and in silence, by the operatic volubility and visibility with which he performs the starring role of Captain *agonistes*."[10] While Tom may not be quite so dramatic, the incoherency of the private and public realms is equally well exposed. And this incoherency also returns the narrative back to those incoherencies of visibility which attach themselves to Wilson's substitution of opaque for translucent. The strategy of banishing the war to the category of the "best-not-remembered" and yet constantly talking about it relies upon a confused sense of invisibility and visibility. In many ways Wilson's narrative operates in that terrain of homographesis mapped out by Lee Edelman with which I dealt in chapter 1. The opacity of the glass bricks signal for Tom and for a Cold War logic the possibility for a whole world to carry on invisibly. The task must therefore be to make this world visible. For Tom this means the demolition of the opaque glass brick partitions. In the ideology of the Cold War this meant the exposure of internal threats to capitalism and straight masculinity. And yet Tom's journey to demolish the opaque partitions—this narrative that attempts to write this world and its occupants from the inside—result in an ever-increasing proximity to it that ultimately threatens to undermine rather than consolidate that which is meant to stand in opposition and therefore hierarchical superiority to it: that one world which Tom considers worth a damn.

Next I want to return to the world of United Broadcasting and follow Tom's journey as he gradually gets closer to Ralph Hopkins. A key figure in this process—literally and metaphorically—is Caesar Gardella, a man with whom Tom spent much of his wartime career and whom he meets again when he goes to United Broadcasting for his interview with Walker. Caesar is now an elevator attendant. Tom, however, fails to recognize him. All he recognizes is the capacity for this man to make him "flustered." So much so that he has to go to the men's room to calm down (24). What is important about this first meeting is the keenness of Tom's observational skills when he gets into the elevator. Caesar stands with his back to Tom, and yet with only one glance Tom generates a copious description of him. He even steps to one side to get a better look at him, but still cannot see his face. Eventually Caesar turns so that "their eyes met" during which there "might have been a quickly suppressed flicker of recognition, but Tom couldn't be sure" (23). There clearly is recognition of something on Tom's behalf, hence his visit to the washroom. Quite how one is meant to think about this recognition is problematic, however. In the realms of male sexuality the meeting of eyes — with another man — can be a moment of desire, or it can be a moment of threat. In this instance it seems to be a moment of threat, because we learn later, when Tom realizes the identity of the elevator attendant, just what the consequences of a mutual recognition might be. It is in the remembering of the incident of his brutal murder of the young German soldier that Tom places Caesar as the elevator attendant. Caesar it is who tries to buy the leather jacket that Tom has taken to keep warm. Rather than take money for it, Tom gives the jacket to Caesar.

This moment of wartime camaraderie helps provide a stronger sense of just what is at issue in the brutality involved in Tom's murdering the German and some of the reasons it remains so vivid for him. Caesar is younger than Tom, one of "the young recruits who replaced the men who didn't come back" (76) from the expedition that resulted in Tom killing the German soldier and taking his jacket. Caesar is an inexperienced corporal, Tom an experienced captain. What Tom does by giving Caesar the jacket is to turn it into a sacred homosocial token which can cement his bonds with his male army colleagues even though the jacket is the very object which has been the cause of his shattering of these homosocial bonds beyond the boundaries of the nation-state by killing the German soldier. As David Savran and Elaine Tyler May have both remarked in their comments on the conviviality of the relationship between Nixon and Khrushchev when it came to drinking to the ladies, national boundaries are liable to disappear when it comes to gender and sexuality. The brutality of Tom's murderous assault when the German soldier refuses to die from being choked is an exhibition of the pain that having to kill another man can cause; it is possible that the brutality is not directed at the German soldier, but at the imperatives of war which mean that these homosocial links have to be broken — paradoxically — in order that they can be reinforced. It is the leather jacket, then, that symbolizes all of this during the war, and it is also what connects Tom to Caesar and what confronts Tom each time he enters the elevator on his journey towards Hopkins and the seat of Organization power.

Structurally then, this kind of homosocial discourse is literally part of the Möbius-like elevator shaft that manages to be both phallically and anally symbolic at the same time. Caesar's position at the heart of this piece of architecture, and Tom's inability to avoid him, means that the knowledge Caesar carries about Tom has to be perpetually confronted. On his journeys to see Hopkins and to demolish the opacity surrounding the Organization, Tom journeys closer to demolishing his own organization. Because Caesar knows about the brutality that killed the German soldier, and he knows that Tom killed his best friend, Hank Mahoney, but most important he also knows about Tom's affair with Maria and the likelihood that Tom is the father of her child.

This is clearly important in terms of Tom's relationship with Hopkins because of the way that it is always there with Tom whenever he meets Hopkins in the office building; each time he enters the elevator it reappears for him, and this of course helps to explain just why it is that I want to discuss Hopkins and the Organization he runs in terms of male sexuality.

As I mentioned earlier, rumors about Hopkins circulate freely enough in the world of United Broadcasting. His invisibility to most of the employees means that these rumors cover just about every possibility:

> There are all kinds of stories about him—they used to say he had two children and had been home twice in twenty years. I think his son was killed during the war—anyway, nobody talks about that anymore. They say he needs less sleep than Edison did. They say he's got his whole filing system memorized, practically, and can quote from any important letter or contract in it. Some say he's got a little blond girl who flies in from Hollywood each month. I've heard it said that he's queer. (29)

Every sexual possibility, that is. And while Hopkins's potential queerness stands no higher or lower in this list of possibilities than his straight relationship with a pretty blond, it would be a mistake to discard this piece of hearsay quite so quickly. There is, after all, a clear inequality between the ways in which different types of sexual identification signify in American culture. One can hardly imagine a situation where office gossip in a large corporate organization centered on the question of whether this or that person was *straight* or not. As the whole of this book so far has tried to show, it is non-straight sexuality that is made to bear the burden of its own visibility through inscription and exposure. Cold War America was not just similar in this respect, it was actually more committed to this type of inscription and exposure. And so in a cultural and social arena where hearsay—about one's political sympathies or one's sexual preferences—could lead to consequences far worse than dismissal from one's job, this kind of textual reference carries far more weight than any of the other possibilities that are listed. And Wilson's narrative does nothing to disabuse this rumor about Hopkins; if anything it does all it can to reinforce it.

Wilson uses Hopkins's commitment to his work as the means for bringing the specter of Cold War psychology into the novel. The son of an "ineffectual man" and a strong mother from whom he inherits "the impression . . . that achievement means everything," Ralph Hopkins is told by his analyst that his working so hard is the result of a deep guilt complex based on "a fear of homosexuality." And although Hopkins "had never consciously worried about homosexuality . . . he tried to believe it, for the psychoanalyst had said it was necessary for him to believe [in order] to be cured, and Hopkins had wanted to be cured, in order to make his wife happy" (156). It is hard to say whether the confusing construction of Wilson's sentences here should be put down to him or to the Freudian analysts he is paraphrasing. For instance, surely by fear of homosexuality he means fear of *being* homosexual. And if Hopkins wants to believe that his guilt is based on a fear of being homosexual and that curing this fear would be witnessed by an ability to make his wife happy, what conclusion is the reader to draw from the fact that he fails completely in this task? Might his failure to make his wife happy (and most probably happy in this context means happy in bed) actually position him as a man who is not only *willing to believe* that he is afraid of being homosexual, but as a man who *is* afraid of being homosexual and therefore almost by definition in the logic of Cold War notions of latency *actually* is homosexual. I am not suggesting this judgment should be made concretely at this point in the narrative, but it is perhaps the most blatant way in which the insidious half-accusation or rumor about homosexuality is left to ferment in the novel. In many ways this narrative strategy acts as a kind of literary innuendo to a knowing audience, an audience primed in the nuances of spotting and identifying just who is who, so important has this concept of latency become in the world of the uniform of gray flannel.

Certainly it invites a closer inspection of Hopkins and his motivations. His relationship with his wife is shown to be little more than a marriage of convenience. Hopkins has an apartment in the city, rarely goes home, and has had little to do with bringing up his children. When his daughter is about to elope with an aging playboy, she stands in front of him and tells him that he has never loved anybody. When Tom has dinner in Hopkins's apartment one night, he observes Hopkins fussing about the room "acting for all the world like an anxious housewife entertaining the rector" (104). Hopkins's effeminate style and physique, the way of a morning that he jumps lightly out of his nonmarital bed and steps briskly towards the shower where he removes his white silk pajamas and then comes out of the shower wearing a "warm *Turkish* towel" weighing "a hundred and thirty-eight pounds, including the towel" (150–51, my emphasis), all stand as richly classificatory descriptions in a novel which never ventures into the bathrooms or showers of any of its other characters, including Tom.

Indeed, the only sections of the novel which are not focalized through Tom's point of view are the sections dealing with Hopkins. It is into the realms where Tom cannot go that the narrative ventures in its efforts to provide a picture of what kind of a man Hopkins is. His obsessive and idiosyncratic demands also reinforce some kind of abnormal psychological condition that, while it never concretely places Hopkins as queer, always potentially threatens to build on those rumors about Hopkins's sexuality that are so firmly planted by the narrative. Tom has to make a special trip to Atlantic City to make sure the arrangements for Hopkins's keynote speech are just how he wants them. The lectern has to be "four feet five inches from the floor," the bed in the hotel suite has to have a hard mattress, the flowers have to be goldenrods or long-stemmed roses but not chrysanthemums, and all the rooms must face the sea (165–66).

Much of this closer inspection that the narrative undertakes mirrors an important aspect of the relationship between Tom and Hopkins. When Tom is employed by United Broadcasting, it is for a job that consists partly of helping to write a speech for Hopkins in connection with a new project. The project itself—to start a national mental health committee—resonates with those Cold War concerns about the mental health of the nation. It is also impossible to read this part of the narrative outside of the way in which Hopkins himself has been depicted as someone who may be in need of the kind of help that wider funding and public interest in mental health problems might provide or outside of the way in which Tom is placed so closely to the problem of mental health by his father's death.

Hopkins and Tom, however, stand unequally in relation to the question of mental health. For Tom—who has lived through the horror of war never knowing if the next day might be his last, has killed seventeen men including his best friend, and has then had to reintegrate into and find his way in postwar America—his relation is a legitimate one. For Hopkins, the narrative suggests that his motivation is not entirely sincere. One of Tom's colleagues suggests two reasons for Hopkins's interest in the mental health project. The first is that it is a way of diverting attention from the bad name United Broadcasting is getting for the quality of its programs: "One thing the company could do is actually to improve the programs, but it would be cheaper to tell all the company's top executives, and particularly the president [Hopkins] to go out and acquire a reputation for doing good" (28). The second suggestion is that Hopkins is doing it to acquire national fame outside of United Broadcasting. What Hopkins does, in fact, is turn the mental health project into a public relations exercise. This fact is particularly important when one considers that United Broadcasting is a company that operates at the heart of American mass culture. Here, then, is an Organization which seems to want to get even more involved than it already is with the minds of American citizens, and for all the worst reasons. Tom, of course, is complicit in this process, since he is responsible for helping Hopkins get the project organized. But Tom's complicity is diluted by his role in the project. As he is involved in writing the speech for Hopkins, he is literally involved in *writing Hopkins himself* for the audience who will hear the speech. And while there is no doubt—as Tom is forced to rewrite the speech over and over again—that he is not entirely in control of what will be said, it is in this writing of Hopkins that Tom helps in the closer inspection of him for the reader and the construction of him as a particular kind of man.

All of these narrative effects, then, are constantly positioning Hopkins in relation to Tom, and constantly positioning him as different from Tom. As the narrative of Tom's penetrating journey towards Hopkins proceeds—making him more visible—these differences cross over between and confuse two categories—business and sexuality. What happens is that the strains and tensions Tom feels in his job as Hopkins's mental health project coordinator and then as his personal assistant—as these jobs begin to take up more of his time and make more demands upon him—are articulated in a rhetoric that foregrounds masculinity and sexuality. Tom's uneasiness about being ambitious and about taking risks may manifest themselves in the way that he worries, but with

Betsy constantly beside him they also manifest themselves in terms of his masculinity:

> You're spoiled and you're licked before you start. In spite of all you did in the war, you're not really willing to go out and fight for what you want. You came back from the war, and you took an easy job, and we both bellyached all the time because you didn't get more money. And what's more, you're a coward. You're afraid to risk a god-damn thing! . . . you've got *no guts*. (64)

The problem for Tom, of course, is that the world in which he is expected to be fighting now is one which, in line with the developments set out in the previous chapter, has become an arena so much at odds with that arena he experienced during the war. Where the virtues of dynamic masculinity were required by war, in the corporate world of feminized and bureaucratized work these virtues seem not to provide the same rewards. It is men like Hopkins, after all—effeminate, obsessive, queer, unhappily married, a bad parent, mysterious—who have achieved success. The real estate venture which Tom agrees to go along with provides an alternative avenue for success outside of the corporate world and one more in line with his wartime experiences. The mapping and control of contested terrain on the battlefield is transposed to the mapping and control of land for the real estate venture that he and Betsy will embark upon. And just as Betsy can wound Tom most severely by equating his lack of ambition at work with his cowardly and gutless character, she can revivify him by paying homage to the strength of his manly character: "Do you know why I love you, Tommy? . . . It's because I never saw a man I thought could get away with making you really angry" (64). That Betsy's appraisal of Tom can shift so suddenly within the space of a few sentences is tribute not just to the incoherency of domestic arguments, but also to the incoherency of the construction of Tom's masculinity in the face of the feminized Organization and the heterosexual family. Tom knows that the kind of virtues Betsy wants him to exhibit in the workplace are not suited to the workplace. Indeed, it might even be possible to suggest that what lies beneath Tom's recognition is the belief that the nineteenth- and early twentieth-century oppositions of business and the masculine, set up in contradistinction to the domestic and the feminine, had collapsed to such an extent that the workplace was an uncertain environment for the propagation of traditional masculine virtues. Certainly it is from this moment that Tom has to face the fact that to recuperate his sense of masculinity against the threat of the Organization he will need to resist the increasing ties which link him to Hopkins.

Tom is made to move gradually closer to Hopkins in a physical sense. Eventually he moves offices and occupies a desk in Hopkins's outer office along with Hopkins's personal secretary and two stenographers. The spatial and positional logic of Tom's situation here should not be overlooked. I have already mentioned his discomfort when he is made to sit in the stenographer's chair to type his interview. Here he is literally made to occupy that feminized secretarial space and to perform a secretarial position as Hopkins's assistant. And yet as the novel progresses, the increasingly close working relationship of Hopkins and Tom is matched by an increasing determination on Tom's part (with Betsy's help) to assert his independence.

When Hopkins asks Tom to read a final draft of the speech, Tom realizes that he faces the alternative of being honest or being a yes man. He puts the speech down after reading the introduction—"Our wealth depends on mental health"—and thinks "they're going to sell mental health the way they sell cigarettes" (182). He gets Betsy to read the speech, and they argue over the possibility of integrity in a job like Tom's, where being honest might mean being out of a job, since honesty sometimes means telling the people who employ you what they do not want to hear. Tom's ability to lie shocks Betsy, and she asks him, "How long will it be before you decide it isn't necessary to tell the truth to me?" (187). Since he has been concealing from her the truth about his wartime relationship with Maria, Tom is faced with the disturbing prospect that the way he behaves at work might actually be a way of behaving that threatens his marriage if the truth were ever uncovered, as it may well be if Caesar decides to blackmail him about Maria and her child as Tom considers he might at one point (117). Tom's decision to be honest with Hopkins marks a crucial turning point in the recuperation of his masculinity, and the fact that it is articulated in a rhetoric of sexuality emphasizes just how Tom perceives Hopkins and United Broadcasting:

> "I'm going to play it *straight* [my emphasis] with him and we'll see how it goes. I'm rather looking forward to fixing up that speech."
>
> "Thank God!" Betsy said. "You know, for a while there, I wasn't sure *what* kind of a man I had married."
>
> Tom glanced at her sharply. "Don't let's go into that," he said. (203)

Being honest and playing it "straight," then, go together in this rhetorical construction of Tom's masculinity. And while the comfort of this decision of Tom's allows him to be convinced of Hopkins's sincerity in regard to the mental health project, it is a conviction that is only possible once Tom and Betsy are satisfied about what kind of a man Tom is. And it does not prevent Tom from suspecting Hopkins's advances towards him. Tom is suspicious of Hopkins's motives: "I don't like being the shadow of another man . . . I think he wants to try and create me in his own image and I don't want any part of it" (227–28).

Towards the latter part of the book there is also a sense in which these advances by Hopkins might be construed as sexual. I mentioned earlier that eye contact between men stands precariously balanced between threat and desire. Tom becomes more conscious than during any other part of the novel of the way Hopkins looks at him. "It was disturbing," he remarks, "that steady, unabashed gaze, the eyes tired, the whole face exhausted, yet so curiously intense and kind" (225). When they go to Hollywood together on a business trip, Hopkins invites Tom back to his hotel suite for a nightcap. Tom notices that everything is laid out just the way it was for Hopkins's stay in Atlantic City. Hopkins fixes the drinks, and then "sprawled out on the sofa the way he had the night he and Tom had talked in his apartment. To his increasing discomfort Tom found that Hopkins was staring at him again . . . Tom sipped his drink nervously" (250). Instead of—or perhaps Tom considers it by way of—a sexual advance, Hopkins offers Tom a better job in California.[11] Maintaining his determination to talk straight, Tom turns down the offer on the grounds that he's "not the kind of person who can get all wrapped up in a job" and wants to spend more time with his family, especially if there's another war coming (251–52). Tom, then, represents a clear break with the tradition of *Babbitt*. For Babbitt sanctity was fleeing from the family into the all-male work world; for Tom sanctity involves fleeing from the work world to the family. There is no pleasure in the prospect of a close male relationship for Tom.

And yet his family life is not yet secured, since he still has a secret that he must tell Betsy in order that their marriage may be purged of the threat hanging over it. Tom uses his commitment to straight talking and tells Betsy about Maria and the child that is his son. Having penetrated what he considers to be the opacity of the Organization and of Hopkins, Tom penetrates the opacity of his gray flannel suit to reveal to Betsy the truth that can only become visible once he affirms the virtues of honesty, straight talking, and openness against the deficiencies of strategic lying and concealment. And *The Man in the Gray Flannel Suit* quite explicitly determines the sites where virtues and deficiencies operate.

Explaining what has happened to his wife, Tom locates Caesar as the locus for this determination: "There was Caesar in his purple uniform, staring at me in my gray flannel suit and reminding me, always reminding me, that I was betraying almost everyone I know" (272). So wearing gray flannel—the most symbolic manifestation of corporate allegiance—comes to signify betrayal for Tom, betrayal of family. I want to carry this remark about betrayal into my conclusion to consider just how this logic sums up Cold War attitudes towards the Organization and male sexuality.

In a wider Cold War context, the word betrayal may signify, as Michael Rogin has demonstrated, in two directions: not only can it be associated with a political betrayal connected with communism and the threat to the American nation, but it can also be associated with an overbearing maternal betrayal that threatens the "paternal inheritance" of the American nation, that is, heterosexuality.[12] Lee Edelman has argued that not only are these two types of betrayal yoked together in Cold War America, as witnessed in the Walter Jenkins affair, but that male homosexuality is figuratively represented in Cold War America as that which threatens "the continuation of civilization itself." (Hence comments such as the one he quotes from Norman Mailer: "As civilization dies, it loses its biology. The homosexual, alienated from the biological chain, becomes its center."[13]) I think there are links between this kind of figurative representation and the opaque glass bricks essential to the development of the narrative of *The Man in the Gray Flannel Suit*.

The changing nature of office and corporate culture are vital ingredients to this reading of the novel. The growth in the size of corporations made them dangerously like communist organizations in the way that they utilized methods of surveillance and secrecy, while the shifting gender requirements of office work made them dangerously *unlike* those kinds of business enterprises which produced men like Babbitt. In many ways, the narrative purpose served by the opaque glass bricks and Tom's determination to demolish and penetrate them is to allow, respectively, the accusation of secrecy to be levelled against the Organization and a process of inscription to be undertaken against those men who dwell in that secrecy, men like Hopkins. Yet of course such a logic requires that inscription be carried out by using the same methods as those used by the Organization itself, the methods of surveillance and scrutiny undertaken by Tom—in his role of attentive and observant sign reader and speechwriter for Hopkins—and by the narrative itself. So the very structure of Wilson's penetrating narrative participates in that process of making "visible the aggressive anality of a culture compelled to repudiate the homosexuality it projectively identifies with the very anality it thus itself enacts."[14]

It is possible to see at this point, then, how Tom's keenness to make the opaque transparent would engage him in some sort of de-scription of his own sense of heterosexual male identity. While I would argue that this happens to some extent, it happens not nearly as much as it does in the three previously considered narratives. If homosexuality does open an epistemological gap in maleness, then it is one that is very tightly closed again by Tom Rath. Each of the three previous narratives, featured very close, desirous relationships between men—between the lawyer-narrator and Bartleby, between Silas Lapham and Tom Corey, and between Babbitt and Paul Riesling. In contrast, *The Man in the Gray Flannel Suit* features no such sustained relationship. Tom Rath barely has any male friends in this narrative, and certainly none at work. In fact, if anything, the opposite occurs. Tom reacts against the formation of any close male friendship with Hopkins. It is a testament to the strength of suspicion and criticism of the Organization in the 1950s that it cannot operate as a site for male friendship, and one of the main reasons for this is the fact that male relationships in such a stigmatized—that is communized and feminized—environment would smack of the homosexuality with which both of these terms were associated. The relationship between Tom and Ralph Hopkins, which is the one relationship which carries the potential to be read in a way analogous to the relationships in the three previous narratives, is from beginning to end marked by a discontinuity of identification and a confrontation of demands, expectations, and lifestyles.

Instead, Tom falls back on his memories of wartime, and particularly his relationship with Hank Mahoney whom he inadvertently kills. The description of Tom's disbelief at what he has done, his unwillingness to accept that Hank is dead, and the way that he carries his body forlornly through the battle scene searching for help, is both moving and tragic (91–95). But while Tom's reaction to this event and the other horrors he experiences is touching and human enough, I mentioned earlier that I found it disingenuous the way that Tom used the war as something that needed to be forgotten yet constantly drawn upon as the source of his masculine apathy, depression, and cynicism.

It is worth remembering the brutality with which Tom killed the young German soldier and the way that after killing Hank he throws two hand grenades into "a cave full of Japs," before going into the cave and finding one still alive who "with grim pleasure he had finished off" (92). My point is that, despite all this horror, Tom comes home to America to continue the logic that ratifies the killing of those men who are marginalized as alien. Not this time the "little man with the bayonet" (79) who is in Tom's mind when he is "Lying on the bed naked with Maria" (81) and who is taking Tom away from Maria, but the men who endanger the sanctity of his marriage to Betsy and the inheritance of his children by threatening that "catastrophic undoing of history, national and familial both" about which Edelman writes.[15] It is to these men that Tom is betraying his family and everyone he knows by wearing his gray flannel suit, such are the dangers that complicity with Organization brings.

If Tom's desire "to see, to recognize, to expose the alterity of homosexuality"[16] in the Organization is witnessed by his desire to demolish the opaque glass bricks which surround it, then it only results in the reinscription of a rhetoric of honesty and straight talking which may work to save his marriage and his family's inheritance, but which at the same time rides on the back of a contradictory rhetoric of openness which in Cold War America not only resulted in the ruthless and often false exposure of political sympathies and sexual behavior but also ensured that those people who suspected that they might have something to hide were forced into silence and seclusion.

Chapter Six

"I ascend like a condor, while falling to pieces"

Fear, Paranoia, and Self-Pity in
Joseph Heller's *Something Happened*

There is a moment towards the end of Joseph Heller's *Something Happened* when Bob Slocum, Heller's narrator, plots the trajectory of his life in terms reminiscent of Silas Lapham's experiences in nineteenth-century Boston. Having had his promotion confirmed while his colleague Andy Kagle is demoted, Slocum suggests that: "We rise and fall like Frisbees, if we get off the ground at all, or pop flies, except we rise slower, drop faster. I am on the way up, Kagle's on the way down. He moves faster. Only in America is it possible to do both at the same time. Look at me. I ascend like a condor, while falling to pieces."[1] In one way this situation is the very antithesis of what happens in *Silas Lapham*. That novel is marked by Lapham's failure in business and his subsequent spiritual coming together—"the moral spectacle which Lapham presented under his changed conditions" as the Reverend Sewell puts it with such admiration.[2] For Slocum there is no such redemptive failure. Not even the death, or more accurately the murder, of his son leads to the sort of moral reconfiguration that one finds in *Lapham*.

And yet, of course, both *The Rise of Silas Lapham* and *Something Happened* can be reduced to the same equation. In *Lapham* business failure leads to moral success; in *Something Happened* business success compounds moral failure. The conclusion is the same: one cannot succeed in American business and expect to succeed as an American human being. Or, more precisely, as an American man, since the relationship between business, manhood, and national identity has been constructed so intensely in American culture.[3] There is something about being connected with business that is considered corrupting and dangerous, something that can be regarded as such a threat that it can bring about the very shattering of one's sense of self, that can—as with Bob Slocum—initiate and effect a "falling to pieces." In this chapter I concentrate on the way that *Something Happened*, and to a lesser extent Don DeLillo's novel *Americana*, deal with surveillance and self-surveillance in the office in terms of three categories that dramatize this "falling to pieces": fear, paranoia, and self-pity.

Something Happened takes its place in a historical lineage of fiction about the dangers of office work quite explicitly. Martha, one of the secretaries in Slocum's department, is going crazy like a latter-day Bartleby as "she gazes out over her typewriter roller at the blank wall only a foot or two in front of her face, forgetting what or where she is and the page she is supposed to be copying" (18). There is also the dead record storeroom that becomes prominent in the course of Slocum's relationship with Virginia (95).[4] That the representation of the crazy copyist is now a woman is testament not only to the way that the shift to a white-collar economy has left women doing the menial office jobs (there are no female managers in *Something Happened* or *Americana*), but also to the way that the medicalization of madness from the late nineteenth into the twentieth century has left women to go crazy while men, men like Slocum, suffer from what Heller calls "the willies" (3), a linguistic conjunction that places male sexuality directly beside a nervous, fearful apprehension. "I get the willies" is the title of the first section of the novel, and Slocum expounds the constituent elements of this condition before he does anything else in the book:

> I get the willies when I see closed doors. Even at work, where I am doing so well now, the sight of a closed door is sometimes enough to make me dread that something horrible is happening behind it, something that is going to affect me adversely; if I am tired and dejected

from a night of lies or booze or sex or just plain nerves and insomnia, I can almost smell the disaster mounting invisibly and flooding out toward me through the frosted glass panes. My hands may perspire, and my voice may come out strange. I wonder why. (3)

This is an important opening since all three of the category elements mentioned above are displayed here. Fear obviously enough; paranoia because it is "something that is going to affect *me*"; and self-pity because of the way Slocum describes this condition by using a common vocabulary of feeling "tired and dejected" whether it be booze, sex, nerves, or insomnia that has occupied him the night before, thus making it a state of mind rather than a localized reaction. In addition, the elements reinforce one another, since it is when Slocum pities himself that the fear and paranoia become so apparent that he can almost "smell" them.

Once again, and here *Something Happened* chimes with all the texts looked at so far, this condition is bound up with a logic of visibility thanks to the presence in the passage of the "frosted glass panes." As an interface between the panoptic, surveilling gaze of the upper echelons of the business hierarchy and the subordinate employee conscious of this surveillance and conscious of the need to preempt it through self-surveillance, the frosted glass condenses many of the power effects that are integral to office culture in capitalism. What is important in relation to *Something Happened* is the way that this initial confession of fear and paranoia prompt Slocum to suggest to himself that something must have happened to him to produce the kind of reaction he experiences in the presence of closed doors.

One might argue that two things are achieved by the subsequent possibilities he puts forward as to what this something might be. First that they actually lead him away from any examination of the status-obsessed and power-obsessed corporate culture in which he works, and second that the number of possibilities merely reinforce the very ambiguity that lies at the heart of naming a book *Something Happened* when nothing does. I would argue that neither of these is a viable proposition. What, though, are the possibilities?

Three are very clearly linked to Slocum's opening of closed doors when he was young and finding something unexpected: his father and mother having sex (3), his brother having sex with one of his friend's sisters (4), and his naked older sister (4). The other three, however, have nothing to do with doors at all, but all are triggered by Slocum finding his father and mother having sex:

Maybe it was the day I came home unexpectedly with a fever and a sore throat and caught my father in bed with my mother that left me with my fear of doors, my fear of opening doors and my suspicion of closed ones. Or maybe it was the knowledge that we were poor, which came to me late in childhood, that made me the way I am. Or the day my father died and left me feeling guilty and ashamed . . . Or maybe it was the realization, which came to me early, that I would never have broad shoulders and huge biceps, or be good enough, tall enough, strong enough, or brave enough to be an All-American football player or champion prizefighter . . . (3)

I quote this passage at length because it is worth seeing just how Slocum's imagination is working to piece together his world at this initial stage of the narrative. What strikes me is not the way he veers away from the corporate realm, or the randomness which causes him to leap from one possibility to the next, but the fact that it is the closed doors that so disturb him at work and that act as the bridge to guide him between domains that are meant to be spatially and temporally distinct—office and home, adulthood and childhood—and then, within these domains, between different themes—wealth and status, sex and masculinity. And all this takes place through a process of self-surveillance again inaugurated by the visual logic of closed doors and frosted glass, by the prompting these artifacts of office culture seem almost compelled to inspire. This link between the themes of sex, status, and masculinity and the corporate frosted-glass world in *Something Happened* is not one that has attracted critical attention.

What *Something Happened* does in this initial phase of the narrative is to effect a modulation of the sort that Foucault identified when he wrote about the production of discourse about sex. Slocum effects a modulation from closed doors and frosted glass to sex and masculinity in a looping process that is enabled by the way that the office is historically marked in its construction by an epistemological logic tied very closely to the construction of American male sexuality. What Slocum seems to be doing is reading these epistemologies one against the other: reading sex and masculinity through the architecture of the office and reading the architecture of the office in terms of sex and masculinity. By being common to both sites, fear, paranoia, and self-pity become the elements that structure the novel and Slocum's imagination, and they are established as soon as the novel opens.

Don DeLillo's *Americana* also works to set up a particular epistemo-logical regime, and there is a similar fascination with the meaning that closed doors have in the office. The narrator, David Bell, thinks that "they close their doors just to frighten us. Everybody knows closed doors mean secret discussions and secret discussions mean trouble,"[5] where "they" are managers who are conducting a purge of employees and creating an atmosphere where nobody knows who is next. But as well as the practical consequences that closed doors might have for his career, Bell is also aware of the way that working in this office environ-ment shapes the world of his consciousness. Moving out of the mail-room and forward in his career helps him "learn more about fear" that is part and parcel of the relationship one has in the office with one's su-periors. Bell learns to distrust those of them "who encouraged inde-pendent thinking" because if "you gave it to them, they returned it in the form of terror, for they knew that ideas, only that, could hasten their obsolescence . . . I learned to speak a new language and soon mastered the special elements of that tongue."[6]

Interestingly, then, the institution of relationships of terror and fear between men in the office hierarchy operate in two directions at once. Not only are men who are subordinated in this hierarchy subject to fear from those above, but those above are also fearful—one might say paranoically so—of those below, since it is the men below who can en-sure their "obsolescence." This kind of reversal even operates on the youngest executives. David Bell is intensely conscious of and proud that he is the youngest executive in his company. When he goes west to make his film, he constantly asks his secretary to find out the age of a new ap-pointee. He turns out to be younger than Bell, and she has to console him by saying, "Don't get mad. He looks older."[7] It is almost as if one's future is already over before it starts in the world of office capitalism, and certainly in the world of TV advertising in which Bell works, so de-pendent is it on image. And it is over because of a rhetoric of newness and progress that is naturalized in the ideology of capitalism. This ca-pacity for fear and paranoia to work both ways up and down the office hierarchy is encapsulated in *Something Happened* when Slocum identifies the way fear saturates all relationships between people in his company:

> In the office in which I work there are five people of whom I am afraid. Each of these five people is afraid of four people (excluding overlaps), for a total of twenty, and each of these twenty people is

afraid of six people, making a total of one hundred and twenty people who are feared by at least one person. Each of these one hundred and twenty people is afraid of the other one hundred and nineteen. (13)

What is going on in this process of mutual fear and suspicion is often an attempt by these men to work out what is happening outside of their localized theatre of influence and control, and in particular to know what other men are thinking about them in order to know the consequences if what they are thinking is put into practice. In *Something Happened* Slocum acts as a conduit for both Jack Green and Andy Kagle to find out what their boss Arthur Baron is going to do with them. Both think they are going to be fired (57–58), and when Slocum has a meeting with Baron, both want a report of the conversation and how they figure in future plans. This is the meeting where Baron offers Slocum Kagle's job. Slocum proceeds to lie to both Green and Kagle, so conscious is he of how each will be affected by the news (he will in effect become Green's boss). In Slocum's own words he now has "the whammy" on each of them (45).

Not only this, but he thinks he knows exactly what kind of men Kagle and Green are. Slocum roots through Kagle's character by way of the clothes that he wears and exposes his faults and the reasons why he will not get much further up the office hierarchy. Kagle "shows poor judgement in colors and styles, as well as in fabrics" (46), all of which is far more important in one's business career according to Slocum than "ability and experience." These do not count anymore, whereas "tone" —which includes manners and wit as well as clothes—does.

He does the same with Green, whom Slocum describes as "a clever tactician at office politics whose major mistake has always been to overestimate the value of office politics in getting ahead" (39). Instead of believing in the company and doing everything that the company asks of him, and nothing more than this, Green "still tries to believe in himself." And instead of keeping friction to a minimum and waging battles "sneakily behind each other's back" where the "secret attack can be denied, lied about, or reduced in significance" (40–42), he is renowned for his frankness and confrontational style. None of this works, according to Slocum. What counts is being a diplomat, that is, a liar (58)—a quality which Slocum himself believes he possesses and which Arthur Baron believes he possesses as well (60).

In *Americana* this reading and appraisal of the other men in the office is at one point geared quite explicitly to form a judgment about male sexuality. When a piece of graffiti appears in the men's washroom declaring one of Bell's colleagues, Reeves Chubb, to be a homosexual, a train of events is set in motion that seeks to determine the answer to this question. Weede Denney, Bell's boss, calls Bell into his office to ask him what he knows about the rumor. With the office door firmly closed, Weede declares that "What a man does in his free time is no concern of mine, within reason," and the "within reason" halts here because the company is working on a project about China and the "State Department doesn't want any queers" involved.[8] What is interesting here is the way that *Americana* itself suddenly slips into a lineage that this book has been trying to outline: Weede asks Bell if he knows that Reeves Chubb sleeps in the office two or three nights each week. In terms reminiscent of Bartleby's feminization of the office, Weede rounds off, "Something like that makes you wonder." But Bell's solution to the nature of Chubb's sexuality also echoes the way that Edelman has shown how the delineation of the markers of sexuality works retrospectively. That is, they are construed after the point of revelation to have been obvious all along so as to reinforce the possibility of the homosexual "passing."[9]

> One of the very best ways to arrive at some kind of conclusive determination in a situation like this with a man's whole future at stake is simply to think back on it. Think back on Reeves. Think of small incidents, anecdotes he's told, his reaction to certain words or phrases, the way he holds those little cigars of his, favorite expressions he uses, his sensibilities, his literary preferences, the amount of time he spends in the john, the kind of shoes he wears. It all has a bearing.[10]

The copiousness of Bell's list, its attention to the most minor of details, witnesses the presence of an incredibly skilled and knowing observer. Clearly this passage is different from the passages from *Something Happened*—primarily in the way the passage from *Americana* concentrates on male sexuality—but I would argue that the similarities between both passages are difficult to ignore. Both demonstrate how closely the observation of men by other men is conducted almost subconsciously within the confines of office culture. The fact that Slocum never mentions sexuality in any explicit manner raises an important question: *where* do we think about sexuality? One could argue that the difference between the two passages marks a disjunction, the passage from *Americana* being clearly about sexuality, the passages from *Something Happened* being clearly not about sexuality. And yet how can one be so sure? Where exactly does the boundary of sexuality exist? If it exists only where there is mention of certain "key words and phrases," then coded love letters, innuendo, symbolic language can never be said to have anything to do with sexuality.

It is here that Sedgwick's work is so important and helps to bridge the potential gap between *Americana* and *Something Happened*. Of particular note is the way that she identifies the visual nature of male homosexual panic as it emerged in post-Romantic Gothic fiction in the first half of the nineteenth century, where plots focussed on what she describes as the "transmutability of the intrapsychic with the intersubjective . . . where one man's mind could be read by that of the feared and desired other."[11] Ultimately Sedgwick has pushed this idea to its epistemological limit in her use of the phrase "It takes one to know one." For Sedgwick this phrase represents the "fatal *symmetry* of paranoid knowledge," where "To know and be known become the same process."[12] It is precisely in the conscious and subconscious processes—and in the narratorial confession—of reading other men where thinking about sexuality takes place. So Slocum's surveillance of Green and Kagle, his figuring out of their strengths and weaknesses, or the ways in which they have the whammy on him or in which he has the whammy on them, is where Slocum thinks about sexuality. And his very use of the word "whammy" with its peculiarly American sexual connotations seems to signal this.[13] In many ways, David Bell's suggestion that Weede Denney "think back on" Reeves Chubb's previous behavior gives the game away about what is involved in the fearful, paranoid office workplace. It makes explicit at the level of content what is implicit at the level of epistemology.

In my first chapter about "Bartleby" I remarked on how the doors that separate the lawyer-narrator's side of the office from the side where Turkey and Nippers work operate in two different ways: closed they ensure a sense of privacy for the lawyer-narrator while failing to fulfill a similar function for Turkey and Nippers, since it is the lawyer-narrator who controls the doors and might potentially open them at any moment, thus exposing the shortcomings of his employees unless they work as if the doors were always open, that is unless they surveil their own behavior constantly. What can be seen in both *Something Happened* and *Americana* is the process whereby that early kind of office discipline disperses into the logic of interaction between men, and why the figure of the closed door becomes so important, particularly for Heller. The closed door swings closed under the impetus of a logic of surveillance and exposure that then brings men into competitive and power-drenched proximity with one another. What becomes important is whether or not one has control of this process and whether the door is closed in front of you or behind you. If closed in front of him, Slocum doesn't "know how to cope with it" (58–59). But if closed behind him, Slocum admits that he "always feels very secure and very superior . . . sitting inside someone's office with . . . other people, perhaps Kagle or Green or Brown . . . doing all the worrying on the outside about what's going on inside" (53). To be on the outside, then, induces fear and paranoia, the sort of discipline which regulates not only office workers but also the liminal space between the classification of heterosexuality and homosexuality in American culture. To be on the inside provides a measure of security.

Clearly some connection is building here with the closet door and with the way this metaphor has worked to establish the relationship of knowledge or ignorance to sexuality since at least the end of the nineteenth century. The connection is the way that both the closed door of the office and the closet door work to produce the epistemological framework that is required so that knowledge can be circulated. What I mean by this is that the closed office door is a backdrop without which the information in front of it would be transparent. Just as the rhetoric of the closet creates the linguistic separation of space into private and public realms, and the subsequent invasion of that private space in order that homosexuality can be made public, exposed, and literally invented as a classification, so the closed office door for Slocum—as I showed in Heller's opening to the book—is the means by which all manner of important information is brought into the narrative: information about sex, status, sexuality, and masculinity. And the very fact that the closed office door utilizes an economy of fear, paranoia, and self-pity means that the information can be seen to be operating against the backdrop of the epistemological crisis of homosexual-heterosexual definition, so central to this crisis are these categories.

I also set this kind of representation in *Something Happened* and *Americana* against the background of the discourse of latency in postwar America and of the increasing visibility of sexual subcultures during the 1960s.[14] Edelman's notion of the marking and reading of the visible homosexual body needs to be sensitive enough to incorporate changes of this magnitude. If he is right and the "homosexual is *made* to bear the stigma of writing or textuality . . . *by* a masculinist culture" (my emphasis),[15] and if the result of this is the subsequent de-scription of heterosexual masculinity, then why would masculinist American culture permit and contribute towards the increasing visibility of homosexuality and homosexual culture—in, for example, Hollywood film noir[16]—from the 1950s on-wards? What I would argue is that an epistemological stand-off actually intensifies as sexual classification, and as the means by which classifica-tory groups are recognized, and solidifies during the course of the twen-tieth century, as both the visibility of non-straight cultures *and* the rep-resentation of non-straight cultures within straight cultures increases.[17]

As the physical or spatial boundaries between sexually identified groups are made more visible—by way of the emergence of gay sec-tions of large cities, by way of media representations (approving or dis-approving) of gay and lesbian subcultures, by way of self-representation by gay, lesbian, and bisexual writers, artists, or celebrities—so the episte-mological boundaries start to assume a greater importance in cultural representations. The increased visibility of sexual subcultures does not in itself and does not *necessarily* result in the problematizing of straight masculinity and sexuality, however. What the increased visibility does is firm up the signifiers of sexual classification—through a kind of cultural saturation that is concomitant with the rise of mass culture—leaving the signified of straight male sexuality (because of its fissured nature) at an increasing distance from its signifiers and thus opening up a greater philosophical gap between the taken-for-granted nature of straight male sexuality and the foundational underpinnings of that sexuality.

It is the attempt to fill this gap, and yet the impossibility of doing so, that one can see taking place in *Something Happened*, since it is once the straight male subject begins to turn towards this wider philosophical sta-tus of contemporary American culture—to the relationship between the individual and the corporation—that he is actually turning away from the security of a straight male subjectivity and towards the fissures that run through it. Especially when the novel in question is such a thorough-going and self-surveilling confessional. To observe the effects upon Bob Slocum, his "falling to pieces" in the wake of his relation with the Amer-ican business organization, is to observe the undermining of a sense of security that is actually represented in literary terms in the languages and discourses of a recursive and all-embracing fear and paranoia that can-not be dissociated from the fundamental epistemological construction of straight male sexuality.

It is within this context that self-pity becomes important too. For Sedgwick, writing in the late 1980s and early 1990s during a very specific cultural moment of "backlash" against feminism in America, self-pity takes its meaning in relation to sentimentalism and notions of authenticity. Sedgwick argues that from the end of the nineteenth century "the exemplary instance of the sentimental ceases to be a woman per se, but instead becomes the body of a man who . . . physically dramatizes . . . a struggle of masculine identity with emotions or physical stigmata stereotyped as feminine." Even more important for the purposes of this chapter, she argues that it is not the body of this man which is named as the site of sentimentality, but rather it is "the relations of figuration and perception that circulate around" the male body that work to "enact sentimentality as a trope."[18] For Sedgwick, twentieth-century Western culture is dominated by a Nietzschean notion of pity whereby the "predictable" and "inauthentic" tears of women and gay men are made to stand in poor relation to the revelatory tears of heterosexual men so valued in our culture.

I contend that once the changes in the visibility of non-straight subcultures occur after the Second World War, as the markers of classifications of straight and gay sexuality solidify in the American imagination, and as the epistemological fields that organize knowledge about sex and sexuality establish themselves as the primary sites for contestation of this knowledge, the importance of straight male self-pity takes on a crucial role for two reasons. First it works as a way of admitting failure in the attempt to fill the philosophical gap between the signifiers and the signified of American straight male sexuality. But second, while doing so, it works to refuse the reason for the gap—since such an acceptance would risk the normalization of non-straight male sexuality— by representing itself aesthetically, and being represented critically, as the attendant condition of American man when faced with the "systematic denaturing, by society, capitalism, the war organization, disfiguration, de-identification, dehumanization, and death" of the modern capitalist state.[19] The "relations of figuration and perception" of which Sedgwick writes, I take to be the fear and paranoia which so structure *Something Happened*, and which so structure the architecture of surveillance and self-surveillance which dominate Bob Slocum's working life.

Indeed, when Slocum tells the reader that "sorrow is my skin condition" (363) or when he admits—humiliated by not being able to make a speech at the company's annual conference—that "what I really wanted to do was burst into tears, and I was afraid I would" (36), the reader should bear in mind a couple of Slocum's other wandering thoughts. First this: "I am aware of still one more person who I am not even aware of; and this one watches everything shrewdly, even me, from some secure hideout in my mind in which he remains invisible and anonymous, and makes stern, censorious judgments, about everything, even me" (135). And then this after Slocum tells us he wishes he could cry more: "I hope desperately that my little boy never finds out I'm a fag if that is what I really am" (247). In the light of what I have argued above, it is this concatenation of self-pity, paranoia, surveillance, and homosexuality in the imagination of Slocum that seem to be the cause of his "falling to pieces."

Having mapped out the epistemological status of fear, paranoia, and self-pity in relation to the closed office door so vital to the generation of Slocum's narrative, I will next look at how this background can make sense of Slocum's life outside the office in which he is now working— both of his family life, particularly his relationship with his son, and of his masculinity which is tied into this relationship.

Relatively few of the 560 pages that make up *Something Happened* are set in Slocum's office. Far more of the novel is about his family life with his unnamed wife, his unnamed daughter, his unnamed son, and his disabled son Derek. Mostly the family relationships are antagonistic. Meals at the dinner table turn into petty arguments and power games—particularly between Slocum and his daughter—that disorient Slocum and put him under pressure as he feels "an army of irritations mobilizing too rapidly ... to keep track of and control. I am already replying to them with my slight stammer" (116). The bad temper that quickly affects Slocum on these occasions usually leads to him evacuating the dinner table for the sanctuary of his study where he can at least attempt to feel sorry for himself in private, where he can "sink back for safety again inside my dense, dark wave of opaque melancholy" (118).

Part of the problem for Slocum here is the difficulty of moving between the spaces of work and home. Although the demands are different in each of these environments, Slocum struggles to switch from the demand that he act a certain way at work to the demand that he act a certain other way at home. Instead of relating to his wife and daughter *as* his wife and daughter, he treats them in the same way that he treats his colleagues at work, that is competitively and with suspicion. Engaged in a battle with his daughter after she intrudes into his study, Slocum asks himself, "*Why* must I win this argument? ... Why must I show off for her and myself and exult in my fine logic and more expert command of language and details . . . ?" before he relaxes "complacently, with a momentary tingle of scorn for my inferior adversary" (200).

What Heller achieves through his portrayal of Slocum, however, is an opening up of the fragility of this quest for superiority, be it at work or at home with wife and children. The "slight stammer" which sometimes affects Slocum when he is drawn into these confrontations begins to assume a much broader significance in the light of his later comment that "I think I'm afraid I might start stuttering incurably when I even think that thought of being homosexual" (247). The issue of homosexuality is thematized by Slocum in his narrative, and given what I have written in the earlier sections of this chapter, this is hardly surprising. But it is thematized in the by now classic sense that it is seen to be connected to effeminacy. The stuttering that proceeds from the mere thought of homosexuality for Slocum is also the stuttering that affects him in his run-ins with Jack Green: "I do not trust myself to reply without stuttering disgracefully, effeminately, a sissy" (415). And for Slocum this linking of homosexuality, effeminacy, and stuttering are intimately tied into his sense of masculinity which is in turn tied in with his—not inconsiderable—heterosexual activity. As well as conducting a long-standing and very casual affair with Penny, Slocum visits prostitutes with Kagle during afternoons when he should be at work, and generally goes along with the company policy about getting laid: "It's okay" (65). On business trips Slocum feels "the country, the company, and society expect" him to get laid. Indeed getting laid is one of the factors that determines the site of the company's annual convention, and "the salesmen who succeed in getting laid there soonest are likely to turn out to be the social heroes of the convention" (66).

Within this company policy that getting laid is okay, however, there are certain rules that modify heterosexual conduct. Talking about getting laid is even better than getting laid itself, although talking about getting laid with your wife is improper etiquette; falling in love is not okay, although marrying someone right after a divorce is okay for men but not for women. And of course marriage is important here. According to Slocum, "unmarried men are not wanted in the Sales department" because "it is difficult and dangerous for unmarried salesmen to mix socially with prominent executives and their wives" (27). For David Bell in *Americana* there exists "no place in the world more sexually exciting than the large office. It is like a fantasy of some elaborate woman-maze."[20] The corporate environment, then, is one where compulsory heterosexuality is built into the whole ethos of business life. And yet what remains most fascinating about *Something Happened* is the way that despite all this getting laid, the one relationship that preoccupies Slocum is the one where he did not get laid, his relationship with Virginia.

Slocum is just seventeen when he first meets Virginia in the automobile accident insurance company. Working under the gaze of Mrs. Yerger, "a positive, large woman of overbearing confidence and nasty amiability," Virginia sits underneath the Western Union clock—whose "pointy minute hand" looks like "a long, phallic sword" (369)—and trades dirty jokes with Slocum (14). Although she tells Slocum to book a hotel room for them on several occasions, he never gets round to it, proffering the lame excuse that he does not know how. There is something that for Slocum is both desperately attractive and sensual about Virginia, and yet something too that prevents him from fulfilling the desire that he has for her and that she seems to have for him. Slocum and Virginia do much of their flirting in the insurance company storeroom where all the dead records are kept. "I enjoyed going there," Slocum says, because "descending the two staircases of that one floor to the musty storeroom was like escaping from scrutiny into some dark, cool, not unpleasant underworld, into the safe and soothing privacy of a deep cellar or dusty, wooden coal shed" (95). This dead record storeroom is both a retreat for Slocum when he is on own, somewhere he can read the newspaper and eat his lunch, as well as the crucible of the configuration of his masculinity. Whereas his friend Tom is taken by Marie Jencks down to the storeroom so that they can have sex, the storeroom is the place where Slocum fails to seduce Virginia. She will not have sex with him on the table that Tom and Marie use.

Taking the link with the dead records of "Bartleby" a little further, what is also relevant here is Slocum's stealing of Tom's handwriting. It is a handwriting that Tom practices meticulously during the working day "until he had achieved precisely the effect he thought he wanted" (78). Considering the link between textuality and sexuality discussed in the first chapter and considering that this modification of their handwriting is taking place when both Tom and Slocum are entering the world of office work and at the same time that they are entering the world of adult sexual relationships, it is not any coincidence that Slocum chooses to copy the handwriting of a "mature" young man slightly older than himself (by four years), especially when Tom is getting laid by Marie Jencks. Handwriting is the textual signifier that establishes Tom's heterosexual masculinity. If Slocum cannot get laid by Virginia Markowitz, then he can at least write like a man who is getting laid.

For it is around this issue of sexual maturity—that is, active masculine heterosexuality—that Slocum's relationship with Virginia revolves. At the very beginning of the novel, Slocum confesses to an early realization that he would not grow up with the broad shoulders necessary to turn him into "an All-American football player." It is precisely with images of these kinds of men that Virginia relives her past sexual history for Slocum. She tells him she was laid in a canoe by "the backfield star of the varsity football team" and engaged in group sex with several other football players during her time at Duke (86 and 475). It is against these kinds of men that Slocum is being measured—and falling short: "like flaked stains now in that dreary storeroom for dead records are my own used-up chances for attaining sexual maturity early, for getting laid young" (392). The "flaked stains" here key into a spermatic rhetoric that stretches back at least as far as Melville in American literature. But by landing on the dead records rather than being "spent" inside heterosexual union, Slocum's sperm is generated, it would seem, by masturbation. Gregory Woods has suggested that male masturbation, "since it involves a male hand on a penis . . . is, in a particular sense, already a homosexual act, even if the masturbator is fantasizing about women at the time."[21] Perhaps this is why Heller, rather than providing positive descriptions of masturbation as Melville does, sees masturbation here as waste. It is the homosexual act of masturbation that is "using up"—depleting it as if it were a finite resource—his masculinity and his heterosexuality.

The sense of regret here is compounded when Slocum turns this situation against Virginia and women like her. In a demonizing move, he represents Virginia's forwardness about sex as a means of making him "passive" (475). "I never got what I wanted," he argues, "[s]he did not like me to do things to her; she liked to do things to me" (85). Quite simply—and maybe this attitude stems from his relationship with Virginia —Slocum does not like women "who are that decisive and commanding . . . Those assertive bitches . . . No wonder so many of our virile young men have trouble getting it up nowadays" (366). Ultimately, however, it is for threatening the tenets of a masculinity that has to be fought hard for that Virginia is condemned. Although Slocum says that he misses her, that he loves her, and that he wants her back so that he can have another chance (86), it seems that the chance he wants has nothing to do with Virginia but with satisfying that need for early sexual maturity that would have cemented his heterosexual masculine identity early and saved him the chore of having to make up for it with all those other women he sleeps with the rest of his adult life. Virginia so preoccupies

Slocum because she is the ultimate excuse, the ultimate if-only. Dead now, she is the site upon which Slocum can work through the fissured construction of his masculine sexuality. The fact that she is tied so closely to the office world that will be his future, to that Western Union clock under which she sits and which will regulate the passing of each of his working days at "one damned sterile office desk after another" (362), makes it only fitting, somehow, that he remember her in relation to a rhetoric of fear and threat: when she raises the possibility of sex with him, Slocum says that

> I'd feel dehumanized and castrated; things would feel gone. There'd be a thumping blow in my chest, and my heart would stop. I would feel ill . . . I would long to sneak out of sight for a while, in order to creep back later and begin all over again with her from a distant and more secure footing . . . I would lose my urge, go numb; I would have a lump in my throat instead of my pants. I lost my cock and balls; they'd go away. (367)

It is this parity, then, between the epistemological architecture of male sexuality in the office and the way in which sexual relationships are played out and remembered that make *Something Happened* most striking. Slocum's reaction, as it demonizes the female in this process, also constructs a double discourse which veers away from the explicit treatment of his masculinity. It is a discourse of self-pity that incorporates a discourse about childishness and about the child in the adult.

Slocum declares that his mind "is a storehouse of pain, a vast, invisible reservoir of sorrows as deep as I am old" (535). Closely associated with this is the melancholy of work for Slocum, the way that between each career challenge successfully overcome there is "a large, emotional letdown . . . a kind of empty, tragic disappointment" (33), and also the fact that Slocum feels he no longer counts in the world. He feels he can no longer change his environment and that any disturbance he could cause would quickly be set right, leaving him to be filed away (19). In many ways the novel signals this to be a response to the world of the multinational corporation and big government. Slocum tortures himself "with the ominous speculation that the CIA, FBI, or Internal Revenue Service has been investigating me surreptitiously for years" (15) and is never convinced that his "illegal thoughts and dreams are not apparent to the authorities in the company" (428).

But if Virginia infantilizes Slocum by castrating him and making him lose his "urge," the state of infantilization is one which Slocum welcomes. He says that he wants to be treated like a baby because he wants the "feeling of security" (457–58) that comes with it. Slocum wants to be able to cry, to return to that childhood state that is free from the pressures of institutionalization, of work, of women like Virginia, of the need to fulfill masculine responsibilities—all of the things that Slocum constructs as the onerous tasks of being a man. How much better it would be to retreat to childhood, especially when he can argue that inside every man and woman "is the fully formed, but uncompleted, little boy or girl that once was and will always remain as it always has been, suspended lonesomely inside its own past . . . And hiding inside of me somewhere . . . is a timid little boy" (231). It seems that Slocum is displacing the crisis of masculine definition here onto the transition between childhood and adulthood. This is important in the novel because of the relationship he has with his own son who is struggling to make this transition and who in fact never has an opportunity to do so because his father murders him.

It has been noted by others that Slocum's son acts as his father's double, and Lois Tyson has claimed that Slocum's son is in many ways an uncommodified version of his father and that his murder resolves Slocum's commitment to commodification.[22] I want to take a slightly different approach—while still maintaining a focus on the sense of connection between Slocum and his son—by thinking about how the son provides a lens for observing the nature of his father's masculinity.

Slocum's son, nine years old and "not yet able to deal like an adult with certain kinds of opposition and frustrations" (220), is having difficulties at school. He hates gym and in particular the gym teacher Forgione to whom Slocum goes to speak. This is a key section of the book because of the way that it links several themes that are key to any understanding of American masculinity. Forgione complains to Slocum that his son "doesn't have a good competitive spirit" and that he "lacks a true will to win"—characteristics that everybody should have, he argues (218). Ahead in relay races, Slocum's son has taken to slowing down and letting the others catch up with him; in basketball games he deliberately throws the ball to the opposition. Slocum takes a dislike to Forgione, not least because he is "a dreadful, powerful, broad-shouldered man who is hairy, hard-muscled, and barrel-chested" who "could do whatever he wanted to you. He could do whatever he wanted to me" (238). In a way then, Slocum is coming face to face with the representation of his failure with Virginia, and it is perhaps not surprising that he starts to admire his son for the way that he is not aggressive, competitive, or outstanding (244), since to side with Forgione would mean not only siding with that of which he himself is jealous—the same way he is jealous of the broad-shouldered members of the football team who have sex with Virginia in front of one another (475)—and which would de-script his own incomplete masculinity, but also siding with him against his son. And yet, away from Forgione, Slocum identifies a wider problem with his son and almost inevitably the characteristics that Forgione relates to him get folded from masculinity into sexuality: "My wife does not want my little boy to grow up to be a fag and worries sneakily that he will. I know she does, because I worry often about the same thing . . . I don't want my boy to be a fag" (220). The use of the word "sneakily" here hints at the way this issue is never discussed by Slocum and his wife, yet this withholding of thoughts, endemic in Slocum's life (246), does not prevent him from calling his son a sissy on several occasions (258).

So Slocum's son's difficulties fit easily into a continuum where effeminacy and a lack of those markers of masculinity lead to homosexuality in American thinking. And they are, of course, the same markers that Slocum identifies in himself and which coalesce to make him stutter "disgracefully, effeminately." It is surprising just how much the issue of homosexuality concerns Slocum. He carries with him a "distant childhood fear of homosexual rape" (404); he is conscious on business trips that he has trouble mixing with men in strange cities because the men who start conversations "appear homosexual and drive" him off (429); on these trips he often sleeps with female prostitutes, but when he returns to his hotel room, he has "what might have been the start of a homosexual dream" which he has to stop and switch to a different dream (433); he is convinced that Arthur Baron's secretary is unhappily married because her husband is "perhaps homosexual" (437).

Most telling of all though is Slocum's confessed habit of taking on other people's characteristics. Kagle has a limp, and when Slocum spends any time with him, he starts limping too, and so, he reasons, "I am not comfortable in the presence of homosexuals, and I suspect it may be for the same reason (I might be tempted to become like them)" (73). This potential slippage of his heterosexual identity—and it is slippage at the level of signification, since he fears he might become "like" them rather one *of* them—merely by way of physical proximity, is one of the results of living in a culture where the fear of latency is felt so strongly. It is testament to the way that Slocum is continually living in the presence of a crisis of sexual identity that here represents itself as a kind of comic paranoia. But if this is the condition in which he lives, then his son lives in even closer proximity to it.

For all the protective feelings that Slocum has for his son, he cannot help but "abuse" him. Slocum argues that in wanting to protect him too much, to keep him immune to abuse and defeat from outside the family, it is he who ends up abusing and defeating him: "I could never bear to see him unhappy . . . so I made him unhappier still," he says (285). There are occasions when Slocum is disappointed that his son refuses to fight back, including a time at the beach when his son goes missing and Slocum wants to kill him, so ashamed, enraged, and disgusted is he by his son's "helplessness and incompetence" (336). Slocum wants to disown him. And then, in a prophetic playing out of the murder that will follow, he wants to "clasp him to me lovingly and protectively and shed tears of misery and deepest compassion over him" (336). Yet this deficit of tears and compassion stems directly from the relation these emotions have to the chain of signification that links effeminacy and homosexuality. Slocum, fearful of the stability of his own heterosexual masculine identity, observes much of this in his son's development through childhood and finds himself in a double bind: he wants to love his son, shed tears on him, and display how much he loves him; yet to do this would require that he position himself too closely to those characteristics of which he is fearful and which he sees his son displaying, thus reinforcing the feeling that he might be a "fag" after all, the very thing he hopes "desperately that [his] little boy never find out" (247). One cannot, after all, in American culture be masculine yet also a child at the same time. In this situation Slocum's son becomes the site of Slocum's self-pity because of the way that this double bind works: the narrative represents his inability to love his son properly as a more general inability to feel in the realms of entropic capitalist bureaucracy—and critics have been eager to ratify this stance—or to be able to display his feelings because of the pressures that being masculine brings with it in this world; yet the narrative is seemingly unaware of the way this kind of discourse actually makes women and gay men the "main targets of its scapegoating projections—viciously sentimental attributions of a vitiated sentimentality" as Sedgwick argues.[23]

June Howard, in an essay which tries to alter the terrain of critical approaches to sentimentality, has argued that while in the past the suffering woman and the sentimental man have been the focus for representations of this phenomenon, the contemporary equivalent is the figure of the endangered child.[24] I would argue, however, that it is with the intention of recuperating male self-pity that Heller's narrative treats Slocum's son as an endangered child. Slocum sees his son endangered by a world that will not allow him to cope—all teenage boys "will fail. They've failed already. I don't think they were given a fair chance" (389)—and by the world in which he will have to work amongst other men. His solution, or at least his response, is to prevent his son from suffering in the world that has so made him suffer. In Slocum's confused confession, murder stands as a way of protecting his son while allowing him to gain plaudits for his coping with the death. "Everybody is impressed with how bravely I've been able to move into Kagle's position," he says (565), and yet they do not know the truth, of course, the truth that Slocum has murdered his son at the one moment when he needed his father's love the most and when his father was incapable of dispensing compassion in anything but an inappropriate way. It is not surprising that Slocum can now put his affairs in order: the son that tormented him with clever questions and answers[25] and his strange behavior is dead, and his other son will remain in a wheelchair for the rest of his life. All that are left are his wife and daughter, whose opposition can be dealt with easily enough since such antagonism can be folded into the gender divide.

Like "Bartleby," then, *Something Happened* is a text that establishes a connection between office work and death. Even if the death of Slocum's son seems to occur unexpectedly in the narrative, it has clearly been prepared for well in advance: the ending is the culmination of a series of events that locate in the figure of Bob Slocum a particular attitude towards the crisis of male definition in the early 1970s. The link between his son's death and Slocum's sense of a self that is "falling to pieces" is signalled clearly enough by the nature of the death. It results from a car going out of control and mounting the sidewalk. From here it is but a short side step to the automobile accident insurance office where Slocum starts his working career and where he is introduced to the architecture of surveillance and self-surveillance—the gaze of Mrs. Yerger and the hideaway that is the storeroom—and to the world of adult sexuality that requires him to establish the evidence of his sexual maturity with Virginia. That he fails to establish this evidence to himself—and presumably to others when the systemic surveillance of postwar American culture is so much a part of the popular imagination—leads him into the confused and knotted logic of a masculine heterosexuality that displaces its own insecurity into the paranoia and fear that have, historically, marked the relationship between heterosexuality and homosexuality and which are now encapsulated in Slocum's fascination with closed office doors and the terrain that opens up when these doors enter his confession: the terrain of sex, status, and masculinity.

If there is any doubt as to the importance of this sense of heterosexualized masculinity to the state of Slocum's mind, then I think he should be allowed to speak this importance for himself. Imagining what it would do to him if his wife were to have an affair, Slocum comes up with this:

> I wonder what I *would* feel like if my wife ever did come home smelling of another man's semen. I think I would die a sudden, shriveling death inside. . . . It would fill me with saddest resignation and lifelong disgust. Judgment will have been rendered against me by her and someone else behind another closed door I did not know was even there, and the judgment will be irreversible. (440–41)

It is the thought that the institution of marriage and family which so defines Slocum's masculinity publicly should be contaminated by another man's semen which is too much for him to bear. And it is no coincidence that it is the *smell* of semen that he concentrates on. For Slocum, it is disaster that he can almost smell "mounting invisibly and *flooding* out toward me through the frosted glass panes" (3, my emphasis). To smell semen, to be so close to another man's semen, is for Slocum to smell disaster, to smell the irreversible judgment on his own masculinity that relies on keeping as far away as possible from another man's semen.

Against the background of the increasing visibility of same-sex loving subcultures, and still living with the legacy of a rhetoric of latency, Slocum's narrative works towards an escape valve of self-pity that for heterosexual masculinity in America lays witness to its failures and contradictions while ensuring that it is never *identified* as a cultural and political issue or even a sexual issue. Instead the crisis of male definition, both in the novel and in much critical attention towards *Something Happened*, is represented as a general cultural crisis so that Slocum has been seen to represent "an irresponsible, self-destructive society that itself has lost its identity and ideological bearings," and it is "the loss of history itself . . . that has happened and given Slocum the willies."[26]

Yet were this the case, then the anxiety of Slocum and his wife over their son's sexual development, Slocum's preoccupation with his sexual failure with Virginia, and his nagging failure to eradicate the specter of homosexuality from his thoughts and at times from the very way that he talks, would have to stand in for a less historicized anxiety in which sexuality was only a symptom. The whole emphasis of this book, and the value of the work of Foucault, Sedgwick, Dollimore, and Edelman, is that sexuality—and particularly this crisis of male definition—is a driving force in the very nature of this anxiety. Eve Sedgwick reminds us that it was only in 1973—a year before the publication of *Something Happened*—that the American Psychiatric Association decided to withdraw the pathologizing diagnosis of homosexuality from its Diagnostic and Statistical manual, and the revised version was not published until 1980.[27] Yet welcome as this move was, what replaced homosexuality in the psychiatric manual was a category called "Gender Identity Disorder of Childhood" and a revisionist analysis that could accept gay men as long as they exhibited an acceptable maturity and masculinity.[28] These two qualities stand at the heart of *Something Happened*, and the failure of Slocum's son to display either of them provokes a discomfort in Slocum that suggests, as in "Bartleby," that the narrator is having to deal with something he recognizes to be in close proximity to himself but which he wants to be rid of. That both texts end in death is witness to the violence that the crisis of male definition may cause.

In *Something Happened* Slocum has developed the ability in the corporate community to read the signifiers of masculinity in the men with whom he works every day. So much so that this amounts almost to a skill. It is this skill, and the longevity of his association with the corporate world, that has left him saturated with the epistemological logic of surveillance and self-surveillance, fear and paranoia, which are then turned against his son because he may turn out bad. The self-pity offered almost in justification—Slocum's "falling to pieces"—should not distract us from the fact that the death of Slocum's son is not a symptom of some wider problem, but rather the very means by which Slocum secures the sense of equilibrium that enables him to move forward in his career, since such skills as he possesses are so important in the world of management problem-solving.

Part Three

A Word for Windows

Chapter Seven

"My own plein-air Arnality bared to the sky"

Shoelaces, Social Energy, and
Sexuality in Nicholson Baker's
The Mezzanine and *The Fermata*

Although published within twenty years of Joseph Heller's *Something Happened*, the two works of Nicholson Baker that are the subject of this chapter—*The Mezzanine* (1988) and *The Fermata* (1994)—witness a clear shift in the mode of self-representation of white-collar straight male sexuality. Gone from the first-person narratives of Howie and Arno Strine are the tangible antagonism towards the postwar corporation that so marked Tom Rath's career decisions in *The Man in the Gray Flannel Suit*; gone too are the discourses of fear, paranoia, and self-pity that beset Bob Slocum in his dealings with a company where everybody is afraid of somebody else in the company. In their place Baker provides two narrators who, on the face of it at least, shy away from the broader problems associated with the status of the monolithic American corporation and with the traumatic impact the corporation has on the lives of straight men and their families. Instead Howie and Arno concentrate, respectively, on the trivia of technology and consumer products remembered fondly during the course of a post-lunch escalator ride and on the masturbatory and optical pleasures to be had when one is able to put the world on hold and then wander through it.

This is not to say that the legacy of Wilson and Heller is absent in fiction about office work in this later period. Indeed it may be that this mode of fiction retains its preeminent position. Brett Easton Ellis's movie *American Psycho* and Jay McInerney's *Bright Lights, Big City* and *Brightness Falls*, for example, while attending to the paradoxes and detail of the changing cultural and working landscape of New York in the 1980s, envisage this landscape as one that generates a sense of loss, trauma, and dehumanization. Elsewhere the preponderance in Blank Fiction of feelings of "disaffection, decadence and brutality,"[1] ensured its preeminence because of the way that it so readily fitted into that discourse about the effect of the economic on the individual, which was discussed at the beginning of the previous chapter. It is the fact that Baker deviates from this traditional discourse that makes his work the more interesting in the context of this study. Rather than just a different literary sensibility, however, the changes in narrative dominant that can be located in Baker's texts need to be understood as altered modes of self-representation in a very different world of white-collar work.

The world of office work that had developed in the postwar period was under threat during the 1970s and 80s. Established businesses and corporations that inherited the paradigm of the Organization Man culture of the 1950s and 60s began to leave it behind as wholesale changes in management structure and management methods took place during this period. In management circles this series of changes has recently been characterized as a shift from the culture of the Organization Man to the culture of the Individualized Corporation,[2] where the proper role of management is no longer to treat employees as "replaceable parts in an efficient production process"—a model developed during management's scientific phase from the end of the nineteenth century through to the 1970s—but instead "to build an organization flexible enough to exploit the idiosyncratic knowledge and unique skills of each individual employee."[3] Regardless of the value of these kinds of management ideologies, it is worth remembering that it was the sheer cultural pervasiveness of changes driven by this kind of rhetoric, and of the changes that lay behind buzzwords like Reaganomics, monetarism, total quality management, and downsizing, that turned management gurus like Tom Peters into media celebrities,[4] created the New York yuppie phenomenon explored by Ellis and McInerney, and altered the culture and the experience of work for many, if not all, white-collar workers in the United

States during the 1980s and 90s. In the next chapter, I discuss the ways in which traditional business and management orthodoxies were challenged in the nascent microcomputer industry and how within this industry different attitudes towards work, and work's relationship to leisure, developed. But in more established and traditional organizational domains, the nature of office work was changing too, and through my reading of Baker's work I suggest that it was being realigned within a changing cultural milieu that, as it emphasized the importance of image, style, surface, consumption, and lifestyle, embarrassed to a new degree the seemingly always threatened distinctions of work and leisure, workplace and home, those public and private arenas inside which most working people have to segregate their time, and arenas that directly reflect the constitution of male sexuality.

Although the relationship between this changing cultural organization and the concomitant shifts in capitalism has been well documented and classified as typical of a more general shift into an era of late capitalist postmodernity, it is surprising just how little attention those writing about late capitalism pay to business and to work,[5] to those localities of experience that offer the chance to examine with greater legibility the relationship of groups of individuals to wider social, economic, and cultural movements. It is with this in mind that I approach the work of Nicholson Baker, for while there seems to be a shying away from the bigger picture of what capitalism in its rampantly aggressive consumer phase does to people, there also seems to be a corresponding alertness to the formalities of work and office culture and how they fit into these more abstract changes. While Ellis and McInerney take their position in the central tower in order to administer a panoptic vision of American capitalism that accepts too unquestioningly the Wilson-Heller discourse, Baker offers us confessions from the communion booth of contemporary work and consumption.

Baker's alertness to the concatenation of individual experience at work and in the social world is illustrated quite early in his first novel. When one of his shoelaces comes undone during the course of his working morning, Howie, the narrator of *The Mezzanine*, decides not to retie it. Instead he lets his foot slip "out of the sauna of black cordovan to soothe itself with rhythmic movements over an area of wall-to-wall carpeting" under his desk.[6] He replaces his shoe only when he is ready to go for lunch. But as he leans forward and bends down over his desk to tie the lace, his work colleagues—who are also leaving for lunch—spot him and wave to him through his open office door. His hands occupied, Howie has to reply by shouting back, "Have a good one guys!" At precisely this moment the shoelace snaps. Howie explains it as follows: "I had probably broken the shoelace by transferring the social energy I had to muster in order to deliver a chummy 'Have a good one!' to them from my awkward shoe-tier's crouch into the force I used in pulling up on the shoelace" (13).

Trivial as this moment appears to be, and for reasons that are not immediately apparent, it still produces something that Howie chooses to describe as "social energy." What I want to work towards understanding in the first part of this chapter is both the nature of this "social energy" produced at such a comic, almost farcical, moment of office experience and how and why it gets transferred in the office environment. Using a critical method which operates at some level of equivalence with Baker's stylistic obsession—in this novel and his other writing—with detail and trivia[7] and his capacity to build volume and weight from the most minor incident, this moment is in fact far from insignificant; what the snapping shoelace actually captures and condenses is an enormous amount of information about the way that contemporary office life is still organized through the mutually dependent discursive regimes of surveillance and self-surveillance and of public and private. *The Mezzanine*, in the way that it deals with questions of contemporary corporate space and corporate boundaries, however, confirms how these categorizations of public and private form what Eve Sedgwick has called an "incoherent register."[8] Moving on from this in the second half of the chapter I discuss the ways in which *The Fermata* carries the project of *The Mezzanine* further and in its juxtaposition of temporal hiatus and visual acuity fashions a literary space for straight male sexuality that can be seen to lead away from that legacy of dynamic masculinity so prevalent in American culture.

One of the things that links the work of Karl Marx, Max Weber, and Michel Foucault on capitalism and surveillance is the understanding that what happens in the workplace—the institutionalizing of hierarchies of order, power, and control—is not confined to the workplace.[9] The workplace becomes, in fact, a site for the operation of discursive practices that are the same—although they might not operate in the same way—as those practices operating outside the workplace boundary. Indeed, it is well known that so concerned were early industrialists with having the discipline of the workplace carry over to the nonwork time of their employees that they were often not content with building factories. Many also built whole towns around their factories that reproduced architecturally and socially the hierarchy of order inside the factory. In the early nineteenth century at Lowell, Massachusetts, for example, the Merrimack Manufacturing Company organized their mill settlement so that, while all their workers lived next to the mill, they were carefully divided between houses for skilled workers and their families and boarding houses for the mill girls who lived under the supervision of a matron. A foreman's house was located in each block of housing to ensure that supervision of workers was constant. Pullman, Illinois, built in the 1880s, became the largest company town in the United States, with 12,600 inhabitants, and was perhaps the clearest example of this type of early paternalistic, "naïve," and strictly regulatory capitalist regime. Not content with the same kind of strategic housing provision like that provided in Merrimack to keep employees within sight of their work superiors, George Pullman went so far as to select the plays that could be performed in the town theatre, to charge excessive membership rates to keep workers from joining the town library, and to ensure that alcohol could only be purchased—again at a high price—in the town hotel.[10]

While all this may seem a long way from the American corporate office that forms the setting for Nicholson Baker's *The Mezzanine* and *The Fermata*—and historically and technologically it clearly is—the conceptual legacies of these early stages of capitalist development have remained in place to ensure that the separation of workplace and non-workplace remains something of a myth. It is worth remembering, too, how the conditions of surveillance become inscribed *into* each subject. For Foucault one "who is subjected to a field of visibility, and who knows it, assumes responsibility for the constraints of power. He inscribes in himself the power relation in which he simultaneously plays both roles; he becomes the principle of his own subjection."[11] Clearly this inscription allows these workplace effects to persist beyond the confines of the office building.

But there are two other important ways in which this process works in the contemporary setting. First there are the altered methods of surveillance. The modern corporate office has become the sort of sophisticated surveilling machine that early industrialists could never have imagined. Architecturally this process has a long history, as demonstrated by the importance of glass, doors, and the allocation of space in all the texts discussed so far. Added to this environment in the last two decades, as well as a fashion for hard surfaces such as chrome and steel to help consolidate a code of visibility and reflection, is the cubicle culture of open-plan workspaces and the more intense monitoring of employee performance brought about in the wake of the rise of human resource management. Whether it is through direct supervision, career appraisal interviews and assessments, or empowerment strategies, one of the consequences of the shift from the Organization Man to the Individualized Corporation is that the organization now keeps track of its employees within a rhetoric that suggests it is for their own good, to help them achieve their goals, to make them better trained, to let them show their initiative. Reminiscent of Foucault's argument that power is positive in the modern era, this kind of monitoring is subtler and far removed from the psychological testing that was carried out by organizations in the 1950s and 60s. But it also goes hand in hand with a more invisible and invasive surveillance that now includes computer keystroke counting, the reading of electronic mail messages and web browsing patterns, and the study of itemized telephone bills.[12]

On the one hand, then, corporate America has developed increasingly more elaborate methods, technologies, and machineries for surveilling and organizing workers, and at the same time it has made sure that workers continually surveil and organize themselves as individuals upon which, and through which, these technologies can operate. As part of the more longstanding Puritan attitudes towards work, it is this development that can be seen to be responsible for the process whereby work and the work ethic—and since the Second World War for an ever increasing number of people work has meant office work—have, according to Catherine Casey, "set in place a type of citizen-worker that would subsequently come to typify modern citizenship and undergird modern forms of social organization."[13] Increasingly people have become defined by the type of work they do, by the way that they do it, and by the way that they perform or display themselves through work;[14] for many people—and certainly for white middle-class men—work and occupation have become the primary elements in social organization.

For Casey this development means that contemporary American corporate institutions no longer need to consolidate hierarchies by means of housing provision; instead the process is achieved through what she has called the "corporate colonization of the self."[15] The aim of this process is to produce individuals whose values and attitudes match those promoted by the organization. This process may not be entirely new, but it is the prevalence and the intensification of it during the last two decades, as well as the number of people that it now affects, that are important. Corporate branding applies not just to products but to employ-ees as well, to their very sense of who they are. They become in many ways themselves products of the corporation and constant advertise-ments for it. As Casey discovered when researching life in one large Amer-ican corporation, not "only does the company's marketing material extol the quality of [its] smart machines, it extols the quality of its employees: their knowledge, skills and dedication to excellence are commodified and marketed."[16]

One can begin to see here the links between changes in organization and management culture and the wider cultural changes that mark the transition into a period of intense consumer capitalism. The importance of the image and of the circulation of images in this transition is now well established,[17] and if one of the effects of living in a culture where "the idea that everything *could* be on film" leads one to "see and behave as though everything *were* on film,"[18] then the work of surveillance in the office and elsewhere can be seen to contribute to this production and circulation of images. This is the second way in which the contemporary workplace boundary is problematized.

Surveillance and self-surveillance are modes that perpetuate the im-portance of and the production of images in a postmodern era. Since in the office the surveilling gaze is constant, due to its very architectural na-ture, one could represent this constancy as generating a series of images of oneself that are being stored—for whatever purpose—in a filmic process. In a sense, then, one is not being watched so much in the con-temporary office as being filmed, being turned into an image that can be commodified and used in the company marketing material. This process could be seen as one of the ways in which panoptic structures instituted in traditional Foucauldian locations—prisons, hospitals, factories, and schools—in the eighteenth and nineteenth centuries adapt or mutate as these locations change shape and as other economic or cultural factors —such as the transition to consumer capitalism—change as well. Thus if the image becomes the site for surveillance processes, it is possible to tie surveillance into those capitalist shifts that create the image as the primary medium of exchange in postmodern economic culture.

As far as the consequences for notions of public and private are con-cerned, it is worth pointing out that in many ways the methods of Fou-cauldian pure surveillance used in the workplace are far more intense than methods used outside the workplace; people, it would seem, are on the whole more willing to accept these technologies of surveillance in-side the office than they would be to accept them elsewhere.[19] It is here that one comes up against the awkward question of where work fits into the schema of the binary proposed by a discourse distinguishing between public and private space. Despite the fact that one is employed, paid, and appraised as an individual, work is often constructed in American culture, and certainly within organizational culture, as a public arena where one subsumes private interests, in return for money, to become part of the "family" or "team," part of the "organization."

Casey actually argues that in an era when traditional occupational and professional boundaries are breaking down, one's relationship "to a product, to team-family members and to the company . . . displaces identification with occupation and its historic repository of skills, knowledges and allegiances."[20] This new allegiance may no longer be made apparent through the singing of corporate anthems, as in the old days of IBM— or indeed in satires of the corporate world of the 1960s such as Thomas Pynchon's Yoyodyne[21]—but is institutionalized instead in other ways, like incentive bonuses or company shareholding schemes; participation in collective activities such as office softball teams, parties, and outings; or through the overwhelming rhetoric of loyalty and belonging. In contrast to this pervasive discourse of display in the public arena of work, capitalist culture then provides—rhetorically at least—nonwork leisure time, private time and space most closely associated with the home or with freedom which is meant to be situated outside the workplace.[22]

The paradox of this seemingly straightforward situation becomes clear, however, when one considers that a worker passes more than labor over to an employer in the arena of the workplace. While the legal system upon which capitalism relies upholds the idea of the boundary of the workplace and the idea of the workplace as a public site—by defining one's rights inside it as different (that is, fewer) than those outside it—capitalist practices inside the workplace are permanently eroding and destroying the boundary of public (work) and private (nonwork) by producing citizen-workers, disciplined subjects, and work as an extension of image-driven consumer culture. As early industrialists were aware, the workplace and the non-workplace, although they may be geographically separate, are in fact made inseparable by the operation of disciplinary power.

In Nicholson Baker's *The Mezzanine*, while it is the mutually dependent discursive regimes of surveillance and self-surveillance in the office and the associated discourses of public and private that help forge both the narrator and the narrative structure of the novel, the narration is also constructed in such a way as to embarrass and problematize the apparently straightforward distinction between public (work) and private (nonwork) time and space. And by way of this problematization, the reader is drawn almost silently into the world of male sexuality, so intensely is this subject bound up with these same discursive regimes.

An important feature of *The Mezzanine* is the way that the surveilling regime under which Howie works in his office is not dealt with as a theme in the narrative. It certainly does not exist as a problem against which Howie is battling. It exists instead at a secondary level which Howie signals almost accidentally; it is the novel's subconscious and part of Howie's cognitive regime. Take the first sentence of the novel: "At almost one o'clock I entered the lobby of the building where I worked and turned toward the escalators, carrying a black Penguin paperback and small white CVS bag, its receipt stapled over the top" (3). *Almost* one o'clock is the give-away here. Not *at* one o'clock, not *just after* one o'clock, but at *almost* one o'clock. Howie has presumably left himself just enough time to ride the escalator back to his office so that he can start work on time, having taken his allotted hour. Later, Howie recalls observing one of the secretaries advancing the date on her date stamper "(through the glass wall of my office)" (32), an incident which signifies perfectly but accidentally the visual regime of the office environment, the way that one's work colleagues are constantly in view. Before he leaves for his lunch break, Howie has to announce his absence from the office by using the sign-out board (28). Not only does this enable his fellow workers and his managers to know his whereabouts, it also carries with it a logic of self-monitoring. Should Howie forget to display his absence, then presumably the possibility of censure will stop him from forgetting the next time. There are many such examples that work to place surveillance and disciplinary power at the level of the taken-for-granted in the novel.

The links by which Howie's life is tied to this capitalist heritage of work are, again, not always thematized explicitly in the narrative but appear at key moments of observation, where Howie looks at and sees and describes objects and actions whose importance goes beyond the sum of their parts. The escalator journey and the centrality of this piece of technology to the novel marks out a discourse of circularity, repetition, and regularity upon which capitalism and the regime of disciplinary surveillance are themselves based and which can rotate along any axis, horizontal or vertical: "the black rubber handrails which wavered slightly as the handrails slid on their tracks, like the radians of black luster that ride the undulating outer edge of an LP" (3). This simile clearly more than hints at the grooved regulation of capitalist life, a discourse into which routines, timetables, and time allocation would all fit. Howie's first office act each morning is to turn ahead his Page-A-Day calendar. This is the way that his life is "ratcheted forward" (33). The novel even ends with an acknowledgment of the consumption of circularity:

> At the very end of the ride, I caught sight of a cigarette butt rolling and hopping against the comb plate where the grooves disappeared. I stepped onto the mezzanine and turned to watch it for a few seconds. Its movement was a faster version of the rotation of mayonnaise or peanut butter or olive jars, or cans of orange juice or soup, when they are caught at the end of supermarket conveyor belts, their labels circling around and around—Hellman's! Hellman's! Hellman's!—something I had loved to see when I was little. (135)

In addition, Howie monitors every aspect of his life. He draws up tables and lists—of the eight major advances in his life (16), of the number of times certain thoughts occur to him during the year (128)—and he disaggregates his thoughts—about the "incredulousness and resignation" caused by the disruption of physical routines (13–14), about why it was a good thing brain cells died (23–24), about the images that occur to him as a result of seeing a magazine display (104)—into memo points (*a*), (*b*), (*c*), and (*d*) or (1), (2), (3), and (4). That none of these examples are directly about Howie's office duties or office life is the most telling thing about them. What they witness is an urge to dissect his life that only makes sense in the light of the scopic regimes of surveillance and self-surveillance. In many ways the formal organization of the novel anticipates the surveilling gaze of the workplace, whose priorities and rules it understands, by presenting itself with everything in place, everything as it should be. Like a well-ordered office worker Howie's narration is a model of efficiency and scheduling. Vital information is filed away in footnotes to the text, and the descriptive writing possesses a level of clinical and spatial organization which can only be the result of an exceptionally penetrative and patient gaze, one for which each action and detail must be made separable so that it can be allocated a description and a position.[23] Take this example, where Howie is putting on his shirt, as one of literally dozens that appear throughout the text:

I began buttoning at the second button down from the top, braving the minor pain in my thumb-tip as I pushed that button through and heard the minuscule creaking or winching sound that its edge made in clearing the densely stitched perimeter. From here I progressed right down the central strip of buttons, did up my pants, and moved onto the cuffs. These two cuff buttons were the hardest, because you could only use one hand, and because the starch was always heavier there than elsewhere; but I had gotten so that I could fasten them almost without thinking: you upended the right cuff button with your thumb-nail and cracked the starch-fused buttonhole apart over it, closing your fingers hypodermically to propel it into place; then you repeated the procedure with the other cuff. Sped up, the two symmetrical cuff-buttoning sequences would have looked like a Highland reel. (51)

The echoes of Taylorism and time and motion observations—where each action is broken down into its component parts—reverberate through this and many other of Baker's descriptions. Rather than the thematic referentiality of the novel, it is the formal referentiality[24] and the formal equivalence to the discursive regimes of surveillance and self-surveillance in the office workplace that allows the novel, even when it is evacuated of incidents in some simplistic way "about" or "connected" to the office, to be so acutely saturated by the office. What Baker does in *The Mezzanine* is turn the discursive regimes of the workplace into form.

There are also moments for Howie, though, when the surveillance of the office and his own self-surveillance intersect uncomfortably, and the snapping of his shoelace is perhaps the clearest example. In a surveilled environment, appearance is clearly very important. Here I mean appearance to be both the way one looks (hence Howie's meticulous attention to his shirt) and at the same time the way one interacts socially. One real-life business manager has said that "any man who is careless about his appearance and his dress is thoughtless to others and . . . lacking in one of the managerial attributes."[25] Howie clearly understands this. He knows he has to return his work colleagues' wave in some form when they walk past him, because office etiquette demands it of him. But Howie also knows that self-surveillance in the office should not make itself known. If it does, then what it displays is not how disciplined a subject is, but how *un*disciplined to have to make such adjustments. And it is here that conceptions of public and private begin to interfere with disciplinary surveillance.

One of Howie's strengths as a narrator is the way that he constantly offends—however consciously—the notion of a public/private binary. Many of the things the reader learns about Howie's life are as a result of a narrative methodology that works by opportune digression. The time sequencing of the novel actually takes the reader forward as well as backwards from the escalator journey, a maneuver that highlights the way in which any point in a cycle is both endlessly regressing away from oneself and endlessly progressing towards oneself. Howie narrates, retrospectively, one lunchtime escalator journey and yet has circulating around him all the events both before and after this one journey up until the point of narration. In many ways *The Mezzanine* is a rite-of-passage novel, the story of how a child becomes, or is supposed to become an adult, how one is made into an individual from a blank sheet, and how one moves from a confined world to a wider world. But Howie builds this personal and private life in the context of his relation to the public, very often mass-produced, corporate, multinational objects such as shoelaces, drinking straws, staplers, and doorknobs, which endlessly circulate around him.

This methodology is set in motion with the first few pages of the novel, which are an exhibition of how public and private layers of existence are interconnected. Howie moves from work to lunch break, he moves from the office to the city streets outside the office—from one public realm to another. He then goes shopping, an act that requires that one's personal and private necessities and luxuries be bought in public. Not only this, but Howie asks for a bag to hold his purchases. And the principle reason you need bags, Howie says, is because "they kept your purchases private, while *signaling to the world* that you led a busy, rich life, full of pressing errands run" (4, my emphasis). But Howie does not stop here. He then goes on to reminisce—after a lengthy footnote on straws and why plastic straws float unlike their paper predecessors—about his adolescent experiences of paper bags and how he learned to refuse the offer of paper bags for his purchases from stores because he wanted to show he had nothing to hide, nothing like the soft-core pornography magazines that he bought sometimes and which sales assistants automatically put in paper bags for him. He then inserts a footnote about a relationship he nearly had with one of these sales assistants who sold him the magazines.

What Howie makes clear in this passage is that his very conception of a private life, a life he can surveil and represent in his narrative, is dependent upon the public objects he can see and touch in the world around him and out of which, in the course of his contacts with them, he can shape his life. What he ends up doing is constantly surveilling his private life through his relationship with these objects. Peter Stallybrass has written that

> it is only . . . in a Cartesian and post-Cartesian paradigm that the life of matter is relegated to the trashcan of the "merely"—the bad fetish which the adult will leave behind as a childish thing so as to pursue the life of the mind. As if consciousness and memory were about minds rather than things, or the real could only reside in the permeated impurity of the material.[26]

For Howie, life is nothing without "things." They are the starting points for the representation of his life. A further example can be found in this footnote about corporate doorknobs.

> Why can't office buildings use doorknobs that are truly knob-like in shape? What is this static modernism that architects of the second tier have imposed on us: steel half U handles or lathed objects shaped like superdomes, instead of brass, porcelain or glass knobs? The upstairs doorknobs in the house I grew up in were made of faceted glass . . . My father must have had special affection for them, because he draped his ties over them . . . He taught me the principal [tie] classifications: rep tie, neat tie, paisley tie. And the tie I wore for the job interview at the company on the mezzanine was one he had pulled from a doorknob . . . (27)

Here again Howie shifts spatial realms in an instant. The link appears seamless because of the presence of the doorknob in each realm, but in many ways it is a dramatic narrative juxtaposition. Howie is moving from the realm of the disciplinary arena of surveillance at work to the arena of self-surveillance that is memories of childhood and family anecdote, and then moving back to the disciplinary work world again by his referencing ties, and more particularly the tie he wore for his interview— which is the supreme moment of monitoring your appearance before a surveilling potential employer.[27] It is as if Howie's private world is etched onto public, corporate objects that are all around him, and what he is doing is reading off his private life in his observation of them.

This really brings me back to Sedgwick's description of the public/ private binary as an "incoherent register." What Sedgwick argues—in relation to Herman Melville's construction of the space of the sailing ship in *Moby-Dick* and *Billy Budd*—is how Melville makes graphic "that the difference between 'public' and 'private' could never be stably or intelligibly represented as a difference between two concrete classes of physical space."[28] Instead, the spaces for acts whose importance depends upon their being categorized as private or public have to be mapped out as either private or public. In other words, narrative has to try to do the —impossible—job of epistemologically fixing and organizing space.

Plainly, the doorknob footnote is an instance of the difficulty of this kind of organization in the way that it struggles to keep separate the alienating "static modernism" of the public office building from the private and domestic bonding between father and son which consists of knowledge being passed from one to the other (where else, after all, will Howie use this knowledge except in the "public" realm of work?).

But I want to discuss several connected episodes focussed around one particular location to show that this possibility of organizing the epistemological status of space is complicated and made contradictory when locations represented as private become the space where official —or one might say in Howie's case, corporate—business has to be done and when a designated public space is seen as suited for a private individual. This discussion will lead towards the impact that these considerations of public and private have for male sexuality, especially when *The Mezzanine* is considered to be a confession—a conclusion which seems inescapable when one considers the intimacy of the narrative, its self-surveilling obsession with every detail of Howie's life and existence, and the uncanny sense that this narrator is talking to the individual reader as interlocutor. Baker achieves this effect not so much by talking *directly* to the reader but by shifting knowledge and thoughts—about Howie, about other people, about the world beyond—between public and private domains. The fact that much of this knowledge and these thoughts are "trivial," which one would normally keep to oneself and keep out of a fictional narrative, serves only to emphasize this shifting between domains. It is this confessional status of the narrative that also leads to a modulation on the theme of sex.

The corporate washroom features quite prominently in Howie's narrative. It is also a space that has featured in some of the other texts dealt with. In "Bartleby" the whole office might be considered a washroom because of Melville's description of the space between one of the windows and the outer wall as a "cistern." The washroom is the first place where Paul Riesling goes when he enters the Athletic Club and where Babbitt follows him. When Tom Rath recognizes Caesar Gardella for the first time in the elevator, the washroom is the place to which he retreats to recompose himself. Something of the importance and the legacy of this all-male environment will become apparent also in the importance that this space has for Howie.

The washroom is the place Howie visits before his lunch hour. But he asks himself whether a lunch hour is defined as beginning just as you enter the men's room on the way to your lunch or just as you exit it. He decides "right or wrong that the stop at the men's room was of a piece with the morning's work, a chore like the other business chores I was responsible for" (71). Howie's dilemma here, over whether going to the men's room is part of public, disciplinary work time or whether it is part of his lunch hour, his private nonwork time, is a dilemma which is bound up with how locations are classified as public or private. Where does the men's room fit into this binary? In one way it could be seen as a private space, that space where Howie can legitimately, away from the surveilling office gaze, adjust his tie, make sure that his shirt is tucked in, clear his throat, wash the newsprint from his hands, and then urinate (72). But Howie also understands that things are not so simple. He recognizes that appearance—again, both social interaction and dress—is part of corporate employment and that these adjustments he makes to himself are in themselves part of his working duties and obligations. But, more than this, he points out how new male employees visit the men's room more often than people who have been working there for some time, "Because the corporate bathroom is the one place in the whole office where you understand completely what is expected of you." You may not be able to understand your job, but "in the men's room, you are a seasoned professional; you let your hand drop casually on the flush handle with as much an air of careless familiarity as men who have been with the company for years" (72–73). So, far from being a private space in the midst of the surveilling office, the men's room suddenly becomes a site of public homosocial activity where what is at stake is something beyond—but also intimately connected to—work: manhood.

In a sense, Howie's acceptance that going to the washroom is part of his work time illustrates how this homosocial activity that takes place there is far from simply allowing all men to be men together, however. Hierarchies continue to exist. Howie meets a company vice president in the men's room, but they "were not obliged to greet each other: the noise of the water from his tap . . . defined us as existing in separate realms" (82–83). In this section of the novel Howie carefully maps out the location of both himself and the vice president, and other men in the washroom. It is not a neutral space which yields itself up to one side of the public/private binary but is continually provisional. Which one it is depends upon who is in there and what they are doing, and since this is the case, it is always threatening or denying the notion of privacy. Howie admits to being nervous about farting in the toilet stalls; he admits to being unable to urinate in the urinals when somebody is standing beside him—until, that is, he discovers the trick of imagining he is urinating on that person's head (84–85). Both of these are testament to the way in which surveillance and its power patterns persist inside the men's room, a surveillance which once again operates upon the body and which can be seen to be marking out a very clear brand of masculinity and power and what that masculinity should consist of and how one should behave. For Howie, not being able to empty his bladder in front of other men is a problem he has to find some ingenious way of solving. Urinating behind the closed door of a cubicle—the simplest solution, one imagines—clearly carries with it associations that Howie would much rather avoid, associations which place the privacy of the water closet cubicle close to that gender binarism that has linked privacy with effeminacy and effeminacy with homosexuality. In the men's room this is obviously a live issue for Howie. As he says elsewhere, "I was a man, but I was not nearly the magnitude of man I had hoped I might be" (54).

Loosening the sphincter is, of course, an entirely different matter. By virtue of the conjunction of plumbing and architecture—which themselves witness a cultural prerogative about men and their anuses—this *has* to be done behind closed doors in the cubicle. And yet how private does a closed door make an act?

> One time, while I was locked behind a stall, I did unintentionally interrupt the conversation between a member of senior management and an important visitor with a loud curt fart like the rap of a bongo drum. The two paused momentarily; and then recovered without dropping a stitch—"Oh, she is a very capable young woman, I'm quite clear on that." "She is a sponge, a sponge, she soaks up information everywhere she goes." "She really is. And she's tough; that's the thing. She's got armor." "She's a major asset to us." (83)

Hearing this conversation, Howie must be reminded not only that the cubicle cannot separate itself from the rest of the men's room by merely isolating itself spatially, but also that the men's room is not a space where work stops either. This homosocial discussion—the reduction of a woman to an asset that can be transferred between men—is yet more evidence pushing him to the conclusion that visiting the men's room—

even visiting the men's room to sit in the privacy of the cubicle—is "of a piece with the morning's work" (71). The exchange between the two men is also about the woman's ability to gather and absorb information, that is to surveil. Just as the workplace and the non-workplace are made inseparable by the operation of disciplinary power, so are the workplace and the washroom. Therefore, Howie's narration in these men's room sections disarticulates the notion that the private space and the public space are discreet spaces that are recognized immediately, that the interface between them has collapsed.

This collapse is analogous to that collapsing of the interface between surface and depth in the commodity culture of postmodernism. Phillip E. Simmons has written about *The Mezzanine* in precisely these terms.[29] It is, he argues, a novel where "the existentialist fear of the void beneath has been replaced by the sunny confidence that there *is* no 'beneath,' that life at the surface is all there is, and is not so bad after all" (608). Rather than preventing the novel from fulfilling some historical purpose, Howie's attention to the detail of the everyday actually witnesses a postmodern historical imagination where "the narrator gestures at larger history only to dismiss it" in favor of "a parallel history . . . of consumption that bears the emotional weight of the personal past" (614–15). I do not disagree with any of this analysis, and I would go along with Simmons in his conviction that Howie makes a home of consumption through which he can construct self and history (622). But there is a concomitant question that Simmons does not address: what *kind* of self and what *kind* of history? Howie creates not *the* postmodern historical self, but *a* self. And for all that he collapses distinctions of public and private, surface and depth, he is still unable to reject these terms as the means of spatial organization. This preservation of terms is evident from some of Howie's meditations and habits. He regrets that, although he prefers escalators, "moments of privacy were impossible" on them unlike in elevators (76); and he likes to wear earphones at work (109), on the subway, and in bed (110). At these moments Howie is shutting himself off from the rest of the world that he takes such delight in at other times. But more than anything, this preservation of organizing spatial terms is a process that actually relies upon a visual logic—one that is reminiscent of that figured in Edgar Allan Poe's "The Purloined Letter," of not being able to see the forest for the trees.

I have already written about the way the disciplinary regime of capitalist surveillance and Howie's relation to the capitalist heritage of work exist in the narrative not as explicit themes but as implicit cognitive regimes. Additionally, take the fact that although Howie gives the reader an obsessive, almost fetishistic gaze at his own life and self, at the end of the novel his actual job is still a mystery, his surname remains unknown, and his lover—although discussed using a female pronoun—remains no more than the letter L. Instead, Howie's identity is constructed for the reader through a series of anecdotes and details and from a very particular and very narrowly focussed perspective. Howie's self-surveillance, while a comic parody of self-surveillance and of American neurotic introspection, is at the same time also a deadly serious plea to the reader to understand that his life, his image of himself, is indeed formed from what some might judge to be trivial details.

If Baker were to provide this foreground of Howie's experience without the background of the office and of work, then Howie would perhaps be little more than the geeky voyeur of his own habits and quirks. But in conjunction, these two levels suggest that the infinitely regressing and penetrative surveilling regime of the office and of work *require and produce as their counterpart* an infinitely regressing and penetrative self-surveillance on the narrator's behalf where those factors which might usually serve to create identity—name, job, sexual object choice, social relations—may be easily missed or passed over in the course of the narrative. This rhetorical maneuver is in fact equivalent to that cultural exposition of male sexuality: the capacity of being able to look "straight" at the theme of male sexuality only then to look "straight" past it and thus not thematize it—for to do so would be to denaturalize and destabilize an obvious "straight" male sexuality.[30] Instead, attention is unwittingly displaced onto the discourses and rhetoric which so constitute it, of which surveillance and self-surveillance, the public and private, are two of the most crucial pairings.

This kind of visual logic is the same as that which D. A. Miller has christened the "open secret," whose function is to "conceal the knowledge of the knowledge,"[31] and that Lee Edelman identifies operating in the men's room, a logic that allows straight men to "see, and *not* perceive," where the "dicks that hang out in the men's room may hide themselves in plain sight."[32] Howie's narrative relies upon the same knotted logic of straight male sexuality which insists on one's "private parts"—either genitals or Howie's intimate thoughts and life details—being displayed in "public"—the urinals or the confessional—and yet remaining unseen, either by way of a prohibition which is placed upon men looking at other men's genitals in the urinals or a prohibition against straight male sexuality being considered to be anything other than natural and obvious. All this is structured by that homosocial desire which is regulated through public genital or confessional display but which must go unrecognized. It is this knotted logic which allows Howie to turn to one of his colleagues after they have just finished urinating—Howie has only been able to perform his public urination by imagining himself urinating on this man's head—and look one another in the eye and name and acknowledge each other in the realm of a straight public manhood: "Don." "Howie." (85).

It is also worth noting here that the washroom represents the last vestige of the office as an all-male terrain as it was in its earliest incarnation, and this drives my concentration upon the washroom passages. What Howie's narration articulates is the legacy of this male history and that process whereby male sexuality is constructed, discussed, and monitored at the level of an epistemology that in contemporary American culture has produced a situation where "The law of the men's room decrees that men's dicks be available for public contemplation at the urinal precisely to allow a correlative mandate: that such contemplation must never take place,"[33] certainly not in public. A straight male sexuality which comes to operate under this kind of visual logic is perfectly capable of producing a novel where the absence of sexual contact within the novel at any physical or thematic level in no way precludes male sexuality being one of the novel's major concerns. Indeed, it is the very prerequisite for the kind of agile displacement offered up by *The Mezzanine*. A straight male sexuality need no longer confront itself in the language of sex but in all manner of modulations derived from the capitalist regimes of consumption, surveillance, and self-surveillance, and the public and private which amount to nothing less than a capitalist poetics of male sexuality.

What is startlingly apparent in the light of this is that the moment when surveillance and self-surveillance and public and private all come into conjunction is an incredibly important moment in the life of the male office worker. The shoelace incident, with all its inherent contradictions, is just such a moment. Collected here for Howie is not just an initial realization that to be caught adjusting one's appearance when his colleagues see him in his awkward shoelace-tying crouch actually offends the requirement that self-surveillance—which is precisely what adjusting your appearance is—should take place not in full public view of your surveilling work colleagues, but in that realm designated as private—even though such a separate space clearly does not exist for him.

It is perhaps more important that what becomes apparent at this moment is the impossibility of separating those things which work hard to maintain an illusion of separability; this strange form of calculus manages to bring together a whole host of anxieties for Howie, anxieties which are intimately bound up with the epistemological construction of male sexuality. Does he look stupid bending down tying his lace? Is he making the right impression on his colleagues? What will they say to other people? How might being caught tying your shoelace in public make you seem vain? Does vanity mean effeminacy? Will people start to spread rumors about him? What strategies must he use to preserve his image of straight manhood in the corporate environment with its stern surveilling gaze? Howie does not in fact ask himself any of these questions when the shoelace breaks, instead he resents his colleagues for having caused the lace to snap, a displacement which signals not only how he has been forced into recognizing his vulnerable status at this intense conjunction of discursive practices, but also how he denies that a complex transfer of social energy has occurred. Because as integral as the incoherency of separate public and private domains are to Howie's self-construction in the narrative, this unfortunately does not obviate their organizing power both inside and outside the workplace, their ability to work to position oneself and others in a hierarchical binary of normal and abnormal. Surveillance and self-surveillance, the epistemological everyday of the office, ensure that the boundary of public and private —the boundary so intensely connected to the construction of a dual model of male sexuality—has to be constantly and intensely monitored, which is precisely what Howie does. Rubbed together as they are when Howie bends down to tie his shoelace, surveillance and self-surveillance, public and private, silently release and circulate the social energy that Howie identifies. Under this degree of pressure, and under the impetus of discursive practices needing to produce material effects, it is inevitable that the shoelace snap.

There are important connections between Howie in *The Mezzanine* and Arno, the narrator of *The Fermata*. Primary among these are Arno's work in offices and the confessional nature of the narrative. Unlike Howie, though, who has a fixed and permanent office job, Arno is a roaming temp who types his way through downtown Boston offices. Which means that he is "exposed to roughly three thousand names" each year, "of which . . . perhaps five hundred belong to individuals I get to know a little. . . . Over ten years, that makes five thousand personalities, about each of whom I must develop a little packet of emotion."[34] In the context of economic discourses about the casualization of office labor and the resulting effects of this short-term contract culture, not to mention the position of being a man working in a role that traditionally has been classified as a female occupation, Arno would seem to be in a position of social vulnerability. The "little packet of emotion" that he has to generate and dispense for each of the people that he meets would seem to place him in a psychically disorienting landscape. Yet once again Baker, through the opportunities that a confessionalized narrative allows him, resists the temptation to fall back on that long-standing discourse of alienation. "Am I an alienated person?" he asks himself. While admitting, "temps are prima facie alienated by virtue of their vocational rootlessness," he concludes that he does not "see that nasal, sociological-sounding word applying in any useful way to me" (155). Like Howie, what Arno manages to do through his narrative is develop a strategy for coping with the circulating social energy of contemporary life.

Central to the achievement of this effect is Arno's special talent. In *The Fermata* Baker provides us with a narrator who possesses the ability to bring the circulation of social energy to a halt—simply by clicking his fingers. In high school Arno Strine discovers that he can make the rest of the world stand still while remaining animated himself in the midst of this motionlessness. Arno calls this strange time and place the "Fold." His ability to enter it is dependent upon some kind of Fold activator, some small act that triggers a hiatus in the movement of the universe. This act may be the writing of a complicated mathematical formula, turning a transformer on and off, or simply clicking his fingers. Each trigger works for only a certain length of time. When it has expired, Arno loses his powers of "fermation" and has to wait for the next trigger to reveal itself to him.

It might be tempting to envisage *The Fermata*, then, as a text that utilizes this narrative device in order to participate in a dialogue about the nature of time that has long preoccupied science fiction writers. If one of the staples of this genre is the calamitous consequence of meddling with time and altering its natural trajectory, then *The Fermata* clearly stands as an antidote to this discourse. For Arno it is the possibility of experiencing effects disallowed by the natural trajectory of time that so interests him. So, for example, he takes the opportunity to do his last-minute Christmas shopping while the rest of the world is switched off—"it's nice to browse in utter silence" (46)—to catch up on books that he wants to read instead of working (47); and to disarm a gang of muggers (48–49).

It might also be possible to read *The Fermata* in relation to a text like Fyodor Dostoyevsky's *The Idiot*. When Arno admits that he finds himself "in a state of Tourette's syndromish meditativeness that I knew by now often presaged a Fermata discovery" (178), there is some intimation that his entry into the Fold represents a kind of searing psychological connectivity with the rest of the world that enables him to control and see it perfectly.

Yet I prefer to see Arno's strange ability as a way in which Baker continues his fascination with surveillance and self-surveillance, the public and the private, and their relation to sexuality, in a form that is predominantly visual and spatial. When Arno halts the world, what happens is that rather than stopping social energy, he actually moves into the framework of its operation the better to understand it.

And this understanding arises from the very nature of his job, part of which involves the transcribing of tapes. It is the process of stopping and starting these tapes that Arno suggests has made him "unusually sensitive . . . to the editability of the temporal continuum—to the fact that an apparently seamless vocalization may actually elide, glide over, hide whole self-contained vugs of hidden activity or distraction—sneezes, expletives, spilled coffee, sexual adventures—within" (38–39). The social energy that Howie identifies in *The Mezzanine* is here turned into that "hidden activity" that is often edited out of existence by scrupulous dictators who do not wish to expose their sneezes and sexual adventures to the rest of the office. Arno unblushingly reveals just such hidden activity in his confessional narrative. And *reveals* because his "temporal powers have always been linked in a way I don't pretend to understand with my sense of sight" (6–7).

As in *The Mezzanine*, this visual dominant has a double meaning: it is a product of the overarching regime of surveillance and self-surveillance that belongs to the history of surveillance and dates back to the beginnings of office culture and that exists in this contemporary period at such an intense level; and it is also part of that history of *looking back* at the culture of office surveillance that was developed through Henry Miller's *Tropic of Capricorn*, Sloan Wilson's *The Man in the Gray Flannel Suit*, and Joseph Heller's *Something Happened* and that was responsible for certain ideas about a threatened straight masculinity and sexuality. *The Mezzanine*, by modulating to themes of the public and private, engaged those ideas about masculinity and sexuality and to a certain extent provided a

way of moving beyond them even though remaining within their defini-
tional confines. What makes *The Fermata* somewhat different from *The
Mezzanine*, however, is its overt thematization of sex and visuality. Arno
readily admits that the Fold is "just a sexual aid" (22), and *The Fermata*
carries on the turn to sex in Baker's work that began with *Vox* (1992),
the story of two strangers who meet on a chat-line and reveal and play
out their sexual fantasies over the phone. The nonsexual uses that Arno
makes of the Fold are entirely tertiary and account for very little of the
narrative. And it is the subsuming of a temporal discourse by a visual
and sexual one that Baker sets up early in *The Fermata*.

The heterosexual relationship with which the narrative both begins
and ends is Howie's desire for Joyce, one of the people for whom he is
typing in his current assignment. The novel opens with Arno stopping
time as Joyce is walking towards him so that he can rearrange her clothes
and examine her pubic hair. The previous week Joyce has dropped off a
tape for Arno and complemented him on his glasses, and he's "been
nuts about her ever since" (5). His glasses are important to Arno. Not
only do they represent something about which he has private doubts
and so is happy to take complements about and have his doubts eased,
but they also mark that interface where Arno meets the world. The problem with contact lenses for Arno is that they get in the way of what he is
seeing: "I could see things through them, but I wasn't *pleased* to look at
things. The bandwidth of my optical processors was being flooded with
'there is an intruder on your eyeball' messages, so that a lot of the incidental haul from my retina was simply not able to get through" (7). And
this incidental material, as Howie demonstrated in *The Mezzanine*, is very
important. Arno also feels that contact lenses isolate him, "heightening
rather than helping rid me of my—well, I suppose it is proper to call it
my loneliness" (8). Instead, it is the sharp corners of his glasses that help
to dig Arno "into sociability" (8).

Initially it might seem that the Fold represents a deathly and static
kind of space in which Arno moves, the kind of motionless space that
Ralph Waldo Emerson so deplored in photography, which is an artistic
form that he complained robbed life of its temporality and imposed
upon it a kind of rigor mortis.[35] And yet for Arno the Fold provides
some of the "most alive times I've had" (11). One reason for this might
be that as a category of space the Fold is closely correlated to that "incoherent register" that constitutes the public/private divide. Stopping
the world for Arno means being able to wander through a public world
that is temporarily turned into one available for his own private plea-

sure and that will later become a public world again. But also Arno's Fold world turns out to be very much like the fold world described by Gilles Deleuze. He suggests that the "outside is not a fixed limit but a moving matter animated by peristaltic movements, folds and foldings that together make up an inside: they are not something other than the outside, but precisely the inside *of* the outside."[36] Those Fold moments when Arno halts time make a kind of ontological sense then—and take the novel away from the realms of science fiction—if they are seen to be moments of doubling back or looping, when "the whole of the inside finds itself actively present on the outside."[37] In many ways this describes the act of confession, a time when private thoughts become represented in material form externally.

To represent this movement or transition in narrative terms is problematic if one is not just willing to settle for a first-person narrator who talks to the reader, a device that would perhaps trap the narrative into a mode of self-reflection and contemplation and diminish the importance of the public and external, spaces that are so fundamental to Baker. As I mentioned in regard to *The Mezzanine*, what Howie does there is literally to see his personal and private life etched onto the surfaces of public consumer objects. In *The Fermata* the situation is somewhat different. It is when he is in the Fold that Arno actually participates in the inscription of himself *onto* this public world. He is literally involved in the writing of himself during these times, not just through the confession that he is typing during time in the Fold, but also in his interaction with this public world. What the narrative of *The Fermata* dramatizes, in a wholly defamiliarized and formalized way, is the material process whereby private and public, internal and external worlds fold inside and outside of one another. Rather than write a seamless narrative that tries to meld these states together, Baker separates them formally, the better to demonstrate their interwoven condition.

Some evidence of the complex nature of the transition into and out of the Fold is given by Arno himself: "The power seems ultimately to come from within me . . . but as I invoke it I have to believe that it is external for it to work properly" (4). The Fold ultimately fails to make sense either as a private and internal world or as a public and external world in Arno's narrative, but it does so to a degree that surpasses the problematization of these categories that takes place in *The Mezzanine* and that will have consequences for the way Baker can attend to the nature of straight male sexuality.

When Arno casually asks friends and acquaintances what they would do if they had the power to stop the world, he finds that many of their responses relate to sex (76–91). Given the chance to do anything unobserved, those questioned are drawn to the opportunities for sexual performance. Although Arno tries to differentiate the particular nature of these sexual responses from his own, it would appear that what a temporal hiatus might actually represent then—so bound up with surveillance and self-surveillance is the regulation of sexual life—is a hiatus in the operation of surveillance and, concomitantly, in the necessity of self-surveillance. This would certainly account for the way that Arno's narrative so quickly subsumes temporal concerns within visual ones. Obviously this suspension of surveillance and self-surveillance has its negative side. The security guard at one of the offices in which Arno works has no hesitation in saying that he would "find the nicest, best-looking chick I could find and rip her clothes off and plank her right there" (87). And worse. Arno is shocked and outraged and tries to argue that when he is in the Fold he does not try to "insert his small-minded dick into the lives of women" (91). Instead, he says, he wants to "insert some novelty into the lives of women . . . I'm captivated by the simple idea of putting something in the path of a woman, so that she can choose to look at it or read it, or, on the other hand, choose to walk on by" (91–92). He leaves pornographic images and vibrators within their eyesight and turns time on and off briefly so that they catch subliminal glimpses of these things (61–63); he writes pornographic stories and leaves them in places where women will find and read them. But since he also uses the Fold to undress women, and at one point to masturbate over them and on them, Arno's defense is also disingenuous. He admits this himself: "when I try to imagine defending my actions verbally I find that they are indefensible, and I don't want to know that" (24). Arno also imagines himself during his first Fold moment, when he opens the blouse of his schoolteacher, as "a daguerreotypist, crouching and covering my head with a camera cloth to see my subject more completely" (32). There is none of Emerson's reticence here. It is the visualization of the female body, and often the female body at the point of orgasm, that stimulates Arno. The sight of a woman's "come-face . . . was the kind of sight that could enhance your life for a decade" (152), he suggests, and he regrets that nobody had yet launched a magazine called *O-Shots* "devoted exclusively to close-up photographs of women's faces in the midst of orgasm . . . or perhaps an O-shot calendar" (153).

Clearly this kind of visual attention to the female body raises the specter of the male objectification of women through images. There is little doubt that if one wanted to make this argument in relation to *The Fermata* there are solid grounds on which to do so. And yet the parameters of such an argument, in order to avoid a kind of correspondingly reductive objectification of Baker's narrative, would need to be set so that they included some of what I want to discuss in the remainder of this chapter. Because for all that Baker drifts into a boringly clichéd porn-iste style at certain sexually heightened points in the text or when he writes his own pornography—his "rot" as he labels it—there remains an attention to the logic and constitution of vision in contemporary culture that pervades Baker's writing and that provides a self-reflexive commentary on its own construction.

The narrative deployment of the temporal hiatus marks out a spatial regime where the culture of intense surveillance and self-surveillance may be suspended. This in itself represents an original engagement with the disciplinary effects of capitalist culture. In addition, in the Fold it is not possible to develop film. Arno, of course, has tried. He tries himself to take a photograph of a woman at the point of orgasm—"coming stunningly"—but "through some oddity of Fold-chemistry . . . the greens appeared only very faintly, and the oranges and reds did not show up at all, so my own visual memory was all I had" (152–53). The failure of reproductive techniques in the Fold suggest once again that this environment halts that process whereby one is not being watched in the contemporary era of surveillance society so much as being filmed. Taking all this into account, and without wanting to let Baker off the hook for the objectification of women, there is a case for heeding Arno's take on the morality of what he does: "Morals depend in part on consequences; consequences on time; and since my amoralities flourish and expire entirely in momentary pico-states of timeless inconsequence the usual rules don't have the same prohibitive force" (156).

There is also an interesting visual scheme set up by Arno that helps to demonstrate how the narrative deals with the construction of straight male sexuality. Rhody, one of Arno's partners, tells him that when he puts his head between her legs, she prefers it if he is not wearing his glasses. She quite likes the sensation of his ears high on her thighs, but when it comes to his glasses she wants his "sense of her open vadge to be more Sisley than Richard Estes" (10). This is especially pertinent because Baker's writing, in its clinical and super-realistic detail, is clearly the literary equivalent of one of Estes's photo-realist paintings. And indeed much of *The Fermata* and *The Mezzanine,* as well as his other work, are written in just this manner; it is Baker's stylistic calling card. However, I suggest that it is during Arno's time in the Fold that his straight male sexuality becomes much more Sisley than Estes, that it begins to blur and distort to such an extent that what one can make out is not always self-evident. The writing itself remains none the less detailed and precise, but as surveillance and self-surveillance are halted, and as Arno's fantasies become more explicit, from within the clean lines of a sexuality that would seem to be in tune with the clean lines of his prose there appears to emerge an altogether less clear portrait.

The first of Arno's attempts at erotica or "rot" is written on the beach. It is a story about vibrators and dildos. Ostensibly for a woman on the beach whom Arno likes the look of, the act of writing this story about vibrators and dildos leads Arno to focus predominantly on his own anus. He writes on the beach with his ass raised in the air. The "outdoor coolness on my very ass*hole*, and on the usually damp stretched skin high upon the sides of my balls—was most interesting. I didn't want anything to go *in* my asshole, no, no, I just wanted it out in the open, sunlit for once, flaunting wavewards its showered cleanness, exposed in a way that was lewd and vulnerable" (123–24). Several things here suggest that Arno would indeed like something to go *in* his asshole, even if it is just one of the vibrators and dildos he is writing about: the double negative—"no, no"—that makes a positive and also produces a disavowing overemphasis on the "no," and the choice of a word like "lewd" that connotes an obscenity of an irreligious nature and is still used in the American legal system to identify an act for which one can be prosecuted. And just what does Arno want to make his asshole vulnerable *to* as he lies there on hands and knees with his ass in the air? Ostensibly it is the sunlight; he seems to want to bring it out of the cubicle stall of the male washroom where it remains private and secluded and into a realm of visibility. And it is important that he emphasizes the ass*hole* and not just his ass, since bearing one's ass in public is hardly novel behavior in the world of heterosexual masculinity's high jinks. But Baker spreads Arno's cheeks and peers in, to the extent that the exposure of Arno's anus becomes part and parcel of that process whereby Arno is inscribing himself *onto* this public world. Baker registers this process by fusing together Arno's identity *with* his asshole. A little later in this episode it is his "cool and drying Arnus" that becomes "exposed to the sun" (124).

The "rot" story that Arno writes on the beach is about a woman who reaches orgasm in the back of a UPS truck. Doubly penetrated by vibrators that have just been delivered to her, she has the driver find a dirt road so that the truck bounces and lurches to help her on her way. The tenor of Arno's story is very much Richard Estes:

> Marian unbent her knees and sat flatly down on the Van Dilden with her legs extended in front of her. This had the effect of pushing the Royal Welsh Fusilier deeper into her ass. . . . The truck started bumping and jostling. She pulled the length of the Fusilier up against her tailbone and bent it around her hip and found that, as she hoped, the other end easily reached her clit. She pulled back its "foreskin" and held the slick second head against herself. (139)

This kind of writing is overly concerned with coordinates and the positioning of elements in a spatial setting. It relies upon the precise writerly organizing of limbs and sex toys. The same narrative eye that dissects Howie's buttoning up of his shirt in *The Mezzanine* also constructs Arno's "rot." And yet while he is writing this story Arno is lying on the beach—his own asshole open to the sunlight—playing with the anus of the woman he is writing the story for. But rather than applying the same precise style to this scenario, Arno describes it in an entirely Sisley-esque manner. He is, he says, "getting a great deal of pleasure out of feeling my own *plein-air Arnality* bared to the sky and holding hers open at the same time" (125, my emphasis), plein-air designating not only a work of art painted out of doors, but also a style or school of French impressionistic painting in the 1860s. So when it comes to the heterosexual fantasy world of Arno's imagination, the visual and perceptual focus is clear and organized (Estes); when it comes to the anal pleasure that Arno takes from writing these stories—which at these moments constitute his very selfhood—and from looking at and stimulating a female anus, suddenly the territory is much less clear (Sisley). The sunlight that Arno pours upon his asshole by assuming such a passive and receptive position on the beach results not in the clean lines of a photo-realist self-portrait, but an altogether more blurred or plein-air picture.

Rather than envisaging Arno as someone who uses his Fold powers to simply engage in a heterosexual voyeurism, then, the Fold is a time when, with the surveillance and self-surveillance of office and social culture in a state of suspension, Arno is able to indulge the complex desires that focus around the anality that is such an important ingredient of Arnality. "I had never typed the word *butthole* before in my life," he confesses. "It isn't a word that comes up much in business correspondence" (227).

The importance of this anality is very much apparent in a later episode that Arno imagines happening after a woman has read a piece of
his "rot." In this imagined episode, Arno seduces the woman who has
read his story—that not only includes "a great many dildos" but "Actual
out-and-out defecation" (235)—through the connecting door between
two motel rooms. The chain remains on the door thus not allowing
Arno to be in the same room as the woman, Adele. While the two of
them both masturbate on either side of the door, and occasionally
glimpse one another, Adele is reluctant to show Arno her ass because it
would mean showing him her asshole. As a compromise she drapes a
damp washcloth over herself and backs up to the door. To stop the
washcloth from falling, Arno pushes it into Adele's asshole: "White
wrinkles would form in the fabric—a sort of plush terry-cloth sphincter would gather around my stiff middle finger as I forced my way in"
(253). Arno proceeds to ejaculate into this terry-cloth sphincter.

Again, although the writing in this section remains intensely descriptive and aware of the positioning of organs, bodies, and doors, there is
a lack of focus that returns the episode to the plein-air world of Arno's
selfhood. First, this episode is imagined. It is not something that Arno
does; it is not something that Arno even writes about. Second—and
this is where the stimulation derives—the ass that Arno penetrates and
ejaculates over is in view while the gendered body to which it belongs is
very much out of view. So desperate is Arno to have the ass within
touching and shooting distance that it takes up the entire gap in the
doorway. The washcloth even disguises Adele's genitalia: "I would know
more or less where things were underneath, but I wouldn't be able to see
them" (252).

Clearly there is nothing here to suggest that Arno wishes it were a
male asshole that he penetrates with his "stiff middle finger" and then
ejaculates over. And yet what needs to be asked is just how Arno's fascination with the anal stimulation of women, and his own anal and phallic stimulation as he *writes about* the anal stimulation of women, intersect
with the absent sexual combination in *The Fermata*: anal sex between
men. At one level there would appear to be only straight answers here
rather than queer ones. The straightest of them all being that even in the
Fold anal sex between men remains something that Arno cannot confront; in Arno's fantasies it is still locked within the kinds of phobic discourses that have established themselves from the nineteenth century
onwards, those that I have identified throughout this book and that so
dominated the postwar representations of the office provided by Wilson

and Heller. *The Fermata* is a novel about sexual fantasy and sexual pleasure, and no matter how much his own anal gratification is part of this pleasure and fantasy, the intrusion of another man into the scene would seem to bear the potential for destroying this pleasure. It would serve to threaten—or, in Edelman's term, de-script—the kind of gender and sexual identity that Arno has so assiduously inscribed across the face of the public world during the course of his narrative.

And yet despite this, there is something about Arno as a male heterosexual that does not seem to fit with the pronouncements of Edelman and others about this particular species. Discussing Bersani's work on passivity and homosexuality—where Bersani declares that "to be penetrated is to abdicate power"[38]—Edelman points out how this passivity is seen by heterosexual men to place homosexual men in the position of heterosexual women where they both literally and metaphorically get fucked. This positioning, according to male heterosexual ideology, "connotes a willing sacrifice of the subjectivity, the disciplined self-mastery, traditionally attributed only to those who perform the 'active' or penetrative—and hence 'masculine'—role in the active-passive binarism that organizes 'our' cultural perspective on sexual behaviour."[39] It is the fear of being placed in such a position that girds masculine heterosexuality against the possible accusation of passivity or effeminacy and that in turn ensures that anal sex between men, and the gay man's anus, is marked as threatening "the imminent end of an empire, the demise of the imperial subject secure in his centrality to, his identification with, history and civilization."[40]

There is, then, a connection between this kind of narrative about anality and a narrative about degeneration. As Jonathan Dollimore has demonstrated, such degeneration narratives have long been a part of Western culture's fear of decline. At different historical moments, however, this narrative is articulated in more specific theoretical terms. In the early modern period the preoccupation was with cosmic decay; in the late nineteenth century this preoccupation with the cosmic "collapsed into the biological, in a way which intensifies anxiety because decline is now radically interior."[41] It is this biological shift that helps to place sexual perversion at the heart of much late nineteenth- and twentieth-century thinking about degeneration and death and that leads to the violent situation whereby "the gay male anus as the site of pleasure gives birth to 'AIDS' as a figuration of death."[42]

Arno's abbreviation of erotica to "rot" cannot pass unexamined in this context or in the context of his preoccupation with anal pleasure.

"Rot" is a word that is too synonymous with words like decay, degeneration, and disintegration for colloquialisms such as "rotting in hell" or a "rotting corpse" not to take on heavier religious or ontological inferences. If Arno takes pleasure in anything, it is the production of this "rot," in the self-reflexive *writing* of it. It is a part of the sexuality that he inscribes while in the Fold. Indeed the Fold, as a suspension of ordinary work time and of surveillance and self-surveillance, gives him the temporal latitude and the philosophical space to write these stories. Arno's is not a narrative of anxiety about the implications of this "rot" for him and the culture at large; it is not a narrative fearful of threats to that kind of centralized subjectivity that in turn shores up the family, history, and civilization. The narratives in *The Man in the Gray Flannel Suit* and *Something Happened* very much were. Arno does not provide the celebration of gay male sex that for Bersani might produce—because of its marginalized social position—a knowledge of desire unavailable elsewhere, that for Foucault might produce a liberating loss of ego, and that for Dollimore might produce "a moment of intensity so marked by its history yet at the same time internally distanced from it."[43] Yet neither does Arno participate in those maneuvers that homophobically represent his own masculinity or sexuality as being in a state of crisis. Although the Fold can be a lonely place, Arno realizes how "laughably far I was from actual suicide" (60); where for Bob Slocum, Virginia remains as the very source of the deficit in his masculinity and therefore as the subject of constant regret, for Arno the women with whom he fails are a source of masturbatory pleasure. The anal pleasure Arno derives from straight sex and writing about straight sex may be occluded in a Sisley-esque manner and never fully examined in the way that the descriptions of his sexual fantasies are in every Estes-like detail, but when Rhody asks him what he would think if a gay man had the ability to stop time and pulled down Arno's pants to gave him a long slow blow job, Arno concludes that it would be fine, that "it wouldn't be the end of civilization" (174). Arno is a narrator, after all, who takes out from the library *The Memoirs of John Addington Symonds*—the English homosexual and campaigner for homosexual legal reform in the nineteenth century—and who can quote the homosexual philosopher George Santayana's observation that "the mind is a lyric cry in the midst of business" (39).

It is a mistake, and a binarizing mistake, to posit that straight masculinity and straight male sexuality are forever engaged in a struggle to recuperate wholeness through homophobic methods such as the inscription of the homosexual male body as a source of threat. This narrative exists, and it is written and played out with lethal consequences, in many arenas. But it would seem that Arno's narrative is not one of those arenas. Baker, in his homage to John Updike in *U and I*, remarks that he is a member of "the first generation to grow up exposed to the range and subtlety and complexity of distinctively gay interests and ways of acting. These became common knowledge: they were no longer sexual semaphore among a gay elite, but were now a constant subject of discussion, delight, disgust, amusement, and enlightenment."[44] In a kind of literary equivalent of fag-hagging, Baker writes that "Most good novelists have been women or homosexuals" and that the overemphasis on sex in the work of these novelists leads "towards subtler revelations in the . . . arena of social behavior."[45] It is from writers like this that Baker draws inspiration.

This generational shift is important because it adds a measure of local historical experience that witnesses the changing shape of cultural and social engagement with the classification of sexuality into homo and hetero. The plain fact is that the world of Wilson and Heller, while it lingers, may itself be degenerating. I would want to see Howie and Arno not as inheritors of Tom Rath and Bob Slocum's legacy, but as surviving and grown-up versions of the son that Bob Slocum murders and who manage to retain a childlike, bemused, wondering attitude towards the surfaces and textures of the consumerized, image-driven world of work and culture that they find themselves circulating within. Arno's narrative does not mark, then, a reaction against the "postmodernism [that] in its popular version can seem to intend the fall of the West insofar as it would effect the death of the subject."[46] Instead, it opens to the sunlight the black hole that is the anus at the heart of Arno's Arnality, looks inside it, but does not see the impending doom of a straight male sexuality.

If *The Fermata* is a text in the mold of those other texts in which, as Phillip E. Simmons suggests, "gestures toward 'depth' of historical understanding are continually returned to the 'surface' of postmodern image culture with its rejection of epistemological foundations and master narratives,"[47] then one of these rejected master narratives in *The Fermata* might just be the one in which straight masculinity and sexuality see in the phobically constructed homosexual other the "end of civilization." How many other characters in the course of this book could have reached Arno's conclusion that "Rot makes life," as he sighs happily to himself "thinking of lonely old Henry James" (153).

Chapter Eight

"Frank Lloyd Oop"

Microserfs, Modern Migration,
and the Architecture of the 1990s

It has been one argument of this book that despite a discourse within capitalism that has sought to maintain the reality of a boundary between workplace and home that this boundary has always been fragile and incoherent, such is the way that surveillance and self-surveillance operate discursively across space. In *The Rise of Silas Lapham*, *Babbitt*, *The Man in the Gray Flannel Suit*, and *Something Happened* I excavated the incoherency of this distinction as it affected straight male sexuality from beneath what appears to be a solidly binarized separation of workplace and home. The work of Nicholson Baker, I have suggested, performs this deconstruction itself, with important consequences for the representation of straight male sexuality in American culture.

Douglas Coupland's *Microserfs*[1] problematizes this relationship still further, since in the working world that is represented in this novel what is striking is the apparent redundancy of the binary of workplace and home, and the connected binary of work and leisure, in the development of the computing software industry. If the structuring of office life is related to the status and definition of straight male sexuality and the bonds of male friendship, such a redundancy is bound to produce repercussions in these areas.

My thinking on this significant change in the representation of workplace and home in *Microserfs* is driven by a comment made by Abe. The "in-house multimillionaire" (5), who shares his rented house along with a group of other Microsoft employees, one of whom is the novel's narrator and diarist, Daniel Underwood, complains one day about the architecture of the 1990s. "He said," Dan relates, "that because everyone's so poor these days, the '90s will be a decade with no architectural legacy or style—everyone's too poor to put up new buildings. He said that code is the architecture of the '90s" (23). By code Abe means computer code. This is what the occupants of the group house deal with all day in their jobs at Microsoft, the writing of it and the testing of it; it is what has made Bill Gates the richest man in the world. If Abe is right, then it is this architecture—the way that it is put together and the way that it creates graphical effects and interfaces for its users—rather than traditional physical architecture that is assuming preeminence in the virtual world of the 1990s. The important forms of architecture are migrating from the spaces that surround us to the spaces that are very often invisible to us and certainly incomprehensible to anyone who does not understand computer code. It may well be, then, that the obsolescence of the binary of workplace and home is a result of the obsolescence of the physical status of the workplace. The most important office in people's working lives may no longer be the office building in which they work, but the copy of Microsoft Office that they have on their desktop computer . . . and on their portable laptop . . . and on their home computer. Once the workings of the office can be condensed into a software package, there is no limit to where the office can be.

It is this narrative of migration, then, that I develop in this chapter. It is speculative, and it may not apply to all office workers.[2] Yet, in its American setting it operates against another narrative of migration that often gets told about the computing industry and contemporary technology. It is possible to guess the spirit of this other narrative that drives businessmen like Bill Gates when, early in his book *The Road Ahead*, he talks about computing as a journey that "has led us to places we barely imagined."[3] This spirit is all the more evident when he declares later that one of the major forces for economic progress in the next millennium will be the "Internet Gold Rush."[4] In this claim resides the literary confirmation that backs up the circumstantial visual prompt on the book's front cover: Gates posing against a barren West Coast landscape. Not even the domesticated disguise of his casual chinos and open-neck shirt and sweater would seem to mask the fact that the words of the generation's wealthiest, most powerful, and most influential businessman have evolved directly from a discourse about American history that is bound up with the frontier: its establishment, its breeching, and its displacement into the realms of technology. This is also a discourse, quite clearly, with a concomitant notion of gender and masculinity.

Given the circumstances of Microsoft's birth and progress, the invocation of these metaphors of the road, the journey, and the Gold Rush are not surprising. Gates and Microsoft cofounder Paul Allen left Boston for New Mexico to be close to their first customer when they founded Microsoft in 1975.[5] Revenues in the first year of business were sixteen thousand dollars; five years later this figure had reached eight million dollars, and twenty years later nearly six billion dollars.[6] Gates was the richest man in the world and Allen the third richest.

Whatever the details of such a phenomenal business trajectory, this fairy-tale success would seem to prove that the power of cultural narratives lies not only in the way that they enable the writing and rewriting of the past, or the justification of present conditions, but also in the way that they allow historical discourses to organize the conditions of reward in present-day culture. The metaphors of the road, the journey, and the Gold Rush are not myths then; they are the conditions that compelled Gates and Allen to migrate to New Mexico, the conditions that compelled the migration of thousands of people to California in the 1840s, and the conditions that compelled a similar migration to California in the 1990s.

Something of the flavor of this contemporary migration can be found in Po Bronson's account of Silicon Valley hopefuls who stake everything they have in their attempts to get their ideas and their computer code onto the most important road in the world today: the information superhighway.[7] These "Venture Trippers" arrive from Paris, from Salt Lake City, from Taiwan, from Boston, and share, according to Bronson, a sense of unbridled opportunity and excitement. They come from places wallowing in an X–Y-axis attitudinal coordinate, a slow motion way of thinking about one's life that offers a plodding story line they can't manage to suspend their disbelief of. "They come because what they see ahead of them . . . is a working life that seems fundamentally *boring*. . . . And rather than choosing not to work hard, the Venture Trippers are taking the opposite approach from the Slackers."[8]

Just as occurred in the 1840s, for most of the hopefuls the gamble does not pay off, of course, and they either filter into the many companies that service the economics of Silicon Valley or have to return to the world from which they came. And yet there is always the one gambler who makes it big and who can sign a deal that will instantly make another multimillionaire[9] and so ratify the economic culture of individual enterprise.

It is difficult to underestimate the importance of this particular narrative when thinking about the computer industry in the last twenty years, such has been the prevalence of start-up entrepreneurs in these new technological sectors of the economy. From Apple to Yahoo! there is usually the story of a self-made multimillionaire to be told behind the façade of a now hugely stock-market-rich global company.[10] Although he is careful to avoid naming names, one imagines that these entrepreneurs, and their allies in the media and in business, would be part of Arthur Kroker's "Virtual Class," a new economic grouping, he argues, that is "compulsively fixated on digital technology as a source of salvation from the reality of a lonely culture and radical social disconnection from everyday life, and determined to exclude from public debate any perspective that is not a cheerleader for the coming-to-be of the fully realized technological society."[11] Kroker suggests that the information superhighway is authoritarian and antidemocratic, that it stifles political dissent and aesthetic creativity, and that it "represents the disappearance of capitalism into colonized virtual space." Such virtual colonialism represents, he suggests in apocalyptic terms, "the endgame of postcapitalism."[12] Kroker's position is the antithesis of the optimistic McLuhanite attitude towards technology.

And yet for all that it is possible to write the history of Bill Gates and West Coast computing in the light of a narrative of cyber-authoritarianism that is invoked in order to reward those traditional frontier values of entrepreneurial opportunism, foresight, and individuality, there is still something troubling about the words of Gates and about the picture of him standing against the American West landscape. Peter Stoneley has noted that while the most keenly-sought transformation of gold-rush hopefuls in the nineteenth century was the change from being poor to being rich, the literature of those who experienced such attempts often points "toward a much more general sense of change and disorientation."[13]

It is a similar sense of change and disorientation in the contemporary period as it is written in *Microserfs* that interests me. This is a novel, after all, whose narrator turns out to be more interested in old asphalt highways than the information superhighway and who, along with his colleagues, forbids discussion of it because they are so sick of hearing about it (114). It is a novel that takes on and intersects with the narrative of pioneering entrepreneurism only to render that narrative unfocussed and imprecise. In Coupland's world Abe, despite the millions of dollars he has made from computing by the age of thirty, has "nothing to his name but a variety of neat-o consumer electronics and boxes of Costco products purchased in rash moments of Costco-scale madness" (10–11).

This kind of lifestyle is one that remains invisible to Kroker. The problem with his assessment of shifts in the dimensions of capitalist activity, and likewise the optimistic narrative that welcomes these technological changes, is that as critical positions they can never account for the way in which these shifts are experienced by the people directing them or upon whom they are exacted, people like Abe for instance. Dan touches on the importance and the transitional nature of this experience when he is persuaded by his girlfriend to keep his diary more regularly: "Karla got me to thinking that we really *do* inhabit an odd little nook of time and space here, and that odd or strange as this little nook may be, it's where *I* live—it's where *I am*" (63).

This sense of an "odd little nook of time" might provide a better way of thinking about Bill Gates than either the hostile attacks or the applause that are directed towards him. Robert Cringeley begins to sum up something of what is interesting about Gates in the following way: "Gates has gone from being the youngest person to be a self-made billionaire to being the self-made billionaire who acts the youngest."[14] For Cringeley the microcomputer industry was "started to satisfy the needs of disenfranchised nerds like Bill Gates who didn't meet the macho standards of American maleness"—the standards of dynamic masculinity inscribed into frontier narratives—and then turned into "a happy accident that allowed these boys to put off forever the horror age—that dividing line to adulthood that they would otherwise have been forced to cross after college."[15] For Tom Rath and Bob Slocum the organization was deficient precisely because of its lack of dynamic masculinity and for the lack of opportunity of this kind it offered masculinity. Cringeley's analysis suggests something similar about the computing industry of which Gates is a part: that it is not an industry built upon the spirit of successful masculine entrepreneurial activity in the mode of Silas Lapham and George Babbitt. This fact is often ignored when critics write about Gates and the computer industry. So keen are they to pin Gates's success into an American business heritage of masculinity, that the distinction between boyhood and manhood is often obscured. According to Pierre Guerlain:

the world of computer nerds and/or hackers, is a man's world . . . [Gates's] critics call it a "boyish fantasy," and there seems to be no doubt that Gates's vision of applied science-fiction appeals mostly to boys and men. Men also seem to be more interested in virtual reality, computer games, science fiction movies; almost all hackers are young men.[16]

Yet there is little here to suggest that boys might in fact be different from men. Or that behaving like a boy when one is supposed to be a man can have both positive and negative connotations. At the beginning of the twentieth century, as noted in chapter 4, there was a movement to have men rather than women take responsibility for the socializing of boys, such was the fear that society was being "womanized." For Bob Slocum it is the potential danger of a boyishness that is effeminate, questioning, and irrational that prompts him to smother his own son in order that he might smother the same traits in himself. Boyishness and the proper transition into manhood has been a problem in the history of American masculinity.

What is most striking to me about Annie Leibovitz's photograph of Gates is precisely the *incongruity* of Gates's casual and domestic—and decidedly *non-business*—attire and the rugged landscape that surrounds him. For Lapham it was obvious that "the landscape was made for man" to exploit in business; one product of the landscape was that entity for which Lapham had so much passion and which he turned into economic profit. For Gates the landscape provides only a photo opportunity as he tries to market his vision of the future, such is the distance from the actual landscape of the products that he manufactures, built as they are with millions of lines of hieroglyphic code. While the spirit of Lapham and Babbitt may linger in the narrative he propounds, it does not linger in his uneasy, timid, slightly frightened, and boyish posture against this landscape. Gates is reminiscent more of Ralph Hopkins than he is of Babbitt or Lapham. This signals that there are altogether more fascinating aspects to the *cultural* shift associated with the rise of the new economic sector of which he is a part and which is part of the ongoing economics of Silicon Valley.

What interests me in this chapter, then, is not the migration to Silicon Valley of hopeful entrepreneurs and that enduring, mythological frontier discourse, but a different kind of migration. It is one that has seen the products responsible for Gates's huge wealth—computer software —begin to alter the very nature of the capitalist working environment and contribute towards "the general sense of change and disorientation" that is experienced by those people whose lives cross the path of this particular historical moment, those people in Coupland's novel.

In June 1996 the *San Jose Mercury News* ran a feature entitled "Sleepless in Silicon Valley" about the working habits of people employed at local computing companies.[17] Together with the article is a series of photographs taken by Meri Simon. One shows a computer programmer covered by a blanket asleep under his desk in a cluttered office. Papers are strewn across the floor and work surfaces, and a soccer ball lies at the sleeper's feet. This latter-day Bartleby is not in danger, however, of angering his employer. He *is* the employer. The photograph is of David Filo. At the time the picture was taken, he was worth five hundred million dollars. As the cofounder of Yahoo!, the internet directory service, he is now worth several times that amount. Yet he does not even have his own office now. When Po Bronson visits him, he finds him sharing a double cubicle with one other person and "a trash heap of paper . . . forty inches deep of unread memos, promotional literature, office chatter. . . . It was his inbox and filing system." For Bronson the irony of this trash heap, the kind of mess, he says, that "your mom hollers at you to clean up," is that "the guy who has engineered the most popular directory for organizing the morass of the World Wide Web" is someone who is "utterly unable to engineer an organizational system for his own paper flow."[18]

In this working world, then, offices have clearly changed. No longer are they the places where one spends a specific portion of the day and from which one then routinely retreats to the private world of the home. Offices are where one may live for days at a time. Part of the impetus for the alteration in this usage pattern derives from the difficulty in allocating a place for the writing of code and the development of software applications. Is it work, or is it a hobby and a leisure activity that, for these code writers, predates its being turned into work? This is one of the themes that I explore in *Microserfs*.

But it is clear that offices in this world are also no longer places governed by the mantra of organizational efficiency in the Taylorist or Weberian fashion. As another programmer tells Bronson, "Work today has to be half work, half play. We spend our whole lives at the workplace."[19] This is a programmer who had recently been suspended for being caught naked at his desk, something he had been doing for many months in front of his programming colleagues who do not mind it, but that took one of the ancillary employees by surprise. He was reinstated when "everyone he'd met a deadline for" defended him.

It is this office world that Dan and his colleagues occupy at Microsoft, a code factory where the ability to "narrow-focus" makes nerds "so good at code-writing: one line at a time, one line in a strand of millions" (2). With this ability the traditional requirements of office organization can be ignored: "the campus is utterly casual" (25) according to Dan. There are no restrictions on the hours that he keeps or how he organizes or decorates his office, and so he fills it with, among other things, a "black-and-white photo shrine to Microsoft VP Steve Ballmer" that starts as a joke "but is sort of taking on a life of its own now" (26). The office corridors are lined with "*Far Side* cartoons taped to windows, Pepsi can sculptures taped to the walls, and inflatable sharks hanging from the ceilings," and life just would not be the same without the "weekly-ish communal stress-relieving frenzies" that on one occasion consists of punishing "plastic troll dolls with 5-irons, blasting them down the hallway, putting yet more divots in the particle board walls and the ceiling panels" (30).

It goes without saying that this kind of behavior would have been impossible in any of the other offices I have looked at so far. And yet it is behavior that is not just *tolerated* by the Microsoft management structure —a structure that by the standards of the 1960s and 70s corporation is streamlined to a skeletal degree—it is an attitude towards work that is fostered by the company as early as the hiring stages of employment. Advice about self-presentation for job interviews seems to make no sense in the computing software world. Fred Moody describes one interview candidate at Microsoft: "he was wearing a baggy striped T-shirt, boat shoes without socks, and oversized shorts made by tearing the legs off a pair of sweatpants."[20] The interviewer, with rock radio playing in the background, conducts the interview oblivious to dress and purely on the candidate's capacity to solve coding problems on a whiteboard. Once again it is code that counts, the ability to narrow focus, to block out the surrounding architecture and immerse oneself in the architecture of the code.

Working at Microsoft, then, means being caught up in a different culture of work, one in which priorities have radically altered. Meeting deadlines and writing code that performs tasks more quickly and more easily than existing code are the arbiters of success. So important to a company like Microsoft are these work values that there is a tacit recognition that the best way to stimulate them is not to rely upon the working environment that was needed to stimulate a different set of work priorities. Just as with David Filo, what matters is not an ability to organize the space in which one works, but the code that will organize the information with which users will interact. Especially when, according to Dan, everyone he knows at Microsoft "has an estimated time of departure and they're all within five years. It must be so weird—living the way my dad did—thinking your company was going to take care of you forever" (17). Dan's father has worked for IBM since he left his job in education in the mid 1980s, and it is IBM that exists as the embodiment of all that Microsoft has superseded. Dan's father works in an IBM division that has been doing well: "by IBM standards—it's not hemorrhaging money" (8), not a problem that any Microsoft divisions have.

Susan, another of the housemates, is an "IBM brat and hates the company with a passion. She credits it with ruining her youth by transferring her family eight times before she graduated from high school . . . nothing too evil can happen to IBM in her eyes" (9). Camped up in Redmond, Microsoft makes none of these disruptive demands on its employees. It makes them work long days—"In at 9:30 A.M.; out at 11:30 P.M.," or 1:30 A.M. or 2:30 A.M.—but instead of making them move home, Microsoft allows its employees to move their homes inside their own offices, and even provides "employee kitchen[s]" full of "dairy cases of Bill-supplied free beverages" (16). The result is that, working at Microsoft, Dan finds that his "weekends are no different than [his] weekdays" (18).

> Today, while raking the front lawn, Todd [the bodybuilding housemate] said, "Wouldn't it be scary if our internal clocks weren't set to the rhythm of waves and sunrise—or even the industrial toot—but to *product cycles*, instead?"
>
> We got nostalgic about the old days, back when September meant the unveiling of new car models and TV shows. Now, carmakers and TV people put them out whenever. Not the same. (55)

Todd has identified what has happened, even though it may be too scary for him to admit. This erasing of the cycles and the time clock of industrial capitalism, along with the erasing of the notion of career trajectory—either within one firm or between firms (which company does one go to as a coder after Microsoft has had one's best years?)—marks an important change in the way that capitalism interacts with its labor.

Microsoft encouraged this change with its use of stock options when it was employing people in the 1980s. While one might see it as a way of exacting loyalty from staff, the reality has been—and this is due to Microsoft's success—that once the stock has been held for the necessary amount of time, the employees then cash in, sell their stock and leave Microsoft. They celebrate with "vesting parties," just like Susan does. She quits Microsoft the day after she "vests" and unveils her new image to her housemates. Her previous image, "Patagonia-wearing Northwest good girl—had been shed for a radicalized look: bent shades, striped Fortrel too-tight top, Angela Bowie hairdo, dirty suede vest, flares, and Adidases" (62).

This possibility of vesting into richness, however, is beginning to fade at Microsoft. Dan is part of a generation of employees faced for the first time "with reduced stock options and . . . plateauing stock prices. I guess that makes them mere employees, just like at any other company" (17). And without this vesting option, Dan wonders what lies ahead once they reach their "inevitable Seven-Year Programmer's Burnout. . . . Face it," he says, "You're always just a breath away from a job in telemarketing" (16–17).

In addition to this, there are other factors that make Microsoft a less appealing place to work than it once was. Coupland's novel is, after all, called *Micro*serfs. The relentless work into the early hours of the morning is one part of the drudgery, but the working environment is also as alienating as it is tolerant and unsupervised. In terms of the formal kinds of surveillance that are etched into the architecture of offices even in a novel as recent as *The Mezzanine*, the offices in *Microserfs* seem remarkably lax: the lack of dress codes, the personalized and often disorganized offices that nowhere in *Microserfs* are entered by anyone but one's peers and that seem to be self-contained away from any management hierarchy, and the sense that workspaces come to mirror and be treated like homespaces. And yet it still manages to institute an almost *1984*-like sense that one is being watched. By Bill.

Moody has noted how Microsoft's approach to corporate organization —forming small teams around specific products and letting them sort out the work amongst themselves—is a "risky approach, for these crews are left unsupervised to a degree unthinkable in standard American corporations." And he admits that one of the results of this approach is "informality" and "individual freedom." But allied with this, he identifies an "excruciating psychological pressure."[21] While job candidates may dress how they like, the interviews are conducted so as not only to test the applicant's programming ability, "but also their psychological fit with Microsoft." Hence the "grueling immersion in the company's ethos and culture"[22] that was originated by Gates.

All routes in Microsoft lead back to Bill Gates. Gates is noted not just for his tantrums in meetings at Microsoft, but also for his stunning technical ability that means he has a different relationship with his employees and their work. As one employee says, "He'll know some intricate low-level detail about a program, and you wonder, 'How did he know that? He has no reason ever to get to that level!' Some piece of code, or some other technology that Microsoft isn't even involved in. You just shake your head."[23] These exacting standards mean that one must prepare as precisely as possible for encounters with him, and this need for preparation is passed along the management line. Consequently Microsoft becomes a company dominated by the image of one man, "Citizen Gates" as he has become known. This is a situation different from the faceless bureaucracies of companies like the ones for which Tom Rath, Bob Slocum, Howie, and Arno Strine work. And yet it does not mean that the creation of surveillance effects is nullified. In some ways they are heightened.

Microserfs starts off with Michael, another of Dan's housemates, receiving flame-mail from Bill. The subject of the e-mail is "a chunk of code Michael had written," about which Bill just "wailed on" (1). Of course the telephone has always allowed access in a chain of hierarchy from the topmost point to the lowest point of that hierarchy. And yet to equate the two forms of communication is to miss the peculiar qualities of intimacy and distance that e-mail facilitates. E-mail allows Bill to enter the office of any Microsoft employee, and yet to do so with a lack of any personal contact that gives it an institutional force similar in many ways to the advice and admonition of the priest's confession box. Not only this, but e-mail is often one-way communication, a type of pure utterance that leads one not to engage with another person, but engage with oneself instead. E-mails like the one Michael receives work to train one's mind on what one is doing, a classic tactic to instill disciplinary self-surveillance. As Dan points out: "We figured it must have been a random quality check to keep the troops in line" (1). And it certainly has an effect on Michael, especially as he is the most sensitive coder in Building Seven. He locks himself in his office and refuses to come out. Dan

gets so concerned that in the middle of the night he drives to the Safe-
way store to buy flat foods to push under Michael's door—"Kraft sin-
gles, Premium Plus crackers, Pop-Tarts, grape leather, and Greezie-
Pops" (2)—for which Michael is grateful when he finally emerges from
his office the next day after sleeping in there overnight. He determines
not to eat anything that is not two-dimensional thereafter: "Ich bin ein
Flatlander," he declares (7), in a jokey but compelling way. The overt reference here may be to Edwin Abbot's 1884 novel *Flatland: A Romance in
Many Dimensions*, a satirical novel whose characters are two-dimensional
segments, triangles, squares, and polygons, and which is very much a cult
text in computing and scientific subcultures.[24] Yet the particular phras-
ing used have also seems to position Michael and his Microsoft cohorts
in a trajectory of American national technology that was heightened by
a president who not only claimed "Ich bin ein Berliner" but also sanctioned the space race.

Once more, though, the two narratives of migration intersect contra-
puntally, since it is not the frontier of space and other-earthly exploration that concerns this generation, but a textual, coded world that
exists—like flat food—in two dimensions on a computer screen, even
though it can come to mimic a three-dimensional environment. This
mimicking is the project that Michael—and it is significant that it is
Michael—ultimately embarks upon and on which the rest of the housemates join him. I will return to this later. For now it is worth pointing out
the impact that this whole flaming of Michael has on Dan: "I thought
about the e-mail and Bill and all of that, and I had this weird feeling—
of how the presence of Bill floats about the campus, semi-visible, at all
times, kind of like the dead grandfather in the *Family Circus* cartoons. Bill
is a moral force, a spectral force, a force that shapes, a force that moulds.
A force with thick, thick glasses" (3).

So for all its informal and unsupervised management practices, for all
its homely offices, play areas, kitchen facilities, and free drinks, these
benefits are put into perspective by the cult of Bill, the omniscient boss
who imbues himself into the spirit, the landscape, and the architecture
of his company. Big Blue becomes Big Green[25] and hands out to its staff
"Ship-it" awards if products go out on time, inscribed with the company's hymn—"Every time a product ships, it takes us one step closer to
the vision: A computer on every desk and in every home." Like the spirit
of Bill these awards are "awesomely indestructible," even when Todd
and Dan tie them to the back of Dan's AMC Hornet and drag them for
an hour around the suburbs of Bellevue and Redmond (47).

Working at Microsoft, then, gives something of a hint of the nature of how the office environment has changed in the new computing software industry. And yet the company's success, which has led to its increasing size,[26] has also led to the negation of the innovative strategies that threatened to turn Microsoft into the "home" of a new working ethic. The road ahead for Dan and his colleagues and friends (there is little distinction between the two categories in *Microserfs*) does not involve Microsoft. It is Michael who offers them the chance to leave Bill behind. Sent on a trip to Silicon Valley by Microsoft, after his flaming by Bill is followed—hard cop/soft cop-style—by lunch with Bill, Michael never returns. It is hard to distinguish the line of motivation for him not returning since Michael never explains the sequence of events which end up with him staying in Silicon Valley. However, he certainly does not want to return to Microsoft. Perhaps he recognizes, like Todd, that at Microsoft while one may not be a cog in the wheel of industry anymore, one is instead a "cross-platform highly transportable binary object" (60); perhaps his time in Silicon Valley makes him feel that getting away from Microsoft is something of the equivalent of emerging from Biosphere 2, like it will be for Dan (98). Maybe he feels the way Dan feels:

> I got to thinking of my cramped, love-starved, sensationless existence at Microsoft—and I got so pissed off. . . . I wanted to forget the way my body was ignored, year in, year out, in the pursuit of code, in the pursuit of somebody else's abstraction. . . . There's something about a monolithic tech culture like Microsoft that makes humans seriously rethink fundamental aspects of the relationship between their brains and bodies—their souls and their ambitions; things and thoughts. (90–91)

Whichever of these possibilities is the more accurate, there is no doubt that Microsoft and Silicon Valley in *Microserfs* come to represent different working environments. It is not the pursuit of code that Dan objects to *per se*, since his new work in Silicon Valley will be the pursuit of more code. It is code that represents "somebody else's abstraction" that he resents; an abstraction that becomes solidified in the monolithic Microsoft. The code that is written there is enshrined in the campus and in the Microsoft branding that connects everything to Bill. Silicon Valley, on the other hand, is a place that exists as a visual phenomenon on the same level as the computer code on which its importance as a place is built: it is invisible. But, as Dan himself comments, "invisibility is invariably where one locates the ACTION" (137).

The failure of traditional visual techniques sufficiently to capture the nature of Silicon Valley is one way of beginning to think about the status of this invisibility. Following a film crew trying to make a documentary about the place and about the computing industry, Po Bronson finds that after a whole day's shooting they still have not found an opening, establishing shot, something that would serve a similar purpose to the letters on the Hollywood hillside telling the audience where they are. Part of this failure derives from the incoherent intersection of the two migratory narratives defined earlier. Slotted into a traditional frontier narrative, Silicon Valley is a story of high stakes, hard work, sudden wealth, and rapid growth, conditions that would seem to offer copious opportunities for synecdochic visual images, just like, for instance, the stock market and investment banking world of the 1980s had—"Liquid crystal stock tickers rushed quotes along the walls. . . . Men and women . . . screaming into their telephones, standing up amid war-room-like computer monitors."[27] And yet in Silicon Valley all the film crew find is "an endless suburb, hushed and nonchalant, in terrain too flat to deserve the term 'valley.'"[28] There is no Valley architecture to represent to the world the vertiginous impact this location is having upon people's lives, nothing to mark it as a distinctive place with a distinctive relationship to a style of capitalism.

Yet if one follows the other narrative of migration, it is possible to discern instead that here is an industry that marks itself in an altogether different kind of way and in an altogether different place: it is on one's desktop in the "screenful of icons that make computers touch-feely familiar"[29] that the Valley appears. The architecture of Silicon Valley, then, resides in the code it produces. And by migrating its architecture in this way—from the three-dimensional to the two-dimensional, from the material to the hieroglyphic—Silicon Valley has facilitated the flattening of the distinctions between the workplace and the home, between work and leisure, that have stood at the heart of the experience of work in American culture in the last hundred years. Once the architecture of code replaces the architecture of the built environment as the site for the creation of value in a capitalist economy, the need for the workplace to be discretely marked and separated becomes less and less important.

At Netscape a dentist visits the office site several times a week so the employees there do not have to leave work to take care of their teeth; at Excite they have office laundry facilities for workers who do not have the time to do their washing at home. The office park—combining a work environment with a mall environment, a producing with a consuming environment, a work with a leisure environment—has become a Silicon Valley phenomenon that, according to Bronson, is part of a whole design to blur the distinction between work and nonwork, between indoors and outdoors, and between work and rest. Silicon Valley "is this concept taken to the level of a whole region: it's one big office park."[30] At the same time, the migration of architecture in this way provides a means for exporting the structures of this architecture to every desktop across the computerized world.

It is into this invisible powerhouse of American capital that Dan and his Microsoft colleagues move. Crossing the border into California from Washington, Karla remarks that "We live in an era of no historical precedents . . . The cards are being shuffled; new games are being invented. And we're actually *driving* to the actual card factory" (99). The double use of "actual" here—since they are not driving towards a card factory at all—draws attention to the metaphor Karla uses and so to the underlying virtuality of Valley economics.

For Dan, the world of Silicon Valley, while it may have no historical precedents, certainly exists in a continuum of capitalist development. Charting the shift in the relationship between corporation and employee since the 1970s, he notes the gradual "integration of the corporate realm into the private" (211) as corporations provided workplace sweeteners —showers for lunchtime joggers, sculptures—that attempted to "soothe the working soul." The campus model at Microsoft and Apple was the next stage in this process, when "the borderline between work and life blurred to the point of unrecognizability" (211).

The final stage of this process is Silicon Valley in the 1990s: "corporations don't even hire people anymore. People become their own corporations" (211). This transition—or delegation—of the corporate ethos also marks a transition in the location of the production of history. Dan's father belongs to that generation who believed that "history was created by think tanks, the DOE and the Rand Corporation of Santa Monica, California" (203–4); the same paranoid generation to which Tom Rath and Bob Slocum belonged and for whom big business and big government epitomized the control over the individual of the military-industrial complex. While revisiting the IBM plant from which he has now been fired, Dan's father says, "I never thought history was something my kid built in the basement. It's a shock" (204).

Dan's father recognizes at this point that the world of business has come full circle. Just as merchants once worked from their homes, so computer coders can now run businesses from home. Within this context, then, and as if to emphasize the collapsing distinction between the workplace and the home that the shift to a virtual architecture of code helps bring about, Dan's parents' Palo Alto house becomes not only the place where Dan, Karla, and Michael move in to live, but also the place where the new business venture is located and which Susan, Bug, and Todd drive to each day. The product they work on is a game developed by Michael called *Oop!* This game, not coincidentally, is a "virtual construction box," a kind of computerized version of Lego. But whereas Lego bricks have only a small number of "bumps" that can be connected to other Lego bricks, *Oop!* bricks can have thousands of bumps, so the possibilities for creating complex objects is vastly increased. Imagine:

> "Oopenstein"—flesh-like *Oop!* bricks or cells, each with ascribed biological functions that allow users to create complex life forms using combinations of single and cloned cell structures. Create life!
> "Mount Oopmore"—a function that allows users to take a scanned photo, texture map that photo, and convert it into a 3D visualized *Oop!* object.
> "Oop-Mahal"—famous buildings, preconstructed in *Oop!*, that the user can then modify as desired.
> "Frank Lloyd Oop"—architectural *Oop!* for adults. (71)

Oop! is an acronym for Object-Oriented Programming, a particular kind of approach to writing code for contemporary Windows software applications. One of the main benefits of the Windows operating system is that it is device-independent. It separates the specific hardware devices on a computer—the keyboard, monitor, hard disk drive, mouse —from the software programs that run on it. This separation is known as abstraction, and it allows software programmers to work with general categories of hardware rather than specific makes and models. They can write code for whatever printer is attached to the computer system, or whatever monitor or keyboard. Windows—through model-specific drivers for particular hardware devices—does the job of letting the software application communicate with the computer hardware.

Object-oriented programming is important because, as its name suggests, it breaks the programming process down into a series of objects that can be reused, not only in the same software application, but in other applications too. These reusable objects shorten development time, are easily distributable, and facilitate the kind of group coding projects that one finds not only at Microsoft but also on Michael's *Oop!* project where each person is given a discrete task. In one way, then, the division of labor that object-oriented programming requires could be seen as a classic *laissez-faire* or even Taylorist solution to software production.

Oop!'s relation to object-oriented programming is left unexplained in *Microserfs*, but I think that what the use of this acronym suggests is that *Oop!* serves the purpose in the novel of something more than just another computer game on the market. It also has a symbolic value that allows the binding together of the various thematic elements of the novel —work, technology, capitalism, computing—around this central motif of code as the architecture of the 1990s. As the very reason why Michael and Dan and their colleagues migrate to Silicon Valley, it stands as a powerful literary metaphor foregrounding the idea that the ultimate purpose of code is to produce architecture, although not the kind of architecture that will occupy the traditional spaces of the body (Oopenstein/ Frankenstein), the national monument (Mount Oopmore/Mount Rushmore), the tourist attraction (Oop Mahal/Taj Mahal), or the workplace (Frank Lloyd Wright's most famous office design was for the Larkin Building in Buffalo, New York, 1904). Instead it is an architecture that has migrated into the syntax of code, and thus it is here that one should look if one wants to know about work, technology, capitalism, and computing in the 1990s.

Code, then, is the synecdochic image the film crew are looking for. But code is flat and two-dimensional; it is text and not images. It is the failure to recognize that the dazzling visual effects of a program like *Oop!*, of a place like Silicon Valley, are produced not by pioneering technological frontiersmen and their visual baggage but by strictly regulated strings of commands, functions, and syntax in coded textual information that leaves the film crew stumbling around for that one image which they hope can capture the essence of the Valley. In a real sense this image actually resides within the computerized equipment they carry with them during their search.

It is worth stressing here just how important the link is between computer code and an architectural terminology that draws on familiar aspects of office design. The key moment in this development, and the key moment that enabled control over computing software to be passed on to the employee and the consumer, was the shift from a character-based to an icon-based command structure. This development was pioneered by Apple but is dominated now by Microsoft. This was the shift from MS-DOS to Windows operating systems. Before the arrival of the

Windows platform, IBM-compatible PC users were forced to type in "often-obscure commands," as Gates himself puts it, in order to run programs and get these programs to do anything. The thinking behind Microsoft's development of Windows was to create an easier to use interface in order "to realize our vision of widespread personal computer use."[31]

As this book has made clear, the connection between windows and offices has a long history. And while American office work has come a long way since the lawyer-narrator's office in "Bartleby," it is windows (or Windows) that provide one key link. But whereas the windows in "Bartleby" offered an unchanging view of either the "white wall of the interior of a spacious sky-light shaft" on one side, or "a lofty brick wall, black by age and everlasting shade" on the other,[32] the Windows of any contemporary office will offer ever-changing views of all kinds of spreadsheets, databases, word-processed documents, files, folders, and messages. What this new Windows environment facilitates—the new Windows environment that can contain the operations of a whole office—is the migration of huge amounts of information from disparate physical locations to the few square inches of real estate that is a computer monitor, and which is accessed by gazing through a myriad of Windows, since every part of every program interface—the scroll bars, the toolbars, the icons, the menus—is a separate window seamlessly integrated into one big window that contains the program. Concentrated and compacted, this information sits waiting as a collection of binary code until it is given a form and an intelligibility by Windows.

It has been a central argument of my book that office windows, and the visual rhetoric which they institute, are one of the ways in which the discourses of surveillance and self-surveillance come to operate in the capitalist office. I want to carry this idea through to these new kinds of Windows environments as well, since they continue and in some ways intensify, the importance of this visual rhetoric, since now windows are not that distraction by which one is surrounded while performing work tasks, but the means through which one has to look to fulfill these tasks. There is no getting away from Windows now. Furthermore, these Windows through which one is constantly looking are not solely located on one's own desktop and are certainly not self-contained in even the smallest of offices, since the development of network technology means that these Windows are connected to other Windows—not physically, perhaps, but directly nevertheless thanks to the space-altering effects that an architecture of code can produce. This kind of technology means that

Windows are two-way. Not only can you look through them to perform your work, but you can be looked at through them. Once again, this is not a visual relationship—the telescreen of *1984* is still beyond Citizen Gates—but a relationship that is mediated through a two-dimensional architecture of code. Code becomes the language that one writes oneself in at the workplace, and it becomes the language that can be reassembled —because it is a code that is architecturally transportable—elsewhere on the network.

One example of the way this can be achieved is in the field of e-mail. Since the computers people use at work belong to the company, the company has the right to monitor employee e-mail boxes. To have someone sitting and wading through all this information would, however, be impractical. Instead network software exists that can filter e-mails depending on keywords, content, and the sender's address. It can copy any mail that fits these parameters to the mailbox of a supervisor who can then act upon only those messages that appear to warrant the company's attention.[33] The connections between this kind of behavior and the role of the warden in the panopticon is clear enough. What is important is not that every e-mail message is being monitored, but that a system is in place that allows, if only potentially, the monitoring of every e-mail. On networked systems there is in fact little information about what is going on at each computer module that cannot be stored and retrieved by network administrator software.[34]

The importance of Silicon Valley for this study is how it exists in relation to these changes. By itself, the fact that it is a barely discernible location in the Californian landscape is not particularly striking. What *is* striking is the way that this relative invisibility can be seen to be both a consequence of, and a metaphor for, the changing site of economic productivity and value creation in contemporary capitalism: the shift from a visible architecture of material production to an invisible architecture of code. To date, the critical responses to this shift have paid little attention to the issue of code itself. Silicon Valley is usually represented, as Brian Jarvis points out, "as the paradigmatic geography of the postindustrial," although these accounts are marked by "certain strategic omissions, relating to the nature of white-collar labour and the structural and spatial interdependence of forms of economic activity."[35] While Jarvis attempts to redress this imbalance by drawing attention to the exclusionary rhetoric of Daniel Bell, Marshall McLuhan, and Jean Baudrillard and then by discussing the way in which the issue of spatiality has come to play an important part in the attempts of Marxist critics to approach the phenomenon of the postindustrial and to recover some sort of radical political culture from within these altered conditions, it is disappointing that not once does Jarvis recognize the serious impact upon notions of spatiality and upon people's lives that the invisibilized computer code produced in Silicon Valley has had.

To clarify my interest here, then, I should point out that in the context of this book, what interests me most about Silicon Valley as a phenomenon is not the way that its specific products have directly changed office culture—Windows, after all, is a product of Microsoft in Seattle. More relevant is that the principle on which these products and Silicon Valley are founded—code as architecture—has literally altered the epistemological organization of office space because of the intrusion into that space of this new dominant.

One way to approach the impact of this epistemological shift in terms of gender and sexuality in the office would be to focus on the ways in which the re-inscription of these visual effects of surveillance and self-surveillance at such a fundamental and operational level in the contemporary office continues the kinds of effects I identified in "Bartleby," *The Rise of Silas Lapham*, *Babbitt*, *The Man in the Gray Flannel Suit*, and *Something Happened*. In my reading of these texts I demonstrated how the textual representation of the architecture of office space becomes the site where a rhetoric about the organization of male heterosexuality is played out, often one that results in the marginalizing and demonizing of same-sex desire.

This approach could be carried through to other contemporary representations of the office. And yet in the previous chapter I showed how for Nicholson Baker this kind of representation was not his primary concern, that there is in his work a sense of a different relationship between the office and male heterosexuality. Likewise, this approach does not seem particularly relevant to *Microserfs*, for two major reasons. First, the office environments in which Dan and his colleagues work are not of the same order as those to be found in popular novels which later became movies such as *American Psycho*, *Bright Lights, Big City*, or *Bonfire of the Vanities*. *Oop!* is a program that is written in Dan's parents' house; the separation of the workplace from the home that marked the earlier texts and still marks other contemporary texts has ceased to apply here. Second, taking the same approach to Coupland as to the earlier texts would miss something of the nature of that "more general sense of change and disorientation" that Peter Stoneley identified in that other defining moment of American capitalism, the Gold Rush.

In critical terms, the question of what I should do with a text like *Microserfs* has been influenced by Eve Sedgwick's introduction to *Novel Gazing: Queer Readings in Fiction*. Here Sedgwick charts the history of a particular kind of paranoid critical reading, into which, it has to be said, much of this book would in fact fit. She argues that the productive critical consequences embodied by Paul Riceour's "hermeneutics of suspicion" may have actually produced the unwelcome side effect of making "it less rather than more possible to unpack the local, contingent relations between any given piece of knowledge and its narrative/epistemological entailments for the seeker, knower, or teller."[36] In the place of this kind of critical inquiry has developed a suspicious criticism that privileges the concept of paranoia and a quest for systemic oppression so that "to theorize out of anything *but* a paranoid critical position has come to seem naive, pious, or complaisant."[37] Sedgwick also charts the way that this kind of paranoid reading, because of Freud's formulation of paranoia as the repression of homosexuality and because of responses to this position that demonstrated how paranoia helped to show how homophobia and heterosexism worked, was taken up by critics, like Sedgwick herself, in the cause of an anti-homophobic inquiry.

A paranoid reading of *Microserfs* would clearly have to situate its representation of the computing industry very firmly within Arthur Kroker's vision of the Virtual Class. The collapse of the separation between workplace and home would, in this reading, amount to nothing less than the incorporation of the home into the workplace, the turning of all sites—because of the transportability of the software office and the logic of Windows on which it relies—into workplaces and the turning of all time into work time. What in fact this amounts to is the fulfillment of the disciplinary desires that preoccupied those early industrialists who wanted to build regulatory towns and communities in which their workers could live. The McLuhanite global village would assume the status of global workhouse, with all the admonishing attributes in regard to gender, sexuality, and normalcy that were so instituted in the nineteenth-century workhouse. This reading would, of course, in its paranoid logic, seem to anticipate the whole systemic structure of surveillance and discipline it was seeking to expose.[38]

This reading is not entirely untenable. But it becomes difficult to sustain in the face of *Microserfs* for two reasons. First, because *Microserfs* is a novel that so manifestly fails to address the structure of this systemic vision, and second, because such a paranoid reading deals in a logic of exposure that assumes its audience will be surprised or disturbed by that which is exposed. But would anybody who had lived through two terms of Reaganism, Sedgwick argues, be shocked to find out that so-called liberal society does not in fact fulfill a duty of pastoral care over each of its citizens? In a similar fashion, just "How television-starved would someone have to be," she asks, "to find it shocking that ideologies contradict themselves, that simulacra don't have originals, or that gender representations are artificial?"[39] Ultimately such critical approaches, while watertight and impossible to refute, have failed to anticipate future changes and thus are inadequate for the job of coping with the effects of power and for making oppositional strategy.

For Sedgwick, it becomes important to recognize that "to practice other than paranoid forms of knowing does *not*, in itself, entail a denial of the reality or the gravity of enmity or oppression."[40] It is in the space opened up by this claim that she places the essays in the collection she is introducing, essays that she argues present a form of "reparative impulse" that is "additive and accretive. Its fear, a realistic one, is that the culture surrounding it is inadequate or inimical to its nurture; it wants to assemble and confer plenitude on an object that will then have resources to offer to an inchoate self."[41] Building on a point she has made elsewhere in her work,[42] Sedgwick turns to the image of the child or adolescent reader to refine her idea of how this reparative reading operates. It is a kind of interpretive absorption that the young reader displays, at a point in life when personal queerness "may or may not (*yet?*) have resolved into a sexual specificity of object choice, aim, site or identification." For this kind of reader, it is the "recognitions, pleasures, and discoveries" that enter the "speculative, superstitious" reading consciousness that are most compelling.[43]

It is a perverse swing, but one that I am willing to risk in order to link *Microserfs* to the possibilities of this reparative critical position and to Cringeley's assessment of Bill Gates as the "self-made billionaire who acts the youngest." Despite his wealth and power, there is a narrative about Gates, one that Cringeley is happy to perpetuate, that he is "a *young* person" even when he is thirty-six (his age when Cringeley was writing his book). This narrative is tied in to a narrative of inadequacy: Bill is not a proper man, he does not respect his responsibilities, he lives in that "shallow world" that kids live in, full of popular culture, music, and zits.

"William H. Gates III, who is not a bad person," Cringeley concludes, "is two-dimensional."[44]

While this kind of summary is meant to be a reproach, for my purposes it seems only right and proper that someone so responsible for the development of a two-dimensional coded architecture should themselves be so childish and two-dimensional. It is at this congruence then of a critical reading practice that pays tribute to the tactics of a childish perspective and a childish, two-dimensional businessman who deals in the two-dimensional code that has become the architecture of the 1990s, that I want to place *Microserfs*. It is only at this point that the relationships and obsessions and anxieties that dominate Coupland's novel seem to gather and to present an experience of a culture that can surpass the paranoid.

There are two preliminary points to be made that will demonstrate how the very background upon which gender and sexuality are organized in the workplaces of *Microserfs* is one that hangs in stark contrast to all the previously dicussed texts. These points, while they may appear to be obvious, are vitally important in the context of the male representations of working life that have preceded them, and they signal an entirely different terrain of engagement between men and men and between men and women.

The first thing to be said is that despite the reputation computing has for being a male and a masculine form of work and leisure activity,[45] in *Microserfs* there is no gender distinction amongst coders. Karla, Susan, and later Dusty, code just like Michael, Dan, Todd, Abe, and Bug. When they start on the *Oop!* project, they are each given discrete coding tasks, each as vital to the final program as any other. Susan even starts a support group called Chyx "for Valley women who code." The prerequisites for joining are "fluency in two or more computer languages, a vagina, and a belief that Mary Tyler Moore as Mary Richards in a slinky pantsuit is the worldly embodiment of God" (288). Dan suspects Susan will be swamped by women wanting to join, and she duly is. But lest this support group be seen as testament to the raw deal women coders receive in the Valley, Susan ends up on CNN discussing "gender-blindness in the tech world" (314).

It would perhaps be too risky to apply this "gender-blindness" appellation to any industry, and yet where in *Microserfs* is the evidence of that fracturing of the working and office space between male- and female-designated environments? It is difficult to find it anywhere. There are no secretaries in *Microserfs*. From *The Rise of Silas Lapham*, through *Babbitt*, and then through *The Man in the Gray Flannel Suit* and *Something Happened*, the secretary has been the only female member of the workforce who has ever been deemed worthy of representation (with the possible exception of Virginia and Mrs. Yerger in *Something Happened*, a femme fatale and a harridan respectively). The feminization of the office that was such a key narrative discourse for men, particularly in the postwar period, in *Microserfs* does not register in Dan's narrative. This may well be due to two connected developments: the diminishing relevance (although not yet the disappearance in some quarters) of the link between women and domesticity that was such a feature of Cold War family rhetoric and the collapsing of the workplace and home binary. Just as the shift to an architecture of code as the site for the creation of capitalist value decreases the importance of the workplace as a site, the rise of a larger female working population diminishes the association of women with a particular domestic environment, since they now occupy so many other spaces as well.

This first point really feeds into the second, which is the prevalence in *Microserfs* of mixed-gendered friendship. It has been difficult to discern friendship of any kind in virtually all the texts so far, barring those friendships in *The Rise of Silas Lapham* and in *Babbitt* that are of a homoerotic nature. Such has been the importance of the family and of the home as an alternative environment to the world of work for the male protagonists in these previous texts, that the issue of friendship has, if broached at all, hardly generated any positive representations. In *Silas Lapham* and *Babbitt* friendship is portrayed almost as a malign necessity that disciplines both of the main characters. Lapham is kept in his socially inferior place by the citizens of Boston with whom he tries to ingratiate himself and by the delegation from the Athletic Club that "shouldered into Babbitt's office with the air of a Vigilante committee in frontier days" to bring him back into line following his affair with Tanis Judique and his ambivalence toward the strike. In *The Man in the Gray Flannel Suit* and *Something Happened* Tom Rath and Bob Slocum simply alternate between office and home, work colleagues and family. There is never any connection between the two sets of people and no one *outside of* the two sets of people. And in *The Man in the Gray Flannel Suit* Tom is responsible for killing his best friend.

In *Microserfs*, by contrast—and once again the impact of the collapsing of the boundary of work and home does social and cultural work—work colleagues are not only friends, they are also housemates. It is important to remember here, of course, that *Microserfs* deals with a different generation of workers than the other texts do. All of them bar Abe are under thirty, so families and family homes have not yet staked a claim on their emotional time and effort. But it has to be said as well that they show no signs of doing so either. Dusty and Todd have a baby together and yet it seems hardly to affect the way that they interact with the rest of the coders.[46]

These two points, however obvious then, suggest that *Microserfs* marks a definite break with the earlier texts. In many ways it is a text that seems to refuse any attempt to force it to fit into the kinds of discourses I have been applying to those texts. In the light of this, I want to go back to the work of Lee Edelman and suggest that one of the things that *Microserfs* does is necessitate a rereading of his theoretical explanation of inscription, de-scription, and the construction of male sexuality within the visual realm.

It is here that we come back to the question of code, since for Edelman the importance of coding the male body was that the reading of these codes by other men did the job of positioning that body in a particular relation to a classification of sexuality. In the chapter on "Bartleby" I argued that the office needed to be considered a site where this inscription and de-scription of the male body in visual terms took place precisely because the office was—and was to become even more—saturated with those types of visual surveillance that Foucault argued were central to the development of a capitalist, disciplinary society from the eighteenth century onwards. It was the visual apparatus of this regime of surveillance that performed the job of producing working male bodies in relation to the categorizations of homosexual and heterosexual. It should also be remembered that for Edelman it was the textualization of the male *homosexual* body in particular that was crucial for marking a hierarchy of sexual identity—heterosexual over homosexual—since the homosexual male body was produced "in a determining relation to inscription itself" and thus assimilated homosexual identity to the position traditionally held by writing—after Derrida—in Western intellectual history, that is inferior to a phonocentric metaphysics of speech and voice.[47]

I have shown in this chapter how the architectures of surveillance that would call up this process of inscription and de-scription in previous office narratives have, in *Microserfs* and in that computer software world of Silicon Valley, become less and less important. The traditional apparatus of visual surveillance in the workplace that would bear testament to this process has been erased here in this flattened, endless suburb; as code has become the architecture of the 1990s, it is into this textual realm that the site of capitalism is migrating. One question that needs to be asked at some point is just how applicable Derrida's assertion about the marginalizing of writing remains when so much of the productive and wealth-generating capacity of capitalism in Silicon Valley is now generated by the writing of code. One could argue that this migration to value based on code would produce a simple transposition effect where the previous kinds of identity construction in the built environment get passed over into this new realm of coded architecture. It is important to be mindful of the two obvious points mentioned above, however, because if the social and cultural backgrounds—the collapsed boundary of work and home, the mixed-gendered working environment —have changed so radically in this location as well, then it would suggest that this simple transposition effect is unlikely, since many of the traditional structures that held it in place have themselves been dissolved.

And we really have to question how applicable Edelman's contention remains about homosexuality being placed in such close relation to inscription, when so many men and women are involved in the process of inscribing code and elsewhere perform jobs that require an intimate contact with inscription—that is, clerical jobs. It may be that the shift to a service economy based on writing and typing and language—by implicating far more groups of people in the processes of writing—actually results in the loosening of the link between inscription and homosexuality. The historical legacy of this link persists in those ideas—as articulated by someone like Robert Cringeley—about computing nerds being boys still, unformed sexually, and not masculine within a very straight definition of masculinity. Indeed, in Annie Leibovitz's photograph of Bill Gates, it is the straightness of the road on which he stands that contributes to the incongruity of the whole scene. Young boys are not always straight; they are people, as Sedgwick says, whose personal queerness "may or may not (*yet?*) have resolved into a sexual specificity of object choice, aim, site or identification."[48] In Edelman's schema it could be that these nerds, often portrayed as not particularly streetwise, are actually very shrewd in their ability to size up social sexual situations because of their familiarity with the relationship between code and the visual effects that it produces.

But in *Microserfs* there are two particular queernesses that get (temporarily?) resolved during the course of the novel that can help to show how the terrain of marking out sexual classifications has changed in this particular world. These lead back to Dan, the novel's central consciousness, whose narrative actually takes on quite explicitly the issue of code. Dan's deconstruction of it does not, however, lead to that second part of Edelman's concept of homographesis—the de-scription of a secure heterosexual identity that would lead to the marking and disavowal of homosexuality so important in the earlier texts. It leads to something altogether more sentimental.

The first queerness is Bug's. Until halfway through the novel he exists without a sexuality. This is not an unusual occurrence, since as Dan tells us, "Many geeks don't really have a sexuality—they just have work" (227). But then, after fulfilling his dream of visiting the Xerox PARC[49] and returning to Dan's parents' house to carry on working, he announces to his friends that he is gay. Bug says that coming south to California has helped him to "sprout," "like those seeds you used to plant on top of sterile goop in petri dishes in third grade" (193–94). After a couple of questions, Dan announces, "So that was that" (194). And in many ways it is. Nothing really changes except that Bug begins to go out on dates with men. He goes to get his hair cut with Dan's dad (251), who, like the rest of the household and the work team, while not oblivious to Bug's sexual outing, incorporate it seamlessly into a worldview that allows changes and shifts in lifestyles to come and go: "You know, Daniel, I have noticed that people are generally thrilled to have change enter their lives," Dan's father tells him. Todd becomes a Marxist for a while (250), and Susan becomes a militant postfeminist with her Chyx organization. It would be easy just to pigeonhole this kind of rhetoric in the novel into a kind of sterile postmodernism were it not for the fact of all the other social, economic, and cultural changes I have outlined and were it not for Bug's sensitive appraisal of his own situation within—and this point needs to be emphasized—this particular local cultural situation. Silicon Valley is, after all, on the doorstep of San Francisco where "being gay is such a non issue" (301). Bug touches on the changing conceptualization of sexual definition within this culture when he says that "I'm vulnerable to identity changes because I'm so desperate to find a niche" (306).

This idea of the niche has important connotations in a contemporary culture that is dominated by consumption. Dennis Allen has tried to think through some of the consequences for sexuality in just such a culture.[50] Allen is interested in two issues: the rise of lesbian, bisexual, and gay studies in the academy and the discourses available for explaining shifts in sexual identity. In an interesting move, he starts off by asking why it is that the shift from a gay or bisexual identity to a straight one— something he has experienced while teaching lesbigay classes—can only be explained in terms of personal regression, biphobia, or a seduction by straight ideology. The discovery of a lesbigay identity, in contrast, is often explained as self-discovery and as the discovery of a sexual authenticity that the shift to a straight identity lacks. Most queer theorists, he argues, subscribe to this notion, whether one considers heterosexuality as a "cultural norm or as the sexual identity of certain people."[51]

With the change from an industrial economy of production to a post-industrial economy of consumption, the very way in which identity is supposed to be formed is different: "identity categories must now be understood not as the inevitable outcome of individual (sexual) desire but rather as the insertion of that desire into a differentiated structure of social signs that defines identities through consumption."[52] The growth of lesbigay studies in the academy reflects the changing role of education in this economy of consumption—sexual identity becoming a category that one consumes along with many others—and it also suggests a change in the notion of difference within categories of sexual identity. No longer is sexuality represented as a divide between straight and gay with the former exploiting the latter. Now there is a realization that all the possible options are equally valid choices, whether this is consumer goods or identity categories.

The shift from a gay or bisexual to a straight identity is incomprehensible in anything but negative ways, while the coming out narrative assumes an economy of production where it is the role of coming out to demystify the relations of exploitation in this economy. In an economy of consumption, however—and this is where Bug's resolved queerness becomes particularly relevant—the narrative of coming out shifts to one "of finding the right category or *niche*, and, because all identity categories are understood as equally valid . . . corrections of mistakes in self-identification can move in any direction" (my emphasis).[53] It is this situation, then, that first allows Bug's gay identification to be entirely unanticipated by people he has been living and working with for several years and then allows the reaction to it to be so muted and so inconsequential for the rest of the novel in narrative terms.

What this leads to, then, is that Edelman's definition of homographesis is very much a theoretical approach to the hierarchization of heterosexuality and homosexuality in an economy of production, rather than consumption. By emphasizing the production of the inscribed male body, the reading of this marked body in turn is productive because it creates the homosexual and the heterosexual man as discrete and oppositional. Since the apparatus of surveillance in the office is key to the facilitating of this act, as the shift to an economy of consumption occurs, so the less important this apparatus will become, and Silicon Valley can flatten out into a strange collection of invisible suburban architecture where homes are offices, where boys can make millions, where Chyx can discuss gender blindness, and where gay Bug can go to the barber's with a friend's dad. For the first time in the texts studied here, a self-identified homosexual man can make an appearance in the office. If anything, in *Microserfs* code loses its moorings to the kind of sexual categorization that it so successfully managed in the earlier texts. Bill's secret, Dan thinks, is that he knows that "emotion can't be converted into lines of code" (335).

The second queerness is Michael's. Of all the coders in the novel, Michael is the most prodigious. It is his awesome, patentable code that lies behind *Oop!* But of all the coders, Michael is the least interactive and the least vocal—an "elective mute"; he is a mixture of the autistic and the dyspraxic according to the others: "The doors in Michael's brain are wide open to certain things, while simultaneously nailed shut to all others. . . . He has no brakes on certain topics" (159). Dan's mother concludes that "Yes, well you geeks are an odd blend of doors and brakes" (159). Michael often retreats to the seclusion of his part of the home/office that is walled off with sound baffles, so he can geek out on code, which is when he produces his best work. There is no hint of sexual desire, resolved or otherwise. Only later do the rest of his friends and colleagues find out that he has been spending much of his time conducting an e-mail liaison across the internet with someone he knows only as Barcode who lives in Ontario, Canada. Barcode's sex remains a mystery.

Todd's reaction to this discovery deserves to be shared: "You know, if I read *one more* article about cybersex I am going to explode" (280). But e-mails are important to Michael, as his flaming from Bill and his subsequent refuge in his office makes clear. And it is the same intimacy and distance that were part and parcel of Bill's mail that is recognizable in Michael's e-mail relationship. And yet in his e-mail relationship—and this is perhaps what makes such cyber romance difficult to understand for some people and so enticing for others—the question of visibility becomes deeply problematic. A romance-language of "love at first sight" no longer applies in these relationships. It is also worth remembering that for Edelman there is a necessity to not only construct a distinctive homosexual "morphology," but also "an emblem of homosexual difference that will securely situate that difference within the register of visibility."[54] The kind of relationship that Michael builds with Barcode is devoid of this register of visibility, even though their insides have already "blended." The words that they write to one another may be visual in the sense that they are part of the Windows world of visibility, and yet as signs that stand in for an "entity" they operate as a kind of code that has to be interpreted in relation to an identity without any of the visual backing that would normally help to forge a judgment. This principle works at such a basic level that even gender may not be discernible from the correspondence. Barcode exists as "he-slash-she" (323).

All this is reminiscent of the Turing Test devised by Alan Turing, the gay mathematician and decoder who worked at Bletchley Park during the Second World War as part of the team given the task of breaking the German Enigma codes. Turing was later charged with committing homosexual acts and took his own life as a result. The Turing Test was Turing's attempt to find a way of assessing whether it was possible for machines to think. Rather than addressing this question directly, Turing proposed a different approach:

> He imagined a game in which an interrogator would have to decide, on the basis of written replies alone, which of two people in another room was a man and which a woman. The man was to deceive the interrogator, and the woman to convince the interrogator . . . If a computer [taking the place of the man or woman], on the basis of its written replies to questions, could not be distinguished from a human respondent, then . . . it must be "thinking."[55]

Perhaps more important for my purposes here than the intelligent machine aspect to this puzzle are two issues. The first is the way that a gay man—one used to concealing and revealing his gay identity in different situations, since he worked in the field of national security, and indeed was later barred from working in this field because his homosexuality supposedly made him vulnerable—chose to ground his test in gender difference. It is this construction of recognizable gender difference—the discourses of femininity and masculinity—and the matching of biology to these discourses that have underpinned and continue to underpin notions of homosexuality and heterosexuality. Second, and more interesting, is the way that a contemporary form of communication has developed from within the computing software industry that, rather than eliminating the room for any doubt in this association of biology and gender, has made it impossible a lot of the time to make a correct association. The world of e-mail and the internet can be a Turing technology.

Tyler Curtain has demonstrated how *can be* does not always become reality and yet how even within an atmosphere that is very gender-specific and often male-dominated the internet quickly folds into a space very much about a problematized sexuality. Because "the unquestioned identity for Internet characters is 'male,'" she argues, "and the default gender for even female-presenting characters is 'male' . . . all interactions are gender-panicked and . . . potentially homosexual."[56] Again, without a visible register to fix any doubts—and these doubts never can be fixed on the internet, since there is nothing that could be displayed visually that would count as final proof—Edelman's explanation of the development of homographesis becomes less convincing. One of the consequences of the shift from an economic architecture that stresses the importance of the visibility of employees in the working environment to an architecture that stresses the importance of the written code they produce, then, is the production of modes of communication that replicate the preeminence of this code as architecture. Video conferencing notwithstanding, this shift has placed highly non-visible and non-authoritative forms of communication at the heart of its ethos of interactivity.

When he locks himself in his office at the beginning of *Microserfs*, Michael's colleagues, friends, and housemates hear his keyboard chattering away and so guess he must be alive. "The situation really begged a discussion of Turing logic," Dan says; "could we have discerned the entity behind the door was indeed even human?" (2). But the implications of this Turing logic in the realm of gender and sexuality may well be taxing the recipient of words that Michael's chattering keys are producing. Later, Michael tells Dan that he has been communicating with Barcode for over a year, long enough for him to have been writing to her during this episode in his office. The office in *Microserfs*, then, becomes a site not where the male body is marked in a relation to a category of sexuality as it is in the earlier texts nor a site where the homosexual body is separated from the heterosexual body and where the heterosexual man comes to consider the contradictions and the anxieties that this process entails as in the earlier texts. In *Microserfs* the office is a site where the male body is still in the process of—literally—being written and where it is not subject to the kinds of visible architectures that would previously have forced it to be positioned so quickly and so decisively.

In trying to posit an analogy that will crystallize her definition of queer, Eve Sedgwick turns to Christmas. It is a time, she says, "when all institutions are speaking with one voice." Church, state, capitalism, and the media line up with one another to create a monolithic ideological event. "What if instead," Sedgwick posits, "there were a practice of valuing the ways in which meanings and institutions can be at loose ends with each other?"[57] From here she turns to the family—that entity in which the spirit of Christmas is meant to reside—and the way that it too makes so many things line up perfectly. Something of what I have been trying to suggest about *Microserfs* as a novel can be summarized in relation to this analogy of Sedgwick's through the following episode. On Christmas Eve, "Around midnight, December 25, Susan grunted, '*Uhhh*, Merry Christmas.' We all reciprocated, and then went back to work" (206). In the morning Dan gets up and finds that "Outside it was Richie Cunningham weather . . . But where is everybody's family? Why isn't everybody with their *families*?"

Microserfs is a novel where things do not line up. It is certainly a novel where the associations that I have been making in earlier parts of this book seem not to line up anymore. Work and leisure have stopped being discrete domains of one's life; the workplace and the home can now be the same place or different places that look the same; architecture is now not only visible but invisible as well, a virtual space formed by code and not just the space that one is surrounded by. I have attempted to show that it is the shift to an architecture of code that has helped shape this Window-ed world and that *Microserfs* tries to represent. An engagement with this code beats away at the heart of Dan's narrative as Coupland constantly seems to be drawing attention to it. The first hint we get is early on when Todd invents a program called "Prince Emulator" that converts "whatever you write into a title of a song by Minnesotan Funkmeister, Prince" (18). Dan rewrites part of his diary with it: "A few minutz l8r I bumpd in2 Karla walkng akros the west lawn. She walkz rely kwikly & she'z so small, like a litl kid" (18). "I reread the Prince Version," he says, "and realized th@ after a certain point, real language decomposes into encryption code; Japanese" (19).

Dan then begins to keep a file on his computer called "Subconscious" that consists of random words that come into his head, which then begin to appear at the end of his diary entries, creating almost a second level of narrative which might be read as a condensed—although alternative

—account of that day's or week's diary entry (see 46, 49, and 52 for examples). These entries allow a glimpse at the workings of Dan's techie, 1990s-acculturated mind, which is sometimes not a contented place, as when the word "Windows" transforms into "Prozac" within the space of a few lines (182). Coupland even takes to giving the reader encoded messages in his text that suggest the link between technology and violence. On pages 104 and 105, what appears to be a random series of os and 1s actually turns out to read:

I heart Lisa Computers
This is my computer
There are many like it,
but this one is mine.
My computer is my best friend.
It is my life.
I must master it,
as I must master my lif%.
Without me, my computer is useless.
Without my computer, I am useless.
I must use my computer true.
I must com}ute faster than my enemy who is trying to kill me.
I must outcompute him before he outcomputes me.
I will.
Before God, I swear this creed.
My computer and myself are defenders of this country.
We are the masters of our enemy.
We are the saviours of my life.
So be it until there is no ene-y, but peace.
Amen.
Tinned peaches
Yttrium
San Fran[58]

This is actually a rendition of the "war prayer" from Stanley Kubrick's movie *Full Metal Jacket*, with the word "computer" substituted for "rifle."

It is not just Dan, either, who helps to define this relationship between code, the software computing industry of the 1990s, and the people experiencing this world. Ethan, the businessman Michael teams up with to help raise venture capital for the *Oop!* project, first meets Michael "inking out all of the vowels on his menu" in a diner; Michael explains that he was "*Testing the legibility of the text in the absence of information*" (109).

Dan copies this attempt and converts another of his diary entries (308) and then converts it so it has no consonants.

My point here is that in this strange transitional landscape that Dan and his friends are negotiating, code has become not only the engine driving capitalist accumulation and economic expansion, but the very means by which communication proceeds and the way, therefore, by which we—following Dan—might understand how "meanings and institutions can be at loose ends with each other." Code is what links a company like Microsoft—the most successful company in the world and the next in a line of American companies that achieved this position through a monopolistic business strategy—and a relationship like that Michael forms with Barcode. Code is also what puts them at loose ends with one another. Code is important in Coupland's narrative, then, because, by standing in such close relation to the industry and the economy it is trying to engage with and the nonvisual form of communication created by that industry, it comes to form the way that the people in that economy and elsewhere are trying to come to terms with the "general sense of change and disorientation" that can accompany the experience of important economic change. This disorientation may manifest itself as "little fears" as it does for Dan: "fear of not producing enough; fear of not finding a little white-with-red-printing stock option envelope in the pigeonhole" (38). It may manifest itself in the "Perfectville" train set landscape that Dan's father builds or in Bug's desperation to "find a niche" (306) or in Dan's anxiety about the diminishing distance between man and machine (228) and the dangers of computers when used in the service of state violence. Code, because of its encrypted nature, signals in an ambiguous way. Ultimately the different associations of code may not line up behind one another either. But as a form of response to the changes that they are living through, code can be about something other than work for the *Microserfs*: "It's about all of us staying together" (199).

If this sentimental note seems to jar, then it should be remembered just what the "all of us" contains in this novel. It is not just Dan and Karla, but Bug, Todd, Abe, Michael, Dusty, Susan—and Barcode too. And in a culture that has in the past so denigrated the closeness of the relationship between sons and their mothers, how refreshing and how loving it is that, virtually paralyzed after a stroke, Dan's mother is surrounded at her bedside by Dan and his friends. She can find only one way to communicate: "part woman/part machine, emanating blue Macintosh light" she moves her fingers across a computer keyboard. Dan, anxious to confirm that it is his mother typing and not the machine, asks her a question that only she will be able to answer. "Tell me something I never liked in my lunch bag at school." She types "PNUT BUTR." "Here it is," Dan says, "Mom speaking like a license plate . . . like the lyrics to a Prince song . . . like encryption. All of my messing around with words last year and now, well . . . it's real life" (369).

This sentimentality is of a different order to the kind of sentimentality and self-pity that men like Lapham, Babbitt, Tom Rath, and Bob Slocum have hidden behind, the kind of sentimentality that would work to identify the pain of masculinity and then displace anxiety about this pain onto the bodies of gay men. Dan's sentimentality is one that arises from a childish anxiety about transition and is never focussed in terms of gender; it focuses instead on Dan and his friends' place within culture and how they cope with a culture that "is inadequate or inimical to its nurture"[59] and upon the reparative impulses that help them to cope.

This book has explored the links between three specific themes—surveillance, the office, and male sexuality—by demonstrating how the office is a site fundamental in the constitution of the sexual identities of American men who experience its architecturalized and institutionalized discourses. A necessary part of this project has involved making explicit the structure of these discourses. One element has come to stand as crucial in the development of the book: the discourse of visuality.

As a way of concluding my thoughts and trying to provide an overview of what I have achieved, I want to excavate this discourse one last time by emphasizing the preoccupation with glass in all of the texts. As a motif it is one that has cropped up over and over again, and one that I have pointed out from chapter to chapter. There are the "ground-glass" doors that separate the lawyer-narrator from his scriveners in "Bartleby" and later separate Silas Lapham from his bookkeepers. In *Babbitt* there is the boundary of "frosted-glass" between inner and outer offices; in *The Man in the Gray Flannel Suit* the "opaque glass bricks" that Tom Rath must penetrate in order to expose the mechanism of the Organization; and in *Something Happened* there are the "frosted glass panes" that so concentrate Bob Slocum's attention to his current and past masculinity and sexuality. In *The Mezzanine* there is the "glass wall" through which Howie watches the rest of the office, and in *The Fermata* the spectacles that position Arno in relation to the rest of the world. In *Microserfs* all the major protagonists spend their long working days looking at, looking through, and—initially, at least—working for a company that produces Windows, displayed in a glass screen. In each instance this recurring motif condenses a range of issues that the story or novel dramatizes elsewhere—issues of masculinity, sexuality, authority, and the place of the individual in relation to the organization.

But the more specific way that the glass is represented in each of the texts can also be seen as a barometer of how the men in those texts are coping with life in the office as it is entwined with their sexual identity. The ground glass and frosted glass that partition the offices in "Bartleby," *The Rise of Silas Lapham*, and *Babbitt*, although they may appear to be similar to the opaque glass bricks and frosted glass panes that are central to *The Man in the Gray Flannel Suit* and *Something Happened*, actually serve an altogether different purpose. In the first three texts, where the central narrator or character owns the office, the occluded glass acts to demarcate space, a process vital in the more general hierarchization of space in capitalist culture where, as Siegfried Kracauer noted, "Each social stratum has a space that is associated with it."[1] In the latter two texts, with this demarcation suitably consolidated, the opaque glass bricks and frosted panes of glass work to dramatize a sense of fear and anxiety about what lies behind that glass for employees who work at some remove from the men who own or run the office in which they work. What is noticeable about the texts by Nicholson Baker and Douglas Coupland is the way that the glass they describe becomes transparent. Howie can observe one of the secretaries advancing the date on her date stamper "(through the glass wall of my office)," and when one uses Windows on one's computer, transparency is imperative to reveal the text or graphics or spreadsheets behind them.

At the risk of providing an over-schematic conclusion, it would seem to me that the three distinct forms in which the visual motif of the glass reappears can be seen to tie in with the three separate periods of male sexuality that I pointed to in my introduction and which I have explored more fully in my examination of the texts. If, as I suggested, the first period is marked by a fluidity in the nature of male friendship, but also by a closing down of that fluidity—a period when, according to Alan Sinfield, "our idea of 'the homosexual' . . . was in the process of becoming constituted"[2]—then it is possible to see the way that the visual glass motif is actually also a spatial one that performs the task of separation and classification. Indeed, it is just this classification of space that is performed in "Bartleby" when the lawyer-narrator has Bartleby set up his desk on his side of the office behind the screen. In *Silas Lapham* it is the closing of the connecting door between the two offices during the interview with Bartley Hubbard that moves the reader into that private space that is Lapham's past and into the symbolic territory of paint and hole that I argued allows us to view his relationship with Tom Corey as a relationship of desire that is constituted through commerce. In each of the three early texts, there is a clear and discernible retreat from the sexual fulfillment of male-male desire. Such a retreat performs—in the actual moment of retreat—the same kind of sexual separation and classification that was taking place elsewhere in the consolidation of the "epistemology of the closet," where the closet is, of course, both a visual and a spatial phenomenon.

There is no such process of demarcation in either *The Man in the Gray Flannel Suit* or *Something Happened*. For both Tom Rath and Bob Slocum the boundaries of male friendship—except perhaps during Tom's experiences in the unique circumstances of war—are clearly defined. It is therefore not simply the demarcation of space that is performed by the visual motifs of opaque and frosted glass. Rather, because glass has served the purpose of separation and classification in the past, it becomes the location upon which an anxiety is played out that separation and classification have not been carried out securely enough. This is what haunts Rath and Slocum. While this anxiety might appear to be similar to that retreat from the sexual fulfillment of desire between, successively, the lawyer-narrator and Bartleby, Silas and Tom, and Babbitt and Paul Riesling, there is one crucial difference. For Tom Rath and Bob Slocum their anxiety stems from an *a priori* belief that the sexual fulfillment of male-male desire is antithetical to their constitution as heterosexual men. In the earlier period the retreat from sexual fulfillment arises from the *potentially* damaging consequences of the revelation of such a relationship. The fear that dominates Rath and Slocum is a result of the incoherent separation and classification that was only in process in the earlier texts.

What conclusions, then, might we draw from the shift in the mode of representation of glass in *The Fermata* and *Microserfs*? I have made it clear that there are continuities between these two novels and the earlier texts. There is no mileage in trying to claim that the workplace is a less surveilled environment or that the shift in working patterns that one finds in *The Fermata* and *Microserfs* offers an escape from the discourses that seek to discipline the postindustrial sexual subject. Indeed things might even have gotten worse as the technologies of surveillance become increasingly sophisticated. What I emphasized earlier in this conclusion, however, was that the glass motif offers a way of gauging how well the straight male subject is *coping* with the demands made upon him by the surveillance strategies implemented in the office and by the entanglement of surveillance with his sexual definition. For the lawyer-narrator in "Bartleby," for Silas Lapham and Tom Corey, and for George Babbitt, the occluded glass that demarcates capitalist and sexual space brings with it an anxiety about how desire may be formulated in a period when it becomes necessary for one to position oneself on either side of the homosexual/heterosexual divide. For Tom Rath and Bob Slocum, the occluded glass marks a fear of losing this demarcation and having the solidity of their heterosexual identity plunged back into doubt. For Arno Strine, Daniel Underwood, and Michael, transparent glass signifies a removal of homosexuality as the threat and predatory danger that is lurking out of sight yet is always capable of "mounting invisibly and flooding out toward"[3] them through frosted glass panes.

I am not suggesting that this fear does not exist elsewhere in other American cultural representations nor that the demarcation of space is unimportant within the confines of the contemporary office world or elsewhere. It is a fear, though, that has lost its potency in these particular narratives of office life and has lost its potency for organizing the sexual identity of these particular straight men in and around the office. Unlike Tom Rath and Bob Slocum, these characters cope with the pressures of office culture without relying upon occluded visual motifs that are perhaps the results of wanting—contradictorily—two needs to intersect: the need "to bring into focus both the male body and the problem of bringing the male body into focus."[4] This is the dilemma for Tom Rath and Bob Slocum. While they experience the anxiety of their sexual definition in a culture of surveillance in terms that cannot help but be bodily, they have no language with which to negotiate this situation that is not either homophobic or self-pityingly sentimental. The opaque glass bricks and frosted glass panes must be considered, then, as the visualized manifestation of a crisis of straight male definition that is itself a product of the visual culture of surveillance and self-surveillance so constitutive of office experience.

This blurred vision stands in stark contrast to the visually acute and incisive Arno Strine who has little trouble bringing the male body into focus and little trouble in bringing the male anus into focus: "I just wanted it out in the open, sunlit for once, flaunting wavewards its showered cleanness, exposed in a way that was lewd and vulnerable."[5] This is how Arno copes with the regime of surveillance that so disciplines him at work. And it is only fitting that this book should end with a novel in which a self-identified gay male character—Bug Barbecue—is finally considered worthy of the attention of a straight male novelist and is brought into the orbit again of male friendship. "Suddenly I look around at Bug and Susan and Michael and everybody," Dan concludes the novel, "and I realize, that what's been missing for so long isn't missing anymore."[6] The transparency of the glass in these two final texts stands as testimony to the possibility that straight male sexuality might cope with the imperatives to read and surveil the male body in the office in ways that break a postwar literary tradition of fear.

Such a break offers the potential for some of the themes and issues raised by this book to be developed in broader critical studies of both contemporary and previous fictions. If the discourse of straight male fear and anxiety now seems incredible to Baker and Coupland, then it would certainly be important to observe if and how it is equally incredible to other writers whose work is less closely focussed around work and to consider if the late 1980s and the 1990s mark a watershed in the cultural and social construction of a straight male sexuality. This period has often been categorized as a period of "backlash" against women. It is also a period that saw the rebirth of a discourse about the primitive cult of manhood.[7] It may well be, however, that such moments are only the most visible manifestations of—and reactions to—much more subtle and long-lasting shifts in the patterns of gender and sex alignment. It would be interesting, for instance, to set alongside the writings of Coupland and Baker the novels and stories of gay male writers like Edmund White, Dennis Cooper, and Dale Peck to identify the ways in which the boundaries and intersections of gay and straight male writing might be reforming in this end-of-the-century era.

Finally, although this book concentrates on the office, it addresses issues that are pertinent to other types of working situations and relationships, especially issues of gender and sexuality and of the close association between narrative and the architecture of the working environment. The representation of work in American fiction in the nineteenth and twentieth centuries remains underexplored. As a way of balancing the stress so often placed upon consumption, work needs to be approached as a site where history and economics meet the life stories of American men and women, where representation in fiction opens access to a wide range of related issues and themes. One in particular that perhaps needs to be considered more closely is the ideological position of business and the business entrepreneur in an American culture where individual advancement carries such positive connotations but where the means by which one achieves such advancement can become the object of social and legal attacks.[8] From the state sanctions against Standard Oil following the work of muckraker Ida Tarbell at the beginning of the century to the Department of Justice's battle with Bill Gates and Microsoft, the American corporation has crystallized many of the contradictions and complexities that result from the clash of individual and institution. Putting businessmen and their businesses into fiction has been one way in which the novel in America has tried to serve the social and political purpose of questioning and determining the acceptable limits of capitalist enterprise.

Introduction

1. Jeremy Lewis, *Chatto Book of Office Life: or Love among the Filing Cabinets* (London: Chatto & Windus, 1992).

2. Eve Kosofsky Sedgwick, *Between Men: English Literature and Male Homosocial Desire* (New York: Columbia University Press, 1985), 1–2.

3. Eve Kosofsky Sedgwick, *Epistemology of the Closet* (Harmondsworth: Penguin, 1994 [1990]), 72.

4. Michel Foucault, *Discipline and Punish* (Harmondsworth: Penguin, 1991 [1977]).

5. Penitentiary designs based on the Benthamite model were to be found in the Walnut Street Jail, Philadelphia (1790); the State Prison, Richmond (1800); and the Western Penitentiary, Pittsburgh (1826). For more on the comparisons between American and European prisons, see Norval Morris and David J. Rothman, *The Oxford History of the Prison: the Practice of Punishment in Western Society* (New York and Oxford: Oxford University Press, 1996).

6. See Dana Nelson, *National Manhood: Capitalist Citizenship and the Imagined Fraternity of White Men* (Durham and London: Duke University Press, 1998).

7. Ralph Waldo Emerson, "Nature," in Nina Baym et al., *The Norton Anthology of American Literature Fourth Edition* (New York and London: W. W. Norton and Company, 1994), 1005–6.

8. This report is available at http://www.defenselink.mil/pubs/rpt040798.html.

9. Lee Edelman, *Homographesis: Essays in Gay Literary and Cultural Theory* (New York and London: Routledge, 1994).

10. Jonathan Goldberg, *Sodometries: Renaissance Texts, Modern Sexualities* (Palo Alto: Stanford University Press, 1992), 2.

11. Goldberg, 5.

12. Goldberg, 5.

13. Calvin Thomas, ed., *Straight with a Twist: Queer Theory and the Subject of Heterosexuality* (Urbana and Chicago: University of Illinois Press, 2000), 17.

14. George Chauncey has argued that gay history, in New York at least, does not fall easily into the "progressive" history of steady liberation. Instead he suggests that "gay life in New York was less tolerated, less visible to outsiders, and more rigidly segregated in the second third of the century than the first, and that the very severity of the postwar reaction has tended to blind us to the relative tolerance of the prewar years." George Chauncey, *Gay New York: The Making of the Gay Male World, 1890–1940* (London: Flamingo, 1995 [1994]), 9.

15. James Annesley, *Blank Fictions: Consumerism, Culture and the Contemporary Novel* (London: Pluto Press, 1998), 1.

1. "Dead letters . . . dead men?"

1. As far as antebellum economic change is concerned see Louise K. Barnett, "Bartleby as Alienated Worker," *Studies in Short Fiction* 11 (1974), 379–85; Stephen Zelnich, "Melville's 'Bartleby, the Scrivener': A Study in History, Ideology, and Literature," *Marxist Perspectives* 2 (1979–80), 74–92; David Kuebrich, "Melville's Doctrine of Assumptions: The Hidden Ideology of Capitalist Production in 'Bartleby,'" *New England Quarterly* 69 (1996), 381–405. For male sexuality see Robert K. Martin, *Hero, Captain, and Stranger: Male Friendship, Social Critique, and Literary Form in the Sea Novels of Herman Melville* (Chapel Hill and London: University of North Carolina Press, 1986); Eve Kosofsky Sedgwick, *Epistemology of the Closet*, (Harmondsworth: Penguin, 1994 [1990]), 91–130; James Creech, *Closet Writing/Gay Reading: The Case of Melville's* Pierre (Chicago: University of Chicago Press, 1993); Gregory Woods, *A History of Gay Literature: The Male Tradition* (New Haven and London: Yale University Press, 1998), 163–66.

2. Michael T. Gilmore, *American Romanticism and the Marketplace* (Chicago and London: University of Chicago Press, 1985), 135.

3. Herman Melville, "Bartleby, the Scrivener: A Story of Wall-Street," in Herman Melville, *The Piazza Tales and Other Prose Pieces 1839–1860* (Evanston and Chicago: Northwestern University Press, 1987), 36 and 45. All further page references to this text appearing in this chapter will be presented in parentheses following the reference in the text.

4. Melville, "The Paradise of Bachelors and the Tartarus of Maids," in *The Piazza Tales*, 331.

5. The most interesting comment on the office to date remains Leo Marx, "Melville's Parable of the Walls," *Sewanee Review* 61 (1953), 602–27.

6. Sedgwick, *Epistemology*, 72.

7. For more on the mid-century bachelor, his place in American urban sexual culture, and spermatorrhea see Vincent J. Bertolini, "Fireside Chastity: The Erotics of Sentimental Bachelorhood in the 1850s," *American Literature* 68 (1996), 707–37.

8. Michel Foucault, *Discipline and Punish* (Harmondsworth: Penguin, 1991 [1977]), 221.

9. This information is taken from Peter Cowan et al., *The Office: a facet of urban growth* (London: Heinemann Educational Books, 1969), 25–29. The subtitle of

"Bartleby"—"A Story of Wall Street"—clearly ties it into this growing special-ized office and administrative world. For the way in which American business became more and more office-based and more and more an economy based upon management after 1840, see Alfred D. Chandler, Jr., *The Visible Hand: The Managerial Revolution in American Business* (Cambridge, Mass., and London: Har-vard University Press, 1977). For a detailed treatment of the relationship of Karl Marx, Max Weber, and Foucault to questions of surveillance see Christo-pher Dandeker, *Surveillance, Power and Modernity* (Cambridge: Polity, 1990).

10. Foucault, *Discipline and Punish*, 306–7.

11. Foucault, *Discipline and Punish*, 217.

12. See E. Anthony Rotundo, *American Manhood: Transformations in Masculinity from the Revolution to the Modern Era* (New York: Basic Books, 1993), especially 167–93 and 194–221. Rotundo identifies the growing importance of work and the workplace as one of the two revolutions in thinking about masculinity in the last two hundred years, the other being the association of masculinity with aggression, combativeness, and sexual desire, all of which of course are impli-cated in questions of homosexual/heterosexual definition. For a discussion of the contradictions and complicated effects of this public/private gender or-ganization, see Glenna Matthews, *The Rise of Public Woman: Woman's Power and Woman's Place in the United States 1630–1970* (New York and Oxford: Oxford Uni-versity Press, 1992); for particular attention to the office, see 119–50. As to how this shift affected male homosocial desire and the role of women in the family in Britain, see Eve Kosofsky Sedgwick, *Between Men: English Literature and Male Homosocial Desire* (New York: Columbia University Press, 1985), 134–60.

13. Sedgwick, *Epistemology*, 110–14.

14. Just as Melville was familiar with the position of men inside sailing ships, so he was familiar with men inside offices. At work by the age of twelve in a New York bank, according to Hershel Parker, his most recent biographer, Melville "filed, copied, ran errands, and made himself as inconspicuous as pos-sible . . . a captive clerk." See Hershel Parker, *Herman Melville: A Biography, Vol-ume 1, 1819–1851* (Baltimore and London: The John Hopkins University Press, 1996), 71–72. Melville was also well acquainted with law offices. One of his clos-est friends, Eli Fly, was "an excellent scrivener as well as a law clerk," and Mel-ville's brothers Gansevoort and Allan were both lawyers, for whom Fly worked in their own law offices on Wall Street. Indeed, Parker has even suggested that Melville actually began his writing of *Typee* in these offices (355).

15. For a more detailed explanation of this idea of retrospective reordering and its implications for questions of male sexuality, see Lee Edelman, *Homo-graphesis: Essays in Gay Literary and Cultural Theory* (New York and London: Rout-ledge, 1994), 173–91.

16. What one in fact sees in "Bartleby" is the representation of the same structural relationship one was likely to find in a New York male brothel of the period: the relationship between an older man and a young man whose manli-ness is decidedly boyish. That this kind of relationship circulated in the cultural as well as the social world can be seen from the sensationalist novels of the time. See Woods, 151–54. Although the depiction of Bartleby as boyish is

achieved implicitly—by his being young, passive, pale and lean, and not in the least muscular—it is nevertheless done effectively enough. References by the lawyer-narrator to the bust of Cicero which sits above him, his description of Wall Street being as deserted as Petra, and his characterization of Bartleby as being "a sort of innocent and transformed Marius brooding among the ruins of Carthage!" (21 and 27–28) tie Melville's lawyer-narrator into the developing Victorian homoerotic attachment to Hellenism, those periods of Greek and Roman history where such tutelary relationships between men of different generations—adult men and their catamites—incorporated same-sex activity as a matter of course. For more on this See K. J. Dover, *Greek Homosexuality* (New York: Random House, 1980); Michel Foucault, *The Use of Pleasure: Volume 2 of The History of Sexuality* (Harmondsworth: Penguin, 1992 [1985]); Woods, 17–40. It is the classical, almost statuesque quality that the lawyer-narrator starts to identify in Bartleby, a figure of boyish manhood, that distresses but touches.

17. Michel Foucault, *The History of Sexuality Volume 1: An Introduction* (Harmondsworth: Penguin, 1990 [1978]), especially 48 and 139–40.

18. Edelman, *Homographesis*, 4.

19. This was the transition from the moment when sodomy as a discontinuous act did not necessarily preclude other forms of sexual relations to the moment when the homosexual became a distinct category of person. This is the thesis as set out by Michel Foucault, *History of Sexuality*, and subsequently reinforced to varying degrees by Jonathan Goldberg, *Sodometries* (Palo Alto: Stanford University Press, 1992); Ed Cohen, *A Talk on the Wilde Side* (New York: Routledge, 1993); and Alan Sinfield, *The Wilde Century* (London: Cassell, 1994). Goldberg is also keen to point out the importance of the continuation of the terminology of sodomy in the modern period. For a more skeptical approach to the chronology upon which Foucault's work rests see Alan Bray, *Homosexuality in Renaissance England* (London: Gay Men's Press, 1982), but more particularly Rictor Norton, *The Myth of the Modern Homosexual* (London: Cassell, 1997). I take the view that the medicalized and psychologized shifts in attitudes towards homosexuality that occur in the second half of the nineteenth century—and they clearly do—are part of the same disciplinary and classificatory project outlined by Foucault in *Discipline and Punish* and *The Order of Things: An Archaeology of the Human Sciences* (London and New York: Pantheon, 1970) which stretches back into the seventeenth and eighteenth centuries. The crucial point about the end of the nineteenth century, I believe, has been made by Sedgwick: "What was new from the turn of the century was the world-mapping by which every given person, just as he or she was necessarily assignable to a male or a female gender, was now considered necessarily assignable as well to a homo- or a heterosexuality," Sedgwick, *Epistemology*, 2. As far as my argument is concerned, I see "Bartleby" as existing in a zone of discourse where the metaphoric and metonymic approaches to identity—reductive as these categories are—are woven tightly together, and hence my concentration on the text as standing at the threshold of developments that were to follow.

20. Edelman, *Homographesis*, 4.

21. Edelman, *Homographesis*, 11.

22. While as a cultural phenomenon effeminacy has a long history, the relationship between effeminacy and same-sex passion has generated considerable discussion. Randolph Trumbach has made a case for the early eighteenth century as the time when effeminacy came to be seen as a marker of sodomy between men, especially in subcultural environments, but Alan Sinfield has suggested that "Up to the time of the Wilde trials—far later than is widely supposed—it is unsafe to interpret effeminacy as defining of, or as a signal of, same-sex passion," *The Wilde Century*, 27. See Randolph Trumbach, "Sodomitical Subcultures, Sodomitical Roles, and the Gender Revolution of the Eighteenth Century: the Recent Historiography," in Robert Purks Maccubin, ed., *'Tis Nature's Fault* (Cambridge: Cambridge University Press, 1987); Trumbach, "Gender and the Modern Homosexual Role in Western Culture: the 18th and 19th Centuries Compared," in Dennis Altman et al., *Homosexuality, Which Homosexuality?* (London: Gay Men's Press, 1989). What seems apparent is that effeminacy and same-sex passion are intricately related to notions of gender in Western culture, and it might be that one cannot discuss homosexuality and effeminacy without discussing the cultural discourses defining gender divisions. This is Edelman's approach.

23. Edelman, *Homographesis*, 11. For the way that the discourse of sex actually contributed the development of gender binarism in the eighteenth and nineteenth centuries, see Thomas Lacquer, *Making Sex* (Cambridge, Mass. and London: Harvard University Press, 1992 [1990]). This equation of sex-organizing and gender-organizing sexuality is one which remains underexplored theoretically.

24. Edelman, *Homographesis*, 12.

25. Foucault, *Discipline and Punish*, 201.

26. This emphasis on the visual nature of society since the Renaissance is mapped out by Martin Jay's *Downcast Eyes* (Berkeley and London: University of California Press, 1993), chapters 1 and 2. The subtitle of the book, *The Denigration of Vision in Twentieth-Century French Thought* refers to the way in which French thinkers have criticized the effects of this emphasis on vision and presented anti-ocular discourses. For the increasing interest in visual technologies and phenomena and for the importance of vision as a discourse in the nineteenth century, see Daniel Pick, "Stories of the Eye," in Roy Porter, ed., *Rewriting the Self: Histories from the Renaissance to the Present* (London: Routledge, 1997),186–99; Suren Lalvani, *Photography, Vision, and the Production of Modern Bodies* (New York: State University of New York Press, 1996); and Jonathan Crary, *Techniques of the Observer: On Vision and Modernity in the Nineteenth Century* (Cambridge, Mass.: Harvard University Press, 1990).

27. Jonathan Dollimore, *Sexual Dissidence* (Oxford: Oxford University Press, 1991), 141. Original in italics.

28. See Bartleby's, albeit terse, dialogue on pages 21, 31, 32, 34, 40, 41, 43, and 44.

29. Gilles Deleuze, "Bartleby; or, The Formula," in Gilles Deleuze, *Essays Critical and Clinical*, trans. Daniel W. Smith and Michael A. Greco (London: Verso, 1998), 68. Rather too conveniently, since he ignores the prose that forms the rest of *The Piazza Tales*, *Israel Potter* (1855), and *The Confidence-Man* (1857),

Deleuze wants to see Bartleby as the story that "announces the long silence, broken only by the music of poems, into which Melville will enter and from which, except for *Billy Budd*, he will never emerge" (72). Deleuze is also alert, however, to the emotional attachment between the lawyer and Bartleby, describing it as "a nearly acknowledged homosexual relation" (75).

30. I don't think that the secret which Bartleby is supposed to be keeping is as well determined in relation to male-male sexual contact as that identified by critics in relation to secrets and secrecy in other texts. I am thinking here of Sedgwick's work on Henry James's *The Wings of the Dove* and "The Beast in the Jungle." See, respectively, Eve Kosofsky Sedgwick, "Is the Rectum Straight?: Identification and Identity in *The Wings of the Dove*," in *Tendencies* (London: Routledge, 1994), 73–106, and Sedgwick, *Epistemology*, 182–212. One of the things that I think is happening instead with "Bartleby" as it was written in the 1850s is the hollowing out of the epistemological space of privacy—in both Bartleby and the lawyer-narrator—that comes to be the home where such secrets can be made to reside, and the space that can then be examined or interrogated discursively. And the impetus for this process is both Bartleby's refusal to read and his refusal to participate in a more speech-centered way with his fellow workers and the lawyer-narrator.

31. Many of the descriptions of Bartleby make an anachronistic reading of him as "homosexual" quite possible because of the way in which in the twentieth century these descriptions hint at those markers which have become related to a particular style of tragic, upper class, effeminate homosexuality. I list them here in the order they appear in the story: strangest (13), motionless, pallidly neat, pitiably respectable, incurably forlorn, sedate (19), silently, palely, leanly composed (20), flute-like tone (22), involuntary, strange wilfulness (23), passiveness (24), lean, penniless weight (25), great stillness, unalterableness of demeanour, strangely tattered dishabille (26), cadaverously gentlemanly nonchalance, wonderful mildness, dismantled condition, decorous (27), pallid, pallid haughtiness, austere reserve (28), morbid moodiness, forlornness (29), calm disdain, perverseness, mildly cadaverous (30), afflictive (32), mute and solitary (33), strange creature (38), apparition, intolerable incubus, poor, pale, passive mortal, helpless creature, innocent pallor (38).

32. The Oxford English Dictionary provides three definitions of "incontinence":

> 1. Lack of restraint with regard to sexual desire; promiscuity. LME
>
> 2. Med. Lack of voluntary control over the passing of urine or faeces. (Foll. by of.) M18.
>
> 3. gen. Lack of constraint; inability to contain or restrain. (Foll. by of.) M19.

My reading of this section of "Bartleby" clearly suggests a link, then, between the first and second definitions.

33. See Edelman, *Homographesis*, 148–70, and Lee Edelman, "Men's Room," in Joel Sanders, ed., *Stud: Architectures of Masculinity* (New York: Princeton Architectural Press, 1996), 152–61.

34. Indeed, this link between the desk and the anus has been made directly,

because the reader has been told already that Nippers's struggle to accommo-
date his too tightly controlled sphincter is dramatized by his inability to find a
comfortable height for his desk (16–17).

35. For a more detailed reading of the link between money and anality, see
Sedgwick, *Between Men*, 161–79.

36. Martin, 7.

2. "And that paint is a thing that will bear looking into"

1. This "circulation" between two (or more) differently classified locales is
clearly a metaphorical concept and probably owes much to those scientific the-
ories which posit the transfer of energy between, for instance, hot and cold
areas, or—climatically—between areas of high and low pressure. In cultural
terms it has been addressed most closely by Stephen Greenblatt in *Shakespearean
Negotiations* (Oxford: Oxford University Press, 1997 [1988]), 1–20. I take on
board Greenblatt's ideas and also posit the idea—working under the proviso
that this thinking is a metaphorical response to material conditions—that circulation arises as a result of culturally organized differences and the tensions
which result from these differences.

2. Michel Foucault, *Discipline and Punish* (Harmondsworth: Penguin, 1991
[1977]), 203–4.

3. All this may undermine the argument that has been put forward that the
ship is the *locus classicus* of modernity and sexuality. See Michel Foucault, "Of
Other Spaces: Utopias and Heterotopias," in Neil Leach, ed., *Rethinking Architecture: a Reader in Cultural Theory* (London and New York: Routledge, 1997),
350–56; Cesare Casarino, "Gomorrahs of the Deep; or, Melville, Foucault and
the Question of Heterotopia," *Arizona Quarterly* 51 (1995), 1–25; Cesare Casarino, "The Sublime of the Closet; or, Joseph Conrad's *The Secret Sharer*," *boundary
2* 24 (1997), 199–243. More likely is the conclusion that such a *locus classicus* is
too limiting and that other spaces exhibit similar structuring movements. I don't
deal directly with the office as heterotopia here, although I do think that many
of the arguments I put forward might be reconceptualized using Foucault's six
principles of heterotopias. The office seems to me to fit each one.

4. For the distinction between these two terms and their continued entanglement see Foucault, *The History of Sexuality Volume 1: An Introduction* (Harmondsworth: Penguin, 1990 [1978]), 106–14.

5. For more on which see Diana Fuss and Joel Sanders, "Bergasse 19: Inside
Freud's Office," in Joel Sanders, ed., *Stud: Architectures of Masculinity* (New York:
Princeton Architectural Press, 1996), 112–39. Freud actually died in the office
located in his home.

6. It should also be noted that such are the demands of work in contemporary society that the temporal and spatial boundaries of consulting room and
office are regularly placed in close juxtaposition. Visits to analysts may take
place immediately before work, at lunchtime, or straight after work. Clearly
these visits are more convenient if the consulting room is located near one's
workplace. There are ways in which the boundaries are even more blurred as

well. When, for example, large employers maintain an in-house doctor or analyst to take charge of employees. This raises all sorts of questions about the confidentiality of conversations and diagnoses that take place within the "privacy" of the consulting room. There is also the situation where managers, as part of their pastoral duties, become analysts themselves, recommending that employees visit a counselor if they are having problems.

7. Bartley Hubbard is the major protagonist in Howells's previous novel, *A Modern Instance* (Boston: Houghton Mifflin Company, 1957 [1882]). His first name seems to echo the name of Bartleby, especially with the missing B in his forename doubled up and emphasized in his surname. Other than this, however, there are few similarities. At work he is a sharp operator, and ambitious. The chronologies of *A Modern Instance* and *The Rise of Silas Lapham* are interesting in the way that they intersect. Although Lapham is not mentioned in the first book, the "Solid Men of Boston" series is; it is one of Bartley's jobs to write for it when he moves to Boston. *A Modern Instance* follows Bartley's life further into the future than *Silas Lapham* does Lapham's. Bartley ends up being shot when in one of his articles he "unfortunately chanced upon the domestic relations of 'one of Whited Sepulchre's leading citizens'" (360). Here Bartley pays the ultimate price for transferring information between those domains classified private and public, a theme which—by way of the confession—is also part of the psychoanalytic project, and one which is important in *Silas Lapham*, as I will show.

8. William Dean Howells, *The Rise of Silas Lapham* (Oxford: Oxford University Press, 1996 [1885]), 3. All further page references in this chapter appear in parentheses.

9. I think I should also make it as clear as I possibly can at this point, if it is not clear already, what it is I am *not* saying about the office. I am not saying that the office, as some sort of space, can be read as analogous to the unconscious, as some sort of metaphorical representation of the unconscious. The relationship between the office and the mind is a material relationship: the way in which one experiences the world of the office and its disciplinary practices will have some effect upon one's self, but some effect which is not determinable *a priori*.

10. See Donald E. Pease, ed., *New Essays on* The Rise of Silas Lapham (Cambridge and New York: Cambridge University Press, 1991), 1–28.

11. D. A. Miller, *The Novel and the Police* (Berkeley: University of California Press, 1988), 21 and 24.

12. Wai-Chee Dimock, "The Economy of Pain: Capitalism, Humanitarianism, and the Realistic Novel," in Donald E. Pease, ed., *New Essays*, 79–80. For a slightly different approach to the relationship between economics and *The Rise of Silas Lapham*, see Ian McGuire, "W. D. Howells and the Crisis of Overproduction," *Journal of American Studies* 33 (1999), 459–72. McGuire contends that in *Silas Lapham* Howells is trying to "articulate an emergent cultural logic, the logic of consumption, before it had developed its own, distinct, vocabulary" (472).

13. Foucault, *The History of Sexuality*, 55.

14. See George Spangler, "The Shadow of a Dream: Howells' Homosexual

Tragedy," *American Quarterly* 23 (1971), 110−19; Elizabeth Stevens Prioleau, *The Circle of Eros: Sexuality in the Work of William Dean Howells* (Durham: Duke University Press, 1983); Sam B. Girgus, *Desire and the Political Unconscious in American Literature* (Basingstoke: Macmillan, 1990), chapter 5.

15. And indeed it is with this formulation that Freud reached that point where the distinction between the professional analyst and the literary critic threatens to disappear almost entirely.

16. Here I am thinking particularly of Eve Kosofsky Sedgwick, *Tendencies* (London: Routledge, 1994), 73−103, and her critique of Kaja Silverman's treatment of Henry James in Silverman's article "Too Early/Too Late: Subjectivity and the Primal Scene in Henry James," *Novel* 21 (1988), 147−73. Also of note are Lee Edelman's deconstruction of the spectatorial Freudian analytic scene via his conception of "(be)hindsight" in Lee Edelman, *Homographesis* (New York and London: Routledge, 1994), 173−91 and Michael Warner's deconstruction of the opposition of heterosexuality to homo- and autoerotics, for which see "Homo-Narcissism; or, Heterosexuality," in Joseph A. Boone and Michael Cadden, eds., *Engendering Men: The Question of Male Feminist Criticism* (New York and London: Routledge, 1990), 190−206. Much of the work which has attacked the conceptual status of psychoanalysis as a methodology for interpretation has followed from the earlier analyses of feminist writers and from Foucault. See Kate Millet, *Sexual Politics* (New York: Doubleday, 1970); Juliet Mitchell, *Psychoanalysis and Feminism: Freud, Reich, Laing and Women* (London: Allen Lane, 1974); Jane Gallop, *Feminism and Psychoanalysis: The Daughter's Seduction* (Basingstoke: Macmillan, 1982); Jacqueline Rose, "Femininity and Its Discontents," *Feminist Review* 14 (1982), 5−21; Julia Kristeva, *Revolution in Poetic Language* (New York: Columbia University Press, 1984 [1974]); Luce Irigaray, *Speculum of the Other Woman*, trans. Gillian C. Gill (Ithaca, New York: Cornell University Press, 1985 [1974]) and *This Sex Which Is Not One* (Ithaca, New York: Cornell University Press, 1985). It should also be pointed out that Foucault's neglect of the psychic realm has recently been questioned by Judith Butler in *The Psychic Life of Power* (Palo Alto: Stanford University Press, 1997).

17. Sedgwick, *Tendencies*, 74.

18. Sedgwick, *Tendencies*, 74.

19. Prioleau, 74. This remains the most substantive and the most suggestive treatment of sexuality in *Lapham* to date and hence my concentration on it here. For a biographical treatment of the issues of male sexuality in relation to Howells's life see E. Anthony Rotundo, *American Manhood: Transformations in Masculinity from the Revolution to the Modern Era* (New York: Basic Books, 1993), 186−87, and John W. Crowley, "Howells, Stoddard, and Male Homosocial Attachment in Victorian America," in Harry Brod, ed., *The Making of Masculinities: The New Men's Studies* (Winchester, Mass.: Allen & Unwin, 1987), 301−24. This article is revised and updated with an appendix about the illustrations to Stoddard's *Summer Cruising in the South Seas*, in John W. Crowley's *The Mask of Fiction* (Amherst: University of Massachusetts Press, 1989).

20. Prioleau, 73.

21. Prioleau, 73.

22. Prioleau, 84.

23. For more on this see Patrick Dooley, "Nineteenth Century Business Ethics and *The Rise of Silas Lapham*," *American Studies* 21 (1980), 79–93. The fullest survey of critical approaches is provided in the introduction of Pease, 1–28.

24. Prioleau, xvi.

25. Jonathan Dollimore, *Sexual Dissidence* (Oxford: Oxford University Press, 1991), 228. By taking this risk Dollimore offers one of the most insightful and useful readings of Freudian psychoanalysis. By recovering the idea of perversity from and through Freud, Dollimore uses a procedure he identifies as follows: "(1) attention to formal definitions, provoking (2) a historical enquiry which in turn leads to (3) a conceptual development facilitating (4) a further historical recovery." While my own procedure in this chapter cannot be so clearly defined, I hope that in some small way this checklist has remained intact at the peripheries of my critical focus.

26. Dimock, 67–90.

27. In economic terms an instance of this would be the limited liability companies which in both the United States and Britain developed first in the railway building sector.

28. She is more concerned with the subplots of Miss Dewey and Rogers as "structural complement" to the main plot. I, of course, do not consider Rogers to be a subplot at all. But Dimock makes the point that in these subplots "tenuous ties" of connection to Lapham are precisely what is important about them. They offer a way for negotiating the limits of responsibility. Should Lapham remain responsible for Rogers after so many years; should he continue to support Jim Millon's wife and daughter?

29. It should be remembered that for Sedgwick the suggestion of the potential unbrokenness of this continuum, the continuum between homosocial and homosexual, is intended as "a strategy for making generalizations about, and marking historical differences in the *structure* of men's relations with other men." Eve Kosofsky Sedgwick, *Between Men* (New York: Columbia University Press, 1985), 2.

30. This is the argument Foucault makes in *The History of Sexuality Volume 1* and which has subsequently come to underpin much of the thinking about modern homosexuality. See Jeffrey Weeks, *Sexuality and Its Discontents* (London: Routledge & Kegan Paul, 1985); David Halperin, *One Hundred Years of Homosexuality and Other Essays on Greek Love* (New York: Routledge, 1990); Eve Kosofsky Sedgwick, *Epistemology of the Closet* (Harmondsworth: Penguin, 1994 [1990]); and Ed Cohen, *A Talk on the Wilde Side* (New York: Routledge, 1993). Rictor Norton, *The Myth of the Modern Homosexual* (London: Cassell, 1997), has made the most vigorous attack on this idea and on the idea of social constructionism in the realm of sexuality.

31. Sedgwick, *Between Men*, 164.

32. There is clearly some age-related logic at work in this demand to set up father-son relationships wherever an older man and a younger man come into contact; but an age-related logic which once more can only position itself in the

first instance in relation to the family where, by necessity, a father is at least a generation older than his son. Of course, the compulsion to turn sexual or desirous relations between older and younger men into father-son relations might have more than a little to do with a twisted homophobic logic which has developed in tandem with the strictly policed separation of homo- and heterosexualities and which somehow assumes that male-male passion is a desire for the "same," rather than a desire for the "different" which is supposed to characterize male-female passion. (For more on this in relation to Oscar Wilde, see Eve Kosofsky Sedgwick, *Epistemology*, 157–63; Sedgwick, *Tendencies*, 52–72.) So, two men who may be marked by all manner of differences—age, class, race—cannot be perceived in twentieth-century heterosexist culture to be participating in a relationship of desire because desire is directed towards an object recognizably the "same." Instead, any possible relationship of desire is passed over as the relationship is translated so that the two men become father and son; sexual desire between men is safely covered up by the family. That this is a bizarrely disavowing maneuver can be seen in the fact that the two men's differences have been reduced to sameness—of gender and biology; the kind of sameness which should—in the heteronormative logic that explains homosexual desire—actually precipitate a relationship of desire; homosexual men are homosexual, so this logic goes, because they desire the same rather than the different. It is the structural, familial relationship posited between these two hypothetical men which—by way of the incest taboo—prevents this sameness leading to, or being conceived of as, desire. Even when these two men might not be biologically related. For more on this see Dollimore, *Sexual Dissidence*, 249–75, and also Leo Bersani, *Homos* (Cambridge, Mass., and London: Harvard University Press, 1995), which takes a somewhat different approach from a gay-centered point of view and tries to reconstruct the validity of a same-desiring logic in understanding homosexuality.

33. See Stuart M. Blumin, "The Hypothesis of Middle-Class Formation in Nineteenth-Century America: A Critique and Some Proposals," *The American Historical Review* 90 (1985), 299–338.

34. For more on squeezing and masturbation in this period see Gregory Woods, *A History of Gay Literature: The Male Tradition* (New Haven and London: Yale University Press, 1998), 163–64. It is also worth pointing out at this point, I think, the intimate connection between male sexuality and the language of money and business. As I have just mentioned, the connection between spending and sperm is one of the most obvious. (And one that is continued in the language of the "money shot" of hard-core pornography.) In addition, there are phrases like "doing business," "doing *the* business," "on the job," "rough trade," and, of course, the whole rhetoric of "partnership" which is clearly important in the plot development of *Silas Lapham*.

35. In many ways, one of the key tasks of queer theory in its deconstructive manifestation is to think about how categories add up in the logic of heteronormativity and how they might add up differently. This is certainly the attitude of Eve Sedgwick in *Tendencies*, 1–20. "What if instead there were a practice of valuing the ways in which meanings and institutions can be at loose ends with

each other?" she argues. "What if the richest junctures weren't the ones where *everything means the same thing? . . .* That's one of the things that 'queer' can refer to: the open mesh of possibilities, gaps, overlaps, dissonances and resonances, lapses and excesses of meaning when the constituent elements of anyone's gender, of anyone's sexuality aren't made (or *can't* be made) to signify monolithically."

36. Another incident which might help place these asterisks in some relation to male sexuality is the reporting of the Oscar Wilde trials ten years after *Silas Lapham* was published, when of course the acts of which Wilde was accused were left blank in the newspaper reports. For more on this see Ed Cohen, *A Talk on the Wilde Side,* and Alan Sinfield, *The Wilde Century* (London: Cassell, 1994), 1–10.

37. Persis's role in her husband's business is important here. While Silas relied on her at the beginning, it is remarked on in the text that her role has gradually reduced to the point where she has no input whatsoever (48).

38. Others might include the sports field and the changing room, the law courts, the pub, the battlefield.

39. Sedgwick, *Epistemology,* 73.

40. I don't want to suggest either that these sentences are simply casual innuendo or that really they are *about* sex. What I want to suggest is that the rhetoric of fiction is one of those places where the cognitive regimes of capitalist sexuality formation cannot help but exist.

41. Sedgwick, *Epistemology,* 145–46.

42. John Seelye, "The Hole in Howells/The Lapse in *Silas Lapham,"* in Pease, 52.

43. This argument becomes even more substantive when viewed in the light of Eve Sedgwick's discussion of Oscar Wilde's *The Picture of Dorian Gray.* Here she utilizes Freud's list of eroto-grammatical slippages that are generated in a homophobic culture where it is impossible for a man to utter "I love him" about another man. She argues that Wilde develops the slippage "I do not love *him,* I *am* him" in *Dorian Gray.* More interestingly for my purposes, is the second of Freud's disavowing utterances: "I do not love *him,* I love *her."* See Sedgwick, *Epistemology,* 157–63.

44. Seelye, 52.

45. See Sedgwick, *Epistemology,* 145.

3. "A dream more romantic than
scarlet pagodas by a silver sea"

1. Quoted in George Chauncey, *Gay New York: The Making of the Gay Male World, 1890–1940* (London: Flamingo, 1995 [1994]), 113–14.

2. For more on Lewis's attitude towards and treatment of his fictional female characters, see Sally E. Parry, "The Changing Fictional Faces of Sinclair Lewis' Wives," *Studies in American Fiction* 17 (1989), 65–79.

3. Anthony Di Renzo, ed., *If I Were Boss: The Early Business Stories of Sinclair Lewis* (Carbondale and Edwardsville: Southern Illinois University Press, 1997), xxxv.

4. T. J. Jackson Lears, *No Place of Grace: Antimodernism and the Transformation of American Culture, 1880–1920* (Chicago and London: University of Chicago Press, 1994 [1983]), 9.

5. Gail Bederman, *Manliness and Civilization: A Cultural History of Gender and Race in the United States, 1880–1917* (Chicago and London: University of Chicago Press, 1995), 13.

6. Jonathan Freedman, "The Affect of the Market: Economic and Racial Exchange in *The Searchers*," *American Literary History* 12 (2000), 585–86.

7. Sinclair Lewis, *Babbitt* (London: Vintage, 1994 [1922]), 180. All further page references in this chapter appear in parentheses.

8. Freedman, 587.

9. Kenneth R. Morefield, "Searching for the Fairy Child: A Psychoanalytic Study of *Babbitt*," *Midwest Quarterly* 37 (1996), 448–58.

10. Henry James, *The Bostonians* (London and New York: Macmillan and Co., 1886), 333.

11. This is an issue that I deal with in terms of office work at greater length in the next chapter.

12. E. Anthony Rotundo, *American Manhood: Transformations in Masculinity from the Revolution to the Modern Era* (New York: Basic Books, 1993), 247.

13. For a demonstration that this is still a live issue see Eve Kosofsky Sedgwick, "How to Bring Your Kids Up Gay: The War on Effeminate Boys," in *Tendencies* (London: Routledge, 1994), 154–64.

14. See Rotundo, 227–32, on primitivism, and Mark C. Carnes, *Secret Ritual and Manhood in Victorian America* (New Haven and London: Yale University Press, 1989).

15. For more on this see Rotundo, 252–53.

16. See George Chauncey, 113.

17. A good introduction to the general subject of sexology is provided by Joseph Bristow, *Sexuality* (London and New York: Routledge, 1997), 12–61. See also Jeffrey Weeks, *Coming Out: Homosexual Politics in Britain from the Nineteenth Century to the Present* (London: Quartet, 1977). The classic European texts of this sexological discourse are Karl Heinz Ulrichs, *The Riddle of "Man-Manly" Love: The Pioneering Work on Male Homosexuality*, 2 vols., trans. Michael A. Lombardi-Nash (Buffalo, New York: Prometheus Books, 1994); Havelock Ellis and John Addington Symons, *Sexual Inversion* (London: Wilson and Macmillan, 1897); and Richard von Krafft-Ebing, *Psychopathia Sexualis, with Especial Reference to Contrary Sexual Instinct: A Medico-Legal Study*, trans. Charles Gilbert Chaddock (Philadelphia: F. A. Davis, 1894). For the importance of these ideas in America see Rotundo, 247–83. In America, the European sexological texts were paralleled by similar, although less well known studies. Chauncey provides a list of such studies in *Gay New York*, 386; for an example of the material in these studies see figure 4.1 on page 98.

18. Chauncey, 47, 47–64.

19. See Dennis W. Allen, "Homosexuality and Narrative," *Modern Fiction Studies* 41 (1995), 609–34.

20. Martin Light, *The Quixotic Vision of Sinclair Lewis* (West Lafayette, Indiana: Purdue University Press, 1975), discusses the tension between the romantic tradition and the realist imperative in Lewis's work.

21. Lee Edelman, *Homographesis: Essays in Gay Literary and Cultural Theory* (New York and London: Routledge, 1994), 6.

22. Chauncey, 9.

4. "The spirit of work weaves a magic wand"

1. Here I am thinking of those social critics who set out to "diagnose" the state of the postwar nation through changes in work and business culture and who I discuss in more detail later, writers like William H. Whyte, C. Wright Mills, David Riesman, Vance Packard, and even J. K. Galbraith.

2. That even Senator Joseph McCarthy became a target of homosexual innuendo through his relationship with his aide Ray Cohn is testament to the way in which homosexuality could be used against even the most apparently solid of citizens once they achieve a position of Organizational power. For a brief survey of the McCarthy-Cohn affair see Neil Miller, *Out of the Past: Gay and Lesbian History from 1869 to the Present* (London: Vintage, 1995), 264–71; for a fuller account see Richard H. Rovere, *Senator Joe McCarthy* (New York: Harcourt Brace, 1959) and Nicholas von Hoffman, *Citizen Cohn* (New York: Doubleday, 1988).

3. Margaret L. Hedstrom, "Beyond Feminisation: Clerical Workers in the United States from the 1920s through the 1960s," in Gregory Anderson, ed., *The White-Blouse Revolution: Female Office Workers since 1870* (Manchester and New York: Manchester University Press, 1988), 143–69.

4. Hedstrom, 149.

5. Hedstrom, 150.

6. Kate Boyer, "Place and the politics of virtue: clerical workers, corporate anxiety, and changing meanings of public womanhood in early twentieth century Montreal," *Gender, Place and Culture* 5 (1998), 263.

7. Ann Douglas, *The Feminization of American Culture* (London: Papermac, 1996 [1977]), 12. Douglas's argument has, of course, come in for a good deal of criticism from feminist critical thinkers who try to carve out a more complex and positive reading of sentimentalism. See in particular Jane Tompkins, "Sentimental Power: *Uncle Tom's Cabin* and the Politics of Literary History," in H. Aram Vesser, ed., *The New Historicism Reader* (New York and London: Routledge, 1994), 206–28.

8. I use this word here simply to stress the way in which women and their associated gender-marked characters were diluting the all-male world of the office.

9. Quoted in Fiona McNally, *Women for Hire: A Study of the Female Office Worker* (London: Macmillan, 1979), 25.

10. Apart from those texts about female office workers already mentioned, see M. W. Davies, *Woman's Place Is at the Typewriter: Office Work and Office Workers, 1870–1930* (Philadelphia: Temple University Press, 1982) and E. J. Rotella, *From Home to Office: U.S. Women at Work, 1870–1930* (Ann Arbor: UMI Research Press, 1981).

11. McNally, 27.

12. Hedstrom, 154.

13. William Dean Howells, *The Rise of Silas Lapham* (Oxford: Oxford University Press, 1996 [1885]), 19.

14. Howells, 108. My emphasis.

15. Glenna Matthews, *The Rise of Public Woman: Woman's Power and Woman's Place in the United States 1630–1970* (New York and Oxford: Oxford University Press, 1992), 148–50.

16. For a classic feminist position on the relationship between women and objectification, or more precisely between the relationship of ocularcentrism and phallogocentrism, see Luce Irigaray, *Speculum of the Other Woman*, trans. Gillian C. Gill (Ithaca, New York: Cornell University Press, 1985). This issue has been particularly important in feminist film theory, following Laura Mulvey's "Visual pleasure and narrative cinema," *Screen* 16 (1975), 6–19. See also Rosemary Betterton, ed., *Looking On: Images of Femininity in the Visual Arts and Media* (London: Pandora, 1987). For a more skeptical approach to Mulvey's legacy see Stella Bruzzi, *Undressing Cinema* (London and New York: Routledge, 1997).

17. Douglas Tallack, *Twentieth-Century America: The Intellectual and Cultural Context* (Harlow: Longman, 1991), 12.

18. Sinclair Lewis, *Babbitt* (London: Vintage, 1994 [1922]), 77.

19. Sinclair Lewis, 265.

20. For more on this see Harry Brod, ed., *The Making of Masculinities: The New Men's Studies* (Winchester, Mass.: Allen & Unwin, 1987); Peter N. Stearns, *Be a Man! Males in Modern Society* (New York: Holmes & Meier, 1979); Elizabeth Pleck and Joseph Pleck, eds., *The American Man* (Englewood Cliffs: Prentice Hall, 1990); David D. Gilmore, *Manhood in the Making: Cultural Concepts of Masculinity* (New Haven: Yale University Press, 1990).

21. Clare Virginia Eby, "*Babbitt* as Veblenian Critique of Manliness," *American Studies* 34 (1993), 5–23.

22. *Eby*, 8–9.

23. *Eby*, 14.

24. Sinclair Lewis, 118.

25. From Strenuous Life Period of strong male bonds (1861–1919) to Period of Companionate Providing (1920–1965), Pleck and Pleck, 23–24.

26. Michael Roper, *Masculinity and the British Organization Man since 1945* (Oxford: Oxford University Press, 1994), 49. Roper argues that in Britain, because of the legacy of family capitalism, the managerial revolution occurred much more slowly and that as a result business organization didn't restructure itself so as to maintain competitive advantage.

27. For the fullest account of this process, see Alfred D. Chandler Jr., *The Visible Hand: The Managerial Revolution in America* (Cambridge, Mass., and London: Harvard University Press, 1977).

28. Tallack, 10 and 4. Many of these changes were apparent in the rise of mass communication forms such as cinema, publishing, and broadcasting. What is clear is that it is not only to the products of these industries that one must look to understand the changes in the social and cultural life of America,

but to the very means by which it was possible for these products to circulate through the social and cultural environment. After all, it was not so much the ability to produce or view a moving image that was important; it was the ability first of all to mass produce it, and—perhaps even more important—to be able to ensure that these copies could be released in hundreds of different towns and cities at the same time along with the concomitant release and dissemination of advertising and secondary media coverage. These feats of organization in the field of mass communications were matched elsewhere in the general areas of product sales, distribution, and advertising, and required whole new industries in themselves and whole new branches to be added to existing corporations. And as these areas grew, so did the need for staff to fill the posts created and for ancillary staff to service these posts, and as staff hierarchies became even more expanded for more ancillary staff to service existing ancillary staff. The growth of the large corporation produced both bureaucracy and a service economy, and at the heart of this development was company organization.

29. Michael Crozier, *The World of the Office Worker* (London and Chicago: University of Chicago Press, 1971 [1965]), 1.

30. For the classic Frankfurt School approaches to capitalism and capitalist culture, see Theodor Adorno, *The Culture Industry* (London: Routledge, 1991); Max Horkheimer and Theodor Adorno, *Dialectic of Enlightenment* (London: Allen Lane, 1973 [1944]); and Herbert Marcuse, *One Dimensional Man* (London: Abacus, 1972). Much of this work has been supplemented in recent years by an increasing attention to Gramscian Hegemony and to the process of consumption and the way that both these approaches help to identify not a capitulation to capitalism but some more complex negotiation with it.

31. Vance Packard, *The Status Seekers* (Harmondsworth: Penguin, 1961 [1959]), 106.

32. Sloan Wilson, *The Man in the Gray Flannel Suit* (New York: Simon and Schuster, 1955), 29 and 26.

33. Henry Miller, *Tropic of Capricorn* (London: Flamingo, 1993 [1939]), 12. All further page references in this section appear in parentheses.

34. Richard Slotkin, *Regeneration through Violence: The Myth of the American Frontier, 1600–1860* (Middletown, Conn.: Wesleyan University Press, 1973); *The Fatal Environment: The Myth of the Frontier in the Age of Industrialization, 1800–1890* (New York: Atheneum, 1985); *Gunfighter Nation: The Myth of the Frontier in Twentieth-Century America* (New York: HarperPerennial, 1993 [1992]).

35. Slotkin, *Gunfighter Nation*, 23.

36. Slotkin, *Gunfighter Nation*, 23.

37. William H. Whyte, *The Organization Man* (Harmondsworth: Penguin, 1960 [1956]), 372.

38. S. J. Kleinberg, *Women in the United States 1830–1945* (Basingstoke and London: Macmillan Press, 1999), 229.

39. Hedstrom, 162.

40. Thomas Hill Schaub, *American Fiction in the Cold War* (Madison: University of Wisconsin Press, 1991).

41. This suspicion is still a running question in the work of Don DeLillo. See

Running Dog (New York: Alfred A. Knopf, 1978) and *White Noise* (New York: Viking Penguin, 1984).

42. Tallack, 225.

43. Daniel Bell, *The End of Ideology: on the Exhaustion of Political Ideas in the Fifties* (Cambridge, Mass.: Harvard University Press, 1988 [1960]).

44. Schaub, 17.

45. Quoted in Tallack, 193.

46. Whyte, 8. All further page references in this section appear in parentheses.

47. Sinclair Lewis, 180.

48. David Savran, *Communists, Cowboys, and Queers: The Politics of Masculinity in the Work of Arthur Miller and Tennessee Williams* (Minneapolis: University of Minnesota Press, 1992), 4.

49. Savran, 35.

50. Lee Edelman, *Homographesis: Essays in Gay Literary and Cultural Theory* (New York and London: Routledge, 1994), 158.

51. Edelman, *Homographesis*, 167.

52. Alan Sinfield, *Cultural Politics—Queer Reading* (London: Routledge, 1994), 42.

53. Alan Bérubé, "Marching to a Different Drummer: Lesbian and Gay GIs in World War II," in Martin Baum Duberman, Martha Vicinus, and George Chauncey Jr., eds., *Hidden from History: Reclaiming the Gay and Lesbian Past* (Harmondsworth: Penguin, 1991 [1989]), 383–94.

54. See R. J. Ellis, *Liar! Liar!: Jack Kerouac—Novelist* (London: Greenwich Exchange, 1999), 36.

55. C. Wright Mills, *White Collar: The American Middle Classes* (New York: Oxford University Press, 1971 [1953]), xv.

56. David Riesman, *The Lonely Crowd* (New Haven and London: Yale University Press, 1970 [1953]), 37.

5. "Opaque glass bricks"

1. William Dean Howells, *The Rise of Silas Lapham* (Oxford: Oxford University Press, 1996 [1885]), 4.

2. Sinclair Lewis, *Babbitt* (London: Vintage, 1994 [1922]), 40.

3. Sloan Wilson, *The Man in the Gray Flannel Suit* (New York: Simon and Schuster, 1955), 7. All further page references in this chapter appear in parentheses. The novel was fifth on the 1955 American bestseller list and was turned into a film starring Gregory Peck the following year.

4. Mention of the confessional is, of course, important in this context, and it is an issue that I pursued at greater length in chapter 2. Like Silas Lapham, Tom Rath is being interviewed; he is being asked to engage in a self-surveilling process that will reveal himself to his employer as he reveals himself to the reader.

5. Their limitations are obvious enough and building authorities generally limited their use to locations where they didn't carry structural loads; in other words, to places where an ordinary window would normally be permitted.

6. William H. Whyte, *The Organization Man* (Harmondsworth: Penguin, 1960 [1956]), 118.

7. Elaine Tyler May, *Homeward Bound: American Families in the Cold War Era* (New York: Basic Books, 1988).

8. May, 11.

9. For more on the novel in relation to the suburban family see Catherina Jurca, "The Sanctimonious Suburbanite: Sloan Wilson's *The Man in the Gray Flannel Suit,*" *American Literary History* 11 (1999), 82–106.

10. Eve Kosofsky Sedgwick, *Epistemology of the Closet* (Harmondsworth: Penguin 1994, [1990]), 116.

11. California, and particularly San Francisco, was already developing its gay and lesbian associations. California was the one state at the time that allowed the public congregation of homosexuals in public places. See John D'Emilio, "Gay Politics and Community in San Francisco since World War II," in Martin Baum Duberman, Martha Vicinus, and George Chauncey Jr., eds., *Hidden from History: Reclaiming the Gay and Lesbian Past* (Harmondsworth: Penguin, 1991 [1989]), 456–73. See also Michael Davidson, *The San Francisco Renaissance: Poetics and Community at Mid-Century* (Cambridge: Cambridge University Press, 1979).

12. Michael Rogin, *Ronald Reagan, the Movie and Other Episodes in Political Demonology* (Berkeley, Los Angeles, and London: University of California Press, 1987), 236–71.

13. Lee Edelman, *Homographesis: Essays in Gay Literary and Cultural Theory* (New York and London: Routledge, 1994), 168.

14. Edelman, *Homographesis,* 169.

15. Edelman, *Homographesis,* 169.

16. Edelman, *Homographesis,* 169.

6. "I ascend like a condor, while falling to pieces"

1. Joseph Heller, *Something Happened* (New York: Alfred A. Knopf, 1974), 527. All further page references in this chapter appear in parentheses.

2. William Dean Howells, *The Rise of Silas Lapham* (Oxford: Oxford University Press, 1996 [1885]), 377.

3. This theme of business success and moral failure is one that has been evident in various textual representations of business in American culture, from Theodore Dreiser's trilogy of novels about Frank Cowperwood—*The Financier* (1912)*, The Titan* (1914)*,* and *The Stoic* (1947)—to F. Scott Fitzgerald's *The Great Gatsby* (1925), to Ralph Hopkins in *The Man in the Gray Flannel Suit.* It is a theme that in the 1980s was reinvented in the wake of Reaganite free-market economics and reached its apotheosis in the movie characters of Gordon Gekko, in Oliver Stone's *Wall Street* (1987), and Patrick Bateman, Brett Easton Ellis's serial-killing, Wall Street yuppie in *American Psycho* (1991).

4. For more on the similarities between *Something Happened* and "Bartleby" see Andrew Gordon, "Dead Letter Offices: Joseph Heller's *Something Happened* and Herman Melville's 'Bartleby, the Scrivener,'" *Notes on Contemporary Literature* 12 (1982), 2–4.

5. Don DeLillo, *Americana* (Harmondsworth: Penguin, 1990 [1971]), 23.

6. DeLillo, *Americana,* 36.

7. DeLillo, *Americana*, 241.

8. DeLillo, *Americana*, 80.

9. Lee Edelman, *Homographesis: Essays in Gay Literary and Cultural Theory* (New York and London: Routledge, 1994), 19.

10. DeLillo, *Americana*, 81.

11. Eve Kosofsky Sedgwick, *Epistemology of the Closet* (Harmondsworth: Penguin 1994, [1990]), 187. See also Eve Kosofsky Sedgwick, *Between Men: English Literature and Male Homosocial Desire* (New York: Columbia University Press, 1985), 83–117 and *The Coherence of Gothic Conventions* (New York: Arno, 1980).

12. Sedgwick, *Epistemology*, 100.

13. According to the Oxford English Dictionary "whammy" is a North American colloquialism that means "An evil or unlucky influence; an unpleasant or problematic effect or situation," and is derived from the word "wham," one of whose meanings in combination with "bam" or "bang" is "quick forceful or violent action (*spec.* w. ref. to sexual intercourse)."

14. I don't have the space to detail the history of this increasing visibility here. Instead, see John D'Emilio, *Sexual Politics, Sexual Communities: The Making of a Homosexual Minority in the United States, 1940–1970* (Chicago and London: University of Chicago Press, 1983); Dennis Altman, *Homosexual Oppression and Liberation* (New York: Avon Books, 1973); and Martin Duberman, *Stonewall* (New York: Dutton, 1993).

15. Edelman, *Homographesis*, 12.

16. Robert J. Corber argues that the representation of gay men in Hollywood film noir of the 1950s both legitimized the gay male gaze and enabled resistance against normative models of Cold War masculinity even as it reinforced homophobic stereotypes. See Robert J. Corber, *Homosexuality in Cold War America: Resistance and the Crisis of Masculinity* (Durham and London: Duke University Press, 1997).

17. House Un-American Activities Committee hearings in the 1950s are perhaps the most obvious example of how the oppression of homosexuality can have the unexpected result of increasing the visibility of sexual behavior and lifestyle. Cindy Patton has identified another in the "problem movies" of the 1950s. See Cindy Patton, "To Die For" in Eve Kosofsky Sedgwick, ed., *Novel Gazing: Queer Readings in Fiction* (Durham and London: Duke University Press, 1997), 330–52.

18. Sedgwick, *Epistemology*, 146.

19. Malcolm Bradbury, *The Modern American Novel* (Oxford: Oxford University Press, 1984 [1983]), 165.

20. DeLillo, *Americana*, 24.

21. Gregory Woods, *A History of Gay Literature: The Male Tradition* (New Haven and London: Yale University Press, 1998), 315.

22. Adam J. Sorkin, "Something Happened to America: Bob Slocum and the Loss of History," *Ball State University Forum* 28 (1987), 48; Lois Tyson, "Joseph Heller's *Something Happened*: The Commodification of Consciousness and the Postmodern Flight from Inwardness," *CEA Critic* 54 (1992), 46.

23. Sedgwick, *Epistemology*, 145.

24. June Howard, "What Is Sentimentality?," *American Literary History* 11 (1999), 76.

25. See Andre Furlani, "'Brisk Socratic Dialogues': Elenctic Rhetoric in Joseph Heller's *Something Happened*," *Narrative* 3 (1995), 252–70.

26. Sorkin, 36 and 39.

27. Eve Kosofsky Sedgwick, *Tendencies* (London: Routledge, 1994), 155.

28. Sedgwick, *Tendencies*, 156.

7. "My own plein-air Arnality bared to the sky"

1. James Annesley, *Blank Fictions: Consumerism, Culture and the Contemporary Novel* (Pluto Press: London, 1998), 5.

2. Sumantra Ghoshal and Christopher A. Bartlett, *The Individualized Corporation* (London: Heinemann, 1999), 3–16.

3. Ghoshal and Bartlett, 8.

4. For the influence of management gurus see A. Huczynski, *Management Gurus* (London: Routledge, 1993) and C. Kennedy, *Guide to Management Gurus* (London: Century Press, 1991).

5. The main culprits here are Fredric Jameson, "Postmodernism, or the Cultural Logic of Late Capitalism," *New Left Review* 146, 53–92; Fredric Jameson, *Postmodernism* (London: Verso, 1991); Fredric Jameson, "Postmodernism and Consumer Society," in Hal Foster, ed., *Postmodern Culture* (London: Pluto Press, 1985 [1983]), 111–25; Jean Baudrillard, *Selected Writings* (Cambridge: Polity Press, 1988), particularly the extracts in chapters 2, 4, and 5. But it is a more general problem that "capitalism" remains an abstract term of reference in much academic writing about the relationship between culture and economics, while in work that is written from a critical management or sociological perspective, the focus is too specialized, model-driven, and policy-oriented.

6. Nicholson Baker, *The Mezzanine* (Cambridge: Granta, 1989 [1988]), 11. All further page references in the first half of this chapter appear in parentheses.

7. Baker's own exposition of the importance of small thoughts and details can be found in the title essay of his *The Size of Thought: Essays and Other Lumber* (London: Chatto & Windus, 1996).

8. Eve Kosofsky Sedgwick, *Epistemology of the Closet* (Harmondsworth: Penguin, 1994, [1990]), 110.

9. For a comprehensive account of the thinking of Marx, Weber, and Foucault in relation to the concept of surveillance and of the way in which their ideas overlap and diverge see Christopher Dandeker, *Surveillance, Power and Modernity* (Cambridge: Polity, 1990).

10. Margaret Crawford, *Building the Workingman's Paradise: The Design of American Company Towns* (London and New York: Verso, 1995), 23–26 and 37–45.

11. Michel Foucault, *Discipline and Punish* (Harmondsworth: Penguin, 1991 [1977]), 202–3.

12. For more on this see David Lyon, *The Electronic Eye: The Rise of Surveillance Society* (Cambridge: Polity, 1994), especially 119–35.

13. Catherine Casey, *Work, Self and Society after Industrialism* (London and New York: Routledge, 1995), 29.

14. This theme has been amplified in much recent work in the field of business and organization sociology. The best summary is in Paul du Gay, *Consumption and Identity at Work* (London: Sage, 1996).

15. Casey, 138–82.

16. Casey, 109.

17. See Baudrillard, *Selected Writings*, 166–84.

18. Phillip E. Simmons, *Deep Surfaces: Mass Culture and History in Postmodern American Fiction* (Athens: University of Georgia Press, 1997), 41.

19. With the introduction of new forms of monitoring in the workplace, such as drugs and alcohol testing, this question of surveillance is obviously a running issue. Clearly, though, the balance of power at work is different than it is elsewhere. The concept of workers' rights and freedoms has been at stake since the very beginning of the trade union movement. I take it that capitalist economic systems and their legal corollaries operate within a logic that stresses the onus of duty and compliance of employee to the employer rather than the other way round. In the United States, the workplace can be seen as one of the key sites where the rhetoric of freedom is exposed; it is where the freedom of businessmen to make themselves rich collides with the constitutional freedom of individuals.

20. Casey, 109.

21. See Thomas Pynchon, *The Crying of Lot 49* (Harmondsworth: Penguin, 1974 [1966]), 61:

Hymn
High above the LA freeways,
And the traffic's whine,
Stands the well-known Galatronics
Branch of Yoyodyne.
To the end, we swear undying
Loyalty to you,
Pink pavilions bravely shining,
Palm trees tall and true.

22. This is the space Babbitt wants to escape to with Paul Riesling.

23. For a discussion of symbolic equivalence in relation to capitalism and writing, and of the writer as resource manager, see Wai-Chee Dimock, "The Economy of Pain: Capitalism, Humanitarianism, and the Realistic Novel," in Donald Pease, ed., *New Essays on* The Rise of Silas Lapham (Cambridge and New York: Cambridge University Press, 1991), 67–90.

24. I take this distinction from Dimock, 80.

25. Rosemary Pringle, *Sexuality, Power and Work* (London and New York: Verso, 1989 [1988]), 112.

26. Peter Stallybrass, "Worn Worlds: Clothes, Mourning and the Life of Things," *Yale Review* 81 (1993), 47.

27. Just how important are one's appearance and one's tie at a job interview is witnessed by this advice given to men seeking professional employment in America: "The lower tip of the tie should come to the top or center of the belt buckle and the back of the tie should go through the label so it cannot escape control and reveal its undisciplined self to the interviewer. The tie relates to the belt symmetrically, producing the body as aesthetically balanced around both vertical and horizontal axes." Quoted in Linda McDowell, *Capital Culture: Gender at Work in the City* (London: Blackwell, 1997), 188.

28. Sedgwick, *Epistemology*, 110.

29. This remains one of only two academic pieces of writing on *The Mezzanine* and forms the basis for Simmons's consideration of the novel in his book *Deep Surfaces*. The other is Ross Chambers, "Meditation and the Escalator Principle (On Nicholson Baker's *The Mezzanine*)," *Modern Fiction Studies* 40 (1994), 765–806. Much of the rest of Baker criticism has been confined to newspapers and magazines. On its publication in the United States in 1988, *The Mezzanine* received widespread acclaim, with most reviewers highlighting Howie's idiosyncratic fascination with details and placing it in a literary heritage that stretches back to Laurence Sterne and continues through Marcel Proust, James Joyce, and Vladimir Nabokov. Most reviewers were won over by what Brad Leithauser in the *New York Review of Books* described as Baker's "mixture of charm, intelligence, and out-and-out weirdness." See Brad Leithauser, "Microscopy," the *New York Review of Books* 36 (1989): 15.

30. Lee Edelman, *Homographesis* (New York and London: Routledge, 1994), 12.

31. D. A. Miller, *The Novel and the Police* (Berkeley: University of California Press, 1988), 206.

32. Lee Edelman, "Men's Room," in Joel Sanders, ed., *Stud: Architectures of Masculinity* (New York: Princeton Architectural Press, 1996), 161.

33. Edelman, "Men's Room," 153.

34. Nicholson Baker, *The Fermata* (New York: Random House, 1994), 43. All further page references in the second half of this chapter appear in parentheses.

35. Ralph Waldo Emerson, *Journals of Ralph Waldo Emerson, 1841–44, Volume 6* (Boston: Forbes, 1912), 100–101.

36. Gilles Deleuze, *Foucault* (London: Athlone, 1988), 97.

37. Deleuze, *Foucault*, 119.

38. Leo Bersani, "Is the Rectum a Grave?" *October* 43 (1987), 212.

39. Edelman, *Homographesis*, 98.

40. Edelman, *Homographesis*, 100.

41. Jonathan Dollimore, *Death, Desire and Loss in Western Culture* (Harmondsworth: Penguin, 1999 [1998]), 129.

42. Edelman, *Homographesis*, 99.

43. Dollimore, *Death, Desire and Loss*, 327.

44. Nicholson Baker, *U and I* (London: Granta, 1991), 135.

45. Baker, *U and I*, 135 and 138.

46. Edelman, *Homographesis*, 101.

47. Simmons, 20.

8. "Frank Lloyd Oop"

1. Douglas Coupland, *Microserfs* (London: Flamingo, 1995). All further references to pages in this text appear in parentheses.

2. It will not, for instance, reduce the ever-increasing number of people working in factory-like call centers who have no choice about where they work or the extreme levels of surveillance that exist in these environments. For more on this aspect of office change see C. Baldry, P. Bain, and P. Taylor, "Bright Satanic Offices: Intensification, Control and Team Taylorism," in C. Warhurst and P. Thompson, eds., *Workplaces of the Future* (London: Macmillan, 1998); Chris Baldry, "Space—The Final Frontier," *Sociology* 33 (1999), 535–53. Although see my later comments about the software they use to perform their jobs.

3. Bill Gates, *The Road Ahead*, rev. ed. (Harmondsworth: Penguin, 1996), xiii.

4. Gates, 262.

5. Robert X. Cringeley, *Accidental Empires*, 2d ed. (Harmondsworth: Penguin, 1996), 55.

6. Michael A. Cusumano and Richard W. Selby, *Microsoft Secrets: How the World's Most Powerful Software Company Creates Technology, Shapes Markets, and Manages People* (London: HarperCollins, 1996), 3.

7. Po Bronson, *The Nudist of the Late Shift: And Other Tales from Silicon Valley* (London: Secker & Warburg, 1999), 3–39.

8. Bronson, 4.

9. Of the five hopefuls whom Bronson follows for several months, only one makes it big. Ben Chiu sells his KillerApp program and company for $46.6 million, of which his share is fifty percent. Of the other four, two manage to keep their start-ups ticking over with small-scale venture capital, while the other two end up working for computer companies.

10. Other examples would include Dell, Hotmail, and Amazon.com.

11. Arthur Kroker, "Virtual Capitalism," in Stanley Aranowitz, Barbara Martinsons, and Michael Menser, eds., *Technoscience and Cyberculture* (New York and London: Routledge, 1996), 168.

12. Kroker, 170 and 178.

13. Peter Stoneley, "Rewriting the Gold Rush: Twain, Harte and Homosociality," *Journal of American Studies* 30 (1996), 189.

14. Cringeley, 95.

15. Cringeley, 8 and 15. Cringeley is too concerned perhaps with the accidental nature of the rise of the microcomputer industry. It can be quite well accounted for in economic terms if one thinks about the way in which the large corporations that came to dominate American capitalism in the 1960s were slowly atrophying in the 1970s during a period of recession and inflation following the removal of the dollar from the gold standard and the oil crisis of 1973 (for more on this see Stephen Paul Miller, *The Seventies Now: Culture as Surveillance* [Durham and London: Duke University Press, 1999], 6–13). Smaller companies with low overheads and new markets to exploit were better able to prosper.

16. Pierre Guerlain, "A Technofreak in Xanadu: Bill Gates and Cool Capitalism," *European Journal of American Culture* 19 (2000), 121.

17. Mark Leibovich, "*Sleepless in Silicon Valley*: Global Competition, Technology's Fast Track Dictates a Lifestyle of Working into the Wee Hours," *San Jose Mercury News*, 21 June 1996, sec. Front: 1A.

18. Bronson, xv.

19. Bronson, xxxiv.

20. Fred Moody, *I Sing the Body Electronic: A Year with Microsoft on the Multimedia Frontier* (London: Hodder and Stoughton, 1996 [1995]), 124–25.

21. Moody, xix.

22. Moody, 123–24.

23. Moody, 80.

24. I am grateful to my copyeditor, Jennifer Usher of Mesa Verde Media Services, for suggesting this connection.

25. Moody, xviii. IBM became known as Big Blue because of the combination of its size, the blue boxes that housed its computers in the early days of production, and the blue suits worn by its executives. Big Green implies that Microsoft has become just as monolithic as IBM, although instead of blue suits it has a reputation for eco-friendly gestures.

26. Although for the world's leading company it is still, in terms of staff, very small. It employed 17,800 people in 1995, the year *Microserfs* was written. See Cusumano and Selby, 3. IBM, in contrast, employs about 320,000 people worldwide. See Cringeley, 121.

27. Bronson, xvii.

28. Bronson, xvii.

29. Bronson, xvii.

30. Bronson, xviii–xix.

31. Gates, 57.

32. Herman Melville, *The Piazza Tales and Other Prose Pieces 1839–1860* (Evanston and Chicago: Northwestern University Press, 1987), 14.

33. Hotmail started out as an attempt to avoid this kind of e-mail surveillance in the workplace. As a web-based method of sending e-mail, it allowed users to bypass network software by posting messages on the web. Although it is possible to follow the tracks of someone's browsing history on the web, since the web browser creates a cache of pages visited—and images downloaded during these visits—it is not possible to monitor text messages sent during this web activity.

34. For more on the details of the surveillance capacities of the contemporary workplace, see David Lyon, *The Electronic Eye* (Cambridge: Polity, 1994), 129–35; Shoshana Zuboff, *In the Age of the Smart Machine* (New York: Basic Books, 1988); and Vincent Mosco and Janet Wasko, eds., *The Political Economy of Information* (Madison: University of Wisconsin Press, 1988).

35. Brian Jarvis, *Postmodern Cartographies: The Geographical Imagination in Contemporary American Culture* (London: Pluto Press, 1998), 17.

36. Eve Kosofsky Sedgwick, ed., *Novel Gazing: Queer Readings in Fiction* (Durham and London: Duke University Press, 1997), 4.

37. Sedgwick, *Novel Gazing*, 5.

38. For more on this, see Sedgwick, *Novel Gazing*, 9–10.

39. Sedgwick, *Novel Gazing*, 17–19.

40. Sedgwick, *Novel Gazing*, 7.

41. Sedgwick, *Novel Gazing*, 27–28.

42. Eve Kosofsky Sedgwick, *Tendencies* (London: Routledge, 1994), 3.

43. Sedgwick, *Novel Gazing*, 2–3.

44. Cringeley, 96–97.

45. See Guerlain, 121.

46. This theme of friendship is one that marks much of Coupland's fiction. *Generation X* (London: Abacus, 1992 [1991]), usually represented as a "slacker" novel, and *Girlfriend in a Coma* (London: Flamingo, 1998) are ensemble pieces that follow the relationships between a group of male and female friends.

47. Lee Edelman, *Homographesis: Essays in Gay Literary and Cultural Theory* (New York and London: Routledge, 1994), 11–12.

48. Sedgwick, *Novel Gazing*, 2.

49. Xerox PARC (Palo Alto Research Center) has been responsible for many of the innovations in personal computing since the early 1970s. It was a pure research center, however, and never attempted to make commercial enterprises out of its innovations. It had a reputation for secrecy and idiosyncratic work practices.

50. Dennis Allen, "Lesbian and Gay Studies: A Consumer's Guide," in Thomas Foster, Carol Siegel, and Ellen E. Berry, *The Gay 90s: Disciplinary and Interdisciplinary Formations in Queer Studies* (New York and London: New York University Press, 1997), 23–50.

51. Allen, "Studies," 24.

52. Allen, "Studies," 31.

53. Allen, "Studies," 40.

54. Edelman, *Homographesis*, 11.

55. Andrew Hodges, *Alan Turing: the Enigma* (Vintage: London, 1992 [1983]), 415.

56. Tyler Curtain, "The 'Sinister Fruitiness' of Machines: *Neuromancer*, Internet Sexuality, and the Turing Test," in Sedgwick, *Novel Gazing*, 145.

57. Sedgwick, *Tendencies*, 5.

58. Each collection of eight digits represents a binary number that can be converted into a decimal number and from there into text. The original idea for this translation was taken from Lawrence You, Microserfs Secret, 1 March 2000, Webpage, S. Chung, Available: http://coupland.tripod.com/msecret1.html, 4 August 2000. I have amended the translated code published on this website to correct some errors.

59. Sedgwick, *Novel Gazing*, 28.

Conclusion

1. Siegfried Kracauer, "On Employment Agencies: The Construction of a Space," in Neil Leach, ed., *Rethinking Architecture: a Reader in Cultural Theory* (London and New York: Routledge, 1997), 59.

2. Alan Sinfield, *The Wilde Century* (London: Cassell, 1994), 8.

3. Joseph Heller, *Something Happened* (New York: Alfred A. Knopf, 1974), 3.

4. Lee Edelman, *Homographesis: Essays in Gay Literary and Cultural Theory* (New York and London: Routledge, 1994), 203.

5. Nicholson Baker, *The Fermata* (New York: Random House, 1994), 123–24.

6. Douglas Coupland, *Microserfs* (London: Flamingo, 1995), 371.

7. See Susan Faludi, *Backlash*, rev. ed. (London: Chatto & Windus, 1992 [1991]) and Robert Bly, *Iron John* (Reading, Mass., and Wokingham: Addison-Wesley, 1990).

8. The only book to deal with this subject at any length is Emily Stipes Watts, *The Businessman in American Literature* (Athens: University of Georgia Press, 1982). Her treatment is based around a belief that almost without exception the literary depictions of American businessmen have been unduly critical.

Adorno, Theodor. *The Culture Industry*. London: Routledge, 1991.

Allen, Dennis W. "Homosexuality and Narrative." *Modern Fiction Studies* 41 (1995): 609–34.

———. "Lesbian and Gay Studies: A Consumer's Guide." In Thomas Foster, Carol Siegel, and Ellen E. Berry, *The Gay 90s: Disciplinary and Interdisciplinary Formations in Queer Studies* (New York and London: New York University Press, 1997): 23–50.

Altman, Dennis. *Homosexual Oppression and Liberation*. New York: Avon Books, 1973.

Altman, Dennis et al. *Homosexuality, Which Homosexuality?* London: Gay Men's Press, 1989.

Anderson, Gregory, ed. *The White-Blouse Revolution: Female Office Workers since 1870*. Manchester and New York: Manchester University Press, 1988.

Annesley, James. *Blank Fictions: Consumerism, Culture and the Contemporary Novel*. London: Pluto Press, 1998.

Aranowitz, Stanley, Barbara Martinsons, and Michael Menser, eds. *Technoscience and Cyberculture*. New York and London: Routledge, 1996.

Baker, Nicholson. *The Mezzanine*. Cambridge: Granta, 1989 [1988].

———. *U and I*. London: Granta, 1991.

———. *The Fermata*. New York: Random House, 1994.

———. *The Size of Thought: Essays and Other Lumber*. London: Chatto & Windus, 1996.

Baldry, C., P. Bain, and P. Taylor. "Bright Satanic Offices: Intensification, Control and Team Taylorism." In C. Warhurst and P. Thompson, eds., *Workplaces of the Future* (London: Macmillan, 1998): 163–83.

Baldry, Chris. "Space—The Final Frontier." *Sociology* 33 (1999): 535–53.

Barnett, Louise K. "Bartleby as Alienated Worker." *Studies in Short Fiction* 11 (1974): 379–85.

Baudrillard, Jean. *Selected Writings*. Cambridge: Polity Press, 1988.

Baym, Nina et al. *The Norton Anthology of American Literature Fourth Edition*. New York and London: W. W. Norton and Company, 1994.

Bederman, Gail. *Manliness and Civilization: A Cultural History of Gender and Race in the United States, 1880–1917*. Chicago and London: University of Chicago Press, 1995.

Bell, Daniel. *The End of Ideology: On the Exhaustion of Political Ideas in the Fifties*. Cambridge, Mass.: Harvard University Press, 1988 [1960].

Bersani, Leo. "Is the Rectum a Grave?" *October* 43 (1987): 197–222.

———. *Homos*. Cambridge, Mass., and London: Harvard University Press, 1995.

Bertolini, Vincent J. "Fireside Chastity: The Erotics of Sentimental Bachelorhood in the 1850s." *American Literature* 68 (1996): 707–37.

Bérubé, Alan. "Marching to a Different Drummer: Lesbian and Gay GIs in World War II." In Martin Baum Duberman, Martha Vicinus, and George Chauncey, Jr., eds., *Hidden from History: Reclaiming the Gay and Lesbian Past* (Harmondsworth: Penguin, 1991 [1989]): 383–94.

Betterton, Rosemary, ed. *Looking On: Images of Femininity in the Visual Arts and Media*. London: Pandora, 1987.

Bly, Robert. *Iron John: A Book about Men*. Reading, Mass., and Wokingham: Addison-Wesley, 1990.

Blumin, Stuart M. "The Hypothesis of Middle-Class Formation in Nineteenth-Century America: A Critique and Some Proposals." *The American Historical Review* 90 (1985): 299–338.

Boone, Joseph A. and Michael Cadden, eds. *Engendering Men: The Question of Male Feminist Criticism*. New York and London: Routledge, 1990.

Boyer, Kate. "Place and the politics of virtue: clerical workers, corporate anxiety, and changing meanings of public womanhood in early twentieth century Montreal." *Gender, Place and Culture* 5 (1998): 261–76.

Bradbury, Malcolm. *The Modern American Novel*. Oxford: Oxford University Press, 1984 [1983].

Bray, Alan. *Homosexuality in Renaissance England*. London: Gay Men's Press, 1982.

Bristow, Joseph. *Sexuality*. London and New York: Routledge, 1997.

Brod, Harry, ed. *The Making of Masculinities: The New Men's Studies*. Winchester, Mass.: Allen & Unwin, 1987.

Bronson, Po. *The Nudist of the Late Shift: And Other Tales from Silicon Valley*. London: Secker & Warburg, 1999.

Bruzzi, Stella. *Undressing Cinema*. London and New York: Routledge, 1997.

Butler, Judith. *The Psychic Life of Power*. Palo Alto: Stanford University Press, 1997.

Carnes, Mark C. *Secret Ritual and Manhood in Victorian America*. New Haven and London: Yale University Press, 1989.

Casarino, Cesare. "Gomorrahs of the Deep; or, Melville, Foucault and the Question of Heterotopia." *Arizona Quarterly* 51 (1995): 1–25.

———. "The Sublime of the Closet; or, Joseph Conrad's *The Secret Sharer*." *boundary 2* 24 (1997): 199–243.

Casey, Catherine. *Work, Self and Society after Industrialism*. London and New York: Routledge, 1995.

Chambers, Ross. "Meditation and the Escalator Principle (On Nicholson Baker's *The Mezzanine*)." *Modern Fiction Studies* 40 (1994): 765–806.

Chandler, Alfred D., Jr. *The Visible Hand: The Managerial Revolution in American Business.* Cambridge, Mass., and London: Harvard University Press, 1977.

Chauncey, George. *Gay New York: The Making of the Gay Male World, 1890–1940.* London: Flamingo, 1995 [1994].

Cohen, Ed. *A Talk on the Wilde Side.* New York: Routledge, 1993.

Cohen, Josh. *Spectacular Allegories: Postmodern Writing and the Politics of Seeing.* London: Pluto Press, 1998.

Corber, Robert J. *Homosexuality in Cold War America: Resistance and the Crisis of Masculinity.* Durham and London: Duke University Press, 1997.

Coupland, Douglas. *Generation X.* London: Abacus, 1992 [1991].

———. *Microserfs.* London: Flamingo, 1995.

———. *Girlfriend in a Coma.* London: Flamingo, 1998.

Cowan, Peter et al. *The Office: a facet of urban growth.* London: Heinemann Educational Books, 1969.

Crary, Jonathan. *Techniques of the Observer: On Vision and Modernity in the Nineteenth Century.* Cambridge, Mass.: Harvard University Press, 1990.

Crawford, Margaret. *Building the Workingman's Paradise: The Design of American Company Towns.* London and New York: Verso, 1995.

Creech, James. *Closet Writing/Gay Reading: The Case of Melville's* Pierre. Chicago: University of Chicago Press, 1993.

Cringeley, Robert X. *Accidental Empires,* 2d ed. Harmondsworth: Penguin, 1996.

Crowley, John W. "Howells, Stoddard, and Male Homosocial Attachment in Victorian America." In Harry Brod, ed., *The Making of Masculinities: The New Men's Studies* (Winchester, Mass.: Allen & Unwin, 1987): 301–24.

———. *The Mask of Fiction.* Amherst: University of Massachusetts Press, 1989.

Crozier, Michael. *The World of the Office Worker.* London and Chicago: University of Chicago Press, 1971 [1965].

Curtain, Tyler. "The 'Sinister Fruitiness' of Machines: *Neuromancer,* Internet Sexuality, and the Turing Test." In Eve Kosofsky Sedgwick, ed., *Novel Gazing: Queer Readings in Fiction* (Durham and London: Duke University Press, 1997): 128–48.

Cusumano, Michael A. and Richard W. Selby. *Microsoft Secrets: How the World's Most Powerful Software Company Creates Technology, Shapes Markets, and Manages People.* London: HarperCollins, 1996.

Dandeker, Christopher. *Surveillance, Power and Modernity.* Cambridge: Polity, 1990.

Davidson, Michael. *The San Francisco Renaissance: Poetics and Community at Mid-Century.* Cambridge: Cambridge University Press, 1979.

Davies, M. W. *Woman's Place Is at the Typewriter: Office Work and Office Workers, 1870–1930.* Philadelphia: Temple University Press, 1982.

Deleuze, Gilles. *Foucault.* London: Athlone, 1988.

———. *Essays Critical and Clinical,* trans. Daniel W. Smith and Michael A. Greco. London: Verso, 1998.

DeLillo, Don. *Americana*. Harmondsworth: Penguin, 1990 [1971].
————. *Running Dog*. New York: Alfred A. Knopf, 1978.
————. *White Noise*. New York: Viking Penguin, 1984.
D'Emilio, John. *Sexual Politics, Sexual Communities: The Making of a Homosexual Minority in the United States, 1940–1970*. Chicago and London: University of Chicago Press, 1983.
————. "Gay Politics and Community in San Francisco since World War II." In Martin Baum Duberman, Martha Vicinus, and George Chauncey, Jr., eds., *Hidden from History: Reclaiming the Gay and Lesbian Past* (Harmondsworth: Penguin, 1991 [1989]): 456–73.
Di Renzo, Anthony, ed. *If I Were Boss: The Early Business Stories of Sinclair Lewis*. Carbondale and Edwardsville: Southern Illinois University Press, 1997.
Dimock, Wai-Chee. "The Economy of Pain: Capitalism, Humanitarianism, and the Realistic Novel." In Donald E. Pease, ed., *New Essays on* The Rise of Silas Lapham (Cambridge and New York: Cambridge University Press, 1991): 67–90.
Dollimore, Jonathan. *Sexual Dissidence*. Oxford: Oxford University Press, 1991.
————. *Death, Desire and Loss in Western Culture*. Harmondsworth: Penguin, 1999 [1998].
Dooley, Patrick. "Nineteenth Century Business Ethics and *The Rise of Silas Lapham*." *American Studies* 21 (1980): 79–93.
Douglas, Ann. *The Feminization of American Culture*. London: Papermac, 1996 [1977].
Dover, K. J. *Greek Homosexuality*. New York: Random House, 1980.
du Gay, Paul. *Consumption and Identity at Work*. London: Sage, 1996.
Duberman, Martin. *Stonewall*. New York: Dutton, 1993.
Duberman, Martin Baum, Martha Vicinus, and George Chauncey, Jr., eds. *Hidden from History: Reclaiming the Gay and Lesbian Past*. Harmondsworth: Penguin, 1991 [1989].
Eby, Clare Virginia. "*Babbitt* as Veblenian Critique of Manliness." *American Studies* 34 (1993): 5–23.
Edelman, Lee. *Homographesis: Essays in Gay Literary and Cultural Theory*. New York and London: Routledge, 1994.
————. "Men's Room." In Joel Sanders, ed., *Stud: Architectures of Masculinity* (New York: Princeton Architectural Press, 1996): 152–61.
Ellis, Havelock and John Addington Symons. *Sexual Inversion*. London: Wilson and Macmillan, 1897.
Ellis, R. J. *Liar! Liar!: Jack Kerouac—Novelist*. London: Greenwich Exchange, 1999.
Emerson, Ralph Waldo. *Journals of Ralph Waldo Emerson, 1841–44, Volume 6*. Boston: Forbes, 1912.
————. "Nature," In Nina Baym et al., *The Norton Anthology of American Literature Fourth Edition* (New York and London: W. W. Norton and Company, 1994): 1005–6.
Faludi, Susan. *Backlash*, rev. ed. London: Chatto & Windus, 1992 [1991].
Foster, Hal, ed. *Postmodern Culture*. London: Pluto Press, 1985 [1983].

Foster, Thomas, Carol Siegel, and Ellen E. Berry. *The Gay 90s: Disciplinary and Interdisciplinary Formations in Queer Studies*. New York and London: New York University Press, 1997.

Foucault, Michel. *The Order of Things: An Archaeology of the Human Sciences*. London and New York: Pantheon, 1970.

———. *Discipline and Punish*. Harmondsworth: Penguin, 1991 [1977].

———. *The History of Sexuality Volume 1: An Introduction*. Harmondsworth: Penguin, 1990 [1978].

———. *The Use of Pleasure: Volume 2 of The History of Sexuality*. Harmondsworth: Penguin, 1992 [1985].

———. "Of Other Spaces: Utopias and Heterotopias." In Neil Leach, ed., *Rethinking Architecture: a Reader in Cultural Theory* (London and New York: Routledge, 1997): 350–56.

Freedman, Jonathan, "The Affect of the Market: Economic and Racial Exchange in *The Searchers*." *American Literary History* 12 (2000): 585–99.

Freud, Sigmund. *The Standard Edition of the Complete Psychological Works of Sigmund Freud, Volume XII*, trans. James Strachey. London: Hogarth Press, 1973 [1958].

Furlani, Andre, "'Brisk Socratic Dialogues': Elenctic Rhetoric in Joseph Heller's *Something Happened*." *Narrative* 3 (1995): 252–70.

Fuss, Diana and Joel Sanders. "Bergasse 19: Inside Freud's Office." In Joel Sanders, ed., *Stud: Architectures of Masculinity* (New York: Princeton Architectural Press, 1996): 112–39.

Gallop, Jane. *Feminism and Psychoanalysis: The Daughter's Seduction*. Basingstoke: Macmillan, 1982.

Gates, Bill. *The Road Ahead*, rev. ed. Harmondsworth: Penguin, 1996.

Ghoshal, Sumantra and Christopher A. Bartlett. *The Individualized Corporation*. London: Heinemann, 1999.

Gilmore, David D. *Manhood in the Making: Cultural Concepts of Masculinity*. New Haven: Yale University Press, 1990.

Gilmore, Michael T. *American Romanticism and the Marketplace*. Chicago and London: University of Chicago Press, 1985.

Girgus, Sam B. *Desire and the Political Unconscious in American Literature*. Basingstoke: Macmillan, 1990.

Godden, Richard. *Fictions of Capital: Essays in the American Novel from James to Mailer*. Cambridge: Cambridge University Press, 1990.

———. *Fictions of Labour: William Faulkner and the South's Long Revolution*. Cambridge: Cambridge University Press, 1997.

Goldberg, Jonathan. *Sodometries: Renaissance Texts, Modern Sexualities*. Palo Alto: Stanford University Press, 1992.

Gordon, Andrew. "Dead Letter Offices: Joseph Heller's *Something Happened* and Herman Melville's 'Bartleby, the Scrivener.'" *Notes on Contemporary Literature* 12 (1982): 2–4.

Greenblatt, Stephen. *Shakespearean Negotiations*. Oxford: Oxford University Press, 1997 [1988].

Guerlain, Pierre. "A Technofreak in Xanadu: Bill Gates and Cool Capitalism." *European Journal of American Culture* 19 (2000): 116–22.

Halperin, David. *One Hundred Years of Homosexuality and Other Essays on Greek Love*. New York: Routledge, 1990.

Hedstrom, Margaret L. "Beyond feminisation: clerical workers in the United States from the 1920s through the 1960s." In Gregory Anderson, ed., *The White-Blouse Revolution: Female Office Workers Since 1870* (Manchester and New York: Manchester University Press, 1988): 143–69.

Heller, Joseph. *Something Happened*. New York: Alfred A. Knopf, 1974.

Hodges, Andrew. *Alan Turing: the Enigma*. London: Vintage, 1992 [1983].

Hoffman, Nicholas von. *Citizen Cohn*. New York: Doubleday, 1988.

Horkheimer, Max and Theodor Adorno. *Dialectic of Enlightenment*. London: Allen Lane, 1973 [1944].

Howard, June. "What Is Sentimentality?" *American Literary History* 11 (1999): 63–81.

Howells, William Dean. *A Modern Instance*. Boston: Houghton Mifflin Company, 1957 [1882].

———. *The Rise of Silas Lapham*. Oxford: Oxford University Press, 1996 [1885].

Huczynski, A. *Management Gurus*. London: Routledge, 1993.

Hutchisson, James M. "'All of Us Americans at 46': The Making of Sinclair Lewis' *Babbitt*." *Journal of Modern Literature* 18 (1992): 95–114.

Irigaray, Luce. *Speculum of the Other Woman*, trans. Gillian C. Gill. Ithaca, New York: Cornell University Press, 1985 [1974].

———. *This Sex Which Is Not One*. Ithaca, New York: Cornell University Press, 1985.

James, Henry. *The Bostonians*. London and New York: Macmillan and Co., 1886.

Jameson, Fredric. "Postmodernism, or the Cultural Logic of Late Capitalism." *New Left Review* 146 (1984): 53–92.

———. "Postmodernism and Consumer Society." In Hal Foster, ed., *Postmodern Culture* (London: Pluto Press, 1985 [1983]): 111–25.

———. *Postmodernism*. London: Verso, 1991.

Jarvis, Brian. *Postmodern Cartographies: The Geographical Imagination in Contemporary American Culture*. London: Pluto Press, 1998.

Jay, Martin. *Downcast Eyes: the Denigration of Vision in Twentieth-Century French Thought*. Berkeley and London: University of California Press, 1994 [1993].

Jurca, Catherina. "The Sanctimonious Suburbanite: Sloan Wilson's *The Man in the Gray Flannel Suit*." *American Literary History* 11 (1999): 82–106.

Kennedy, C. *Guide to Management Gurus*. London: Century Press, 1991.

Kleinberg, S. J. *Women in the United States 1830–1945*. Basingstoke and London: Macmillan Press, 1999.

Kracauer, Siegfried. "On Employment Agencies: The Construction of a Space." In Neil Leach, ed., *Rethinking Architecture: a Reader in Cultural Theory* (London and New York: Routledge, 1997): 59–64.

Krafft-Ebing, Richard von. *Psychopathia Sexualis, with Especial Reference to Contrary Sexual Instinct: A Medico-Legal Study*, trans. Charles Gilbert Chaddock. Philadelphia: F. A. Davis, 1894.

Kristeva, Julia. *Revolution in Poetic Language*. New York: Columbia University Press, 1984 [1974].

Kroker, Arthur. "Virtual Capitalism." In Stanley Aranowitz, Barbara Martin-sons, and Michael Menser, eds., *Technoscience and Cyberculture* (New York and London: Routledge, 1996): 167–79.

Kuebrich, David. "Melville's Doctrine of Assumptions: The Hidden Ideology of Capitalist Production in 'Bartleby.'" *New England Quarterly* 69 (1996): 381–405.

Lacquer, Thomas. *Making Sex*. Cambridge, Mass., and London: Harvard University Press, 1992 [1990].

Lalvani, Suren. *Photography, Vision, and the Production of Modern Bodies*. New York: State University of New York Press, 1996.

Leach, Neil, ed. *Rethinking Architecture: a Reader in Cultural Theory*. London and New York: Routledge, 1997.

Lears, T. J. Jackson. *No Place of Grace: Antimodernism and the Transformation of American Culture, 1880–1920*. Chicago and London: University of Chicago Press, 1994 [1983].

Leibovich, Mark. "*Sleepless in Silicon Valley*: Global Competition, Technology's Fast Track Dictates a Lifestyle of Working into the Wee Hours." *San Jose Mercury News*, 21 June 1996, sec. Front: 1A.

Leithauser, Brad. "Microscopy." *The New York Review of Books* 36 (1989): 15.

Lewis, Jeremy. *Chatto Book of Office Life: or Love among the Filing Cabinets*. London: Chatto & Windus, 1992.

Lewis, Sinclair. *Babbitt*. London: Vintage, 1994 [1922].

Light, Martin. *The Quixotic Vision of Sinclair Lewis*. West Lafayette, Indiana: Purdue University Press, 1975.

Lyon, David. *The Electronic Eye: The Rise of Surveillance Society*. Cambridge: Polity, 1994.

Maccubin, Robert Purks, ed. *'Tis Nature's Fault*. Cambridge: Cambridge University Press, 1987.

Marcuse, Herbert. *One Dimensional Man*. London: Abacus, 1972.

Martin, Robert K. *Hero, Captain, and Stranger: Male Friendship, Social Critique, and Literary Form in the Sea Novels of Herman Melville*. Chapel Hill and London: University of North Carolina Press, 1986.

Marx, Leo. "Melville's Parable of the Walls." *Sewanee Review* 61 (1953): 602–27.

Matthews, Glenna. *The Rise of Public Woman: Woman's Power and Woman's Place in the United States 1630–1970*. New York and Oxford: Oxford University Press, 1992.

May, Elaine Tyler. *Homeward Bound: American Families in the Cold War Era*. New York: Basic Books, 1988.

McCall, Dan. *The Silence of Bartleby*. Ithaca and London: Cornell University Press, 1989.

McDowell, Linda. *Capital Culture: Gender at Work in the City*. London: Blackwell, 1997.

McGuire, Ian. "W. D. Howells and the Crisis of Overproduction." *Journal of American Studies* 33 (1999): 459–72.

McNally, Fiona. *Women for Hire: A Study of the Female Office Worker*. London: Macmillan, 1979.

Melville, Herman. *Moby-Dick*. Harmondsworth: Penguin, 1986 [1851].

———. *The Piazza Tales and Other Prose Pieces 1839–1860*. Evanston and Chicago: Northwestern University Press, 1987.

Miller, D. A. *The Novel and the Police*. Berkeley: University of California Press, 1988.

Miller, Henry. *Tropic of Capricorn*. London: Flamingo, 1993 [1939].

Miller, Neil. *Out of the Past: Gay and Lesbian History from 1869 to the Present*. London: Vintage, 1995.

Miller, Stephen Paul. *The Seventies Now: Culture as Surveillance*. Durham and London: Duke University Press, 1999.

Millet, Kate. *Sexual Politics*. New York: Doubleday, 1970.

Mills, C. Wright. *White Collar: The American Middle Classes*. New York: Oxford University Press, 1971 [1953].

Mitchell, Juliet. *Psychoanalysis and Feminism: Freud, Reich, Laing and Women*. London: Allen Lane, 1974.

Moody, Fred. *I Sing the Body Electronic: A Year with Microsoft on the Multimedia Frontier*. London: Hodder and Stoughton, 1996 [1995].

Morefield, Kenneth R. "Searching for the Fairy Child: A Psychoanalytic Study of *Babbitt*." *Midwest Quarterly* 37 (1996): 448–58.

Morris, Norval and David J. Rothman. *The Oxford History of the Prison: the Practice of Punishment in Western Society*. New York and Oxford: Oxford University Press, 1996.

Mosco, Vincent and Janet Wasko. eds. *The Political Economy of Information*. Madison: University of Wisconsin Press, 1988.

Mulvey, Laura. "Visual pleasure and narrative cinema." *Screen* 16 (1975): 6–19.

Nelson, Dana. *National Manhood: Capitalist Citizenship and the Imagined Fraternity of White Men*. Durham and London: Duke University Press, 1998.

Norton, Rictor. *The Myth of the Modern Homosexual*. London: Cassell, 1997.

Packard, Vance. *The Status Seekers*. Harmondsworth: Penguin, 1961 [1959].

Parker, Hershel. *Herman Melville: A Biography, Volume 1, 1819–1851*. Baltimore and London: The John Hopkins University Press, 1996.

Parry, Sally E. "The Changing Fictional Faces of Sinclair Lewis' Wives." *Studies in American Fiction* 17 (1989): 65–79.

Patton, Cindy. "To Die For." In Eve Kosofsky Sedgwick, ed., *Novel Gazing: Queer Readings in Fiction* (Durham and London: Duke University Press, 1997), 330–52.

Pease, Donald E., ed. *New Essays on* The Rise of Silas Lapham. Cambridge and New York: Cambridge University Press, 1991.

Pick, Daniel. "Stories of the Eye." In Roy Porter, ed., *Rewriting the Self: Histories from the Renaissance to the Present* (London: Routledge, 1997): 186–99.

Pleck, Elizabeth and Joseph Pleck, eds. *The American Man*. Englewood Cliffs: Prentice Hall, 1990.

Porter, Roy, ed. *Rewriting the Self: Histories from the Renaissance to the Present*. London: Routledge, 1997.

Pringle, Rosemary. *Sexuality, Power and Work*. London and New York: Verso, 1989 [1988].

Prioleau, Elizabeth Stevens. *The Circle of Eros: Sexuality in the Work of William Dean Howells*. Durham: Duke University Press, 1983.

Pynchon, Thomas. *The Crying of Lot 49*. Harmondsworth: Penguin, 1974 [1966].

Riemer, James D. "Rereading American Literature from a Men's Studies Perspective: Some Implications." In Harry Brod, ed., *The Making of Masculinities: The New Men's Studies* (Winchester, Mass.: Allen & Unwin, 1987): 289–300.

Riesman, David. *The Lonely Crowd*. New Haven and London: Yale University Press, 1970 [1953].

Rogin, Michael. *Ronald Reagan, the Movie and Other Episodes in Political Demonology*. Berkeley, Los Angeles, and London: University of California Press, 1987.

Roper, Michael. *Masculinity and the British Organization Man since 1945*. Oxford: Oxford University Press, 1994.

Rose, Jacqueline. "Femininity and Its Discontents," *Feminist Review* 14 (1982): 5–21.

Rotella, E. J. *From Home to Office: U.S. Women at Work, 1870–1930*. Ann Arbor: UMI Research Press, 1981.

Rotundo, E. Anthony. *American Manhood: Transformations in Masculinity from the Revolution to the Modern Era*. New York: Basic Books, 1993.

Rovere, Richard H. *Senator Joe McCarthy*. New York: Harcourt Brace, 1959.

Sanders, Joel, ed. *Stud: Architectures of Masculinity*. New York: Princeton Architectural Press, 1996.

Savran, David. *Communists, Cowboys, and Queers: The Politics of Masculinity in the Work of Arthur Miller and Tennessee Williams*. Minneapolis: University of Minnesota Press, 1992.

Schaub, Thomas Hill. *American Fiction in the Cold War*. Madison: University of Wisconsin Press, 1991.

Sedgwick, Eve Kosofsky. *The Coherence of Gothic Conventions*. New York: Arno, 1980.

———. *Between Men: English Literature and Male Homosocial Desire*. New York: Columbia University Press, 1985.

———. *Epistemology of the Closet*. Harmondsworth: Penguin, 1994 [1990].

———. *Tendencies*. London: Routledge, 1994.

———, ed. *Novel Gazing: Queer Readings in Fiction*. Durham and London: Duke University Press, 1997.

Seelye, John. "The Hole in Howells/The Lapse in *Silas Lapham*." In Donald E. Pease, ed., *New Essays on* The Rise of Silas Lapham (Cambridge and New York: Cambridge University Press, 1991): 47–65.

Silverman, Kaja. "Too Early/Too Late: Subjectivity and the Primal Scene in Henry James." *Novel* 21 (1988): 147–73.

Simmons, Phillip E. *Deep Surfaces: Mass Culture and History in Postmodern American Fiction*. Athens: University of Georgia Press, 1997.

Sinfield, Alan. *Cultural Politics—Queer Reading*. London: Routledge, 1994.

———. *The Wilde Century*. London: Cassell, 1994.

Slotkin, Richard. *Regeneration through Violence: The Myth of the American Frontier, 1600–1860*. Middletown, Conn.: Wesleyan University Press, 1973.

———. *The Fatal Environment: The Myth of the Frontier in the Age of Industrialization, 1800–1890*. New York: Atheneum, 1985.

———. *Gunfighter Nation: The Myth of the Frontier in Twentieth-Century America*. New York: HarperPerennial, 1993 [1992].

Sorkin, Adam J. "Something Happened to America: Bob Slocum and the Loss of History." *Ball State University Forum* 28 (1987): 35–53.

Spangler, George. "The Shadow of a Dream: Howells' Homosexual Tragedy." *American Quarterly* 23 (1971): 110–19.

Stallybrass, Peter. "Worn Worlds: Clothes, Mourning and the Life of Things." *Yale Review* 81 (1993): 35–50.

Stearns, Peter N. *Be a Man! Males in Modern Society*. New York: Holmes & Meier, 1979.

Stoneley, Peter. "Rewriting the Gold Rush: Twain, Harte and Homosociality." *Journal of American Studies* 30 (1996): 189–209.

Tallack, Douglas. *Twentieth-Century America: The Intellectual and Cultural Context*. Harlow: Longman, 1991.

Thomas, Calvin, ed. *Straight with a Twist: Queer Theory and the Subject of Heterosexuality*. Urbana and Chicago: University of Illinois Press, 2000.

Tompkins, Jane. "Sentimental Power: *Uncle Tom's Cabin* and the Politics of Literary History." In H. Aram Vesser, ed., *The New Historicism Reader* (New York and London: Routledge, 1994): 206–28.

Trumbach, Randolph. "Sodomitical Subcultures, Sodomitical Roles, and the Gender Revolution of the Eighteenth Century: the Recent Historiography." In Robert Purks Maccubin, ed., *'Tis Nature's Fault* (Cambridge: Cambridge University Press, 1987): 109–21.

———. "Gender and the Modern Homosexual Role in Western Culture: the 18th and 19th Centuries Compared." In Dennis Altman et al., *Homosexuality, Which Homosexuality?* (London: Gay Men's Press, 1989): 149–69.

Tucker, Lindsey. "Entropy and Information Theory in Heller's *Something Happened*." *Contemporary Literature* 25 (1984): 323–40.

Tyson, Lois. "Joseph Heller's *Something Happened*: The Commodification of Consciousness and the Postmodern Flight from Inwardness." *CEA Critic* 54 (1992), 37–51.

Ulrichs, Karl Heinz. *The Riddle of "Man-Manly" Love: The Pioneering Work on Male Homosexuality*, 2 vols., trans. Michael A. Lombardi-Nash. Buffalo, New York: Prometheus Books, 1994).

Vesser, H. Aram, ed. *The New Historicism Reader*. New York and London: Routledge, 1994.

Warhurst, C. and P. Thompson, eds. *Workplaces of the Future*. London: Macmillan, 1998.

Warner, Michael. "Homo-Narcissism: or, Heterosexuality." In Joseph A.

Boone and Michael Cadden, eds., *Engendering Men: The Question of Male Feminist Criticism* (New York and London: Routledge, 1990): 190–206.

Watts, Emily Stipes. *The Businessman in American Literature*. Athens: University of Georgia Press, 1982.

Weeks, Jeffrey. *Coming Out: Homosexual Politics in Britain from the Nineteenth Century to the Present*. London: Quartet, 1977.

———. *Sexuality and Its Discontents*. London: Routledge & Kegan Paul, 1985.

Whyte, William H. *The Organization Man*. Harmondsworth: Penguin, 1960 [1956].

Wilson, Sloan. *The Man in the Gray Flannel Suit*. New York: Simon and Schuster, 1955.

Woods, Gregory. *A History of Gay Literature: The Male Tradition*. New Haven and London: Yale University Press, 1998.

Zelnich, Stephen. "Melville's 'Bartleby, the Scrivener': A Study in History, Ideology, and Literature." *Marxist Perspectives* 2 (1979–80): 74–92.

Zuboff, Shoshana. *In the Age of the Smart Machine*. New York: Basic Books, 1988.

Adorno, Theodor, 73
Afghanistan, xvii
Allen, Dennis, 191
Allen, Paul, 167
anality, 15, 25–28, 34–35, 36, 76, 88–
   89, 98, 106, 159–64, 212n34
Apple, 168, 181

Baker, Nicholson, 133–36, 140, 143,
   146, 150, 153, 155, 156, 158, 159,
   164, 165, 184, 202, 205, 228n29;
   The Fermata, 133, 137, 152–64, 201,
   203, 204; *The Mezzanine*, 133, 135–
   36, 137, 140–52, 154–55, 156,
   158, 160, 174, 201; *U and I*, 164
Baudrillard, Jean, 184
Bederman, Gail, 48
Bell, Daniel, 78, 184
Bersani, Leo, 162–63
Bérubé, Alan, 83
Blank Fiction, 134
Boyer, Kate, 67
Bronson, Po, 167, 171, 178, 179,
   229n9
Bush, George Sr., xvii
business and America, 28–29, 49–
   50, 66, 72–74, 75–76, 78–83,
   109–10, 166–67

Casey, Catherine, 138–39
Chauncey, George, 54, 62, 208n14

Clinton, Bill, xi, xiv, xvi, xvii, xviii,
   xix; on gays in military, xiv–xviii
computer code, 166, 170, 172, 175,
   181–82, 193, 196–98
Cooper, Dennis, 205
Corber, Robert J., 225n16
corporatization, 73–74, 77–82, 138–
   39
Coupland, Douglas, 165, 169, 171,
   174, 184, 187, 196, 198, 202, 205;
   Microserfs, 165–199, 201, 203, 204,
   205, 231n46
Creech, James, 3
Cringeley, Robert, 169, 186–87, 190,
   229n15
Curtain, Tyler, 195

Dead Letter Office, 4, 17–18
Deleuze, Gilles, 13, 156, 211n29
DeLillo, Don, 110, 113; *Americana*,
   110, 113–16, 121
Derrida, Jacques, 189, 190
Di Renzo, Anthony, 48
Dickens, Charles, 27, 35
Dimock, Wai-Chee, 24, 26–27, 35,
   216n28
Dollimore, Jonathan, 12, 13, 16, 44,
   79, 130, 162, 163, 216n25
"Don't Ask, Don't Tell" policy, xv
Dos Passos, John, 80
Dostoyevsky, Fyodor, 154

Douglas, Ann, 68, 220n7
Dreiser, Theodore, 80
Dumas, Alexandre, 68

Eby, Clare, 71
Edelman, Lee, xv, xx, 9–10, 13, 14,
    16, 54, 57, 59, 79, 82, 83, 96, 105,
    107, 115, 130, 150, 162, 189–95,
    215n16
effeminacy, 10, 13, 41–42, 52, 53–54,
    55–56, 82–83, 126, 211n22; Cold
    War, 93, 99–100. *See also* latency
Ellis, Brett Easton, 134, 135
Emerson, Ralph Waldo, xiv, 155, 157
Estes, Richard, 158–59, 160, 163
Excite, 178

Filo, David, 171, 173
Fitzgerald, F. Scott, 80
Foucault, Michel, 5, 6, 9, 10, 21, 22,
    24, 53, 87, 130, 136–38, 163, 189;
    surveillance, 5–6, 11, 139–40
Freedman, Jonathan, 48
Freud, Sigmund, 24, 27, 83, 84, 213n5

Gates, Bill, 166–70, 175, 183, 186,
    190, 206; *The Road Ahead*, 166
Gilmore, Michael, 3
Goldberg, Jonathan, xvii, xviii
Guerlain, Pierre, 169–70

Haskell, Thomas, 26
Hedstrom, Margaret, 67
Hegger, Grace Livingstone, 48
Heller, Joseph, 109, 117, 128, 134,
    135, 162, 164; *Something Happened*,
    109–30, 133, 154, 163, 165, 169,
    170, 179, 184, 188, 201, 202, 203,
    204
heterosexual family, 22, 58, 61, 91–
    95, 102, 104–5, 107
Hofstadter, Richard, 78
homographesis, xx, 9–11, 14, 190–
    93
homosociality, xii, 9, 27, 28, 33, 35–
    36, 57–58, 97–98

Horkheimer, Max, 73
Hotmail, 230n33
Howard, June, 128
Howells, William Dean, 22, 24, 26,
    28, 29, 44, 84; *A Modern Instance*,
    214n7; *The Rise of Silas Lapham*,
    22–45, 51, 62, 69–70, 73, 74, 75–
    76, 84, 87, 88, 106, 109–10, 165,
    169, 170, 184, 188, 201, 202, 203,
    204, 214n7, 216n28
Hussein, Saddam, xvii
Huxley, Aldous, 81

IBM, 140, 173, 179

James, Henry, 53, 164
Jarvis, Brian, 183, 184
Jenkins, Walter, 82, 105
Johnson, Lyndon, 82

Khrushchev, Nikita, 82, 97
Kinsey Report, 83
Kracauer, Siegfried, 202
Kroker, Arthur, 168–69, 185
Kubrick, Stanley, 197

latency, 83, 84, 93, 99–100, 127,
    129
Lawrence, D. H., 76
Lears, T. J. Jackson, 48
Leibovitz, Annie, 170, 190
Lewinsky, Monica, xi, xiv, xviii, xix
Lewis, Jeremy, xii
Lewis, Sinclair, 47, 48, 49, 50, 53, 54,
    56, 57, 61, 71, 76; *Babbitt*, 47–62,
    69, 70–72, 73–74, 76, 87, 88, 104,
    106, 146, 165, 169, 184, 188, 201,
    202, 204; *The Job*, 48; "Honestly—
    If Possible," 48; "A Story with a
    Happy Ending," 48

Mailer, Norman, 105
male self-pity, 41–42, 76, 118–20,
    124–28
Marcuse, Herbert, 73
Martin, Robert K., 3, 19

Marx, Karl, 136
masculinity, 29–30, 31, 50, 53, 84–85, 102, 125–27, 169–70
May, Elaine Tyler, 92, 97
McCarthy, Joseph, 79, 80, 83, 220n2
McInerney, Jay, 134, 135; *Bright Lights, Big City,* 134
McLuhan, Marshall, 184, 185
McVeigh, Timothy, xvi, xvii, xviii
Melville, Herman, 3, 4, 6, 18, 19, 21, 123, 209n14; "Bartleby, the Scrivener," 3–19, 21, 22, 37, 51, 62, 74, 75, 87, 88, 91, 106, 116, 122, 128, 146, 182, 184, 201, 202, 203, 204, 209–10n16, 210n19, 212n30, 212n31, 212n32; "The Paradise of Bachelors and the Tartarus of Maids," 4; *Billy Budd,* 19, 96, 145–46; *Moby Dick,* 4, 145–46; *Pierre,* 3; sexuality, 3–4; *Typee,* 209n14
Merrimack Manufacturing Company, 137
Merwin, Henry Childs, 47, 48, 50
Microsoft, 166, 167, 172–77, 181–82, 184
Miller, D. A., 24, 150
Miller, Henry, 79, 80, 81; *Tropic of Capricorn,* 74–77, 80, 81, 88, 154
Mills, C. Wright, 74, 84, 90
Moody, Fred, 172, 174

Netscape, 178
Niebuhr, Reinhold, 78
Nixon, Richard, 82, 97

office: architecture, 7–8, 23, 49, 50–51; corporatization, 72–73; feminization, 66–72, 77, 91, 102–3, 105, 110, 187–88; historical development, 6; as laboratory, 21–23; in Silicon Valley, 171–73; surveillance, 5–6, 7–8, 12–13, 40–41, 50–51, 60–61, 69–70, 75, 87, 111–12, 137–38, 141, 143; washroom, 55, 146–49, 150–51

Organization Man, 66, 77, 80–82, 134, 138
Orwell, George, 81; *1984,* 174, 183
Oval Office, xi, xiv, xvi, xvii, xix

Peck, Dale, 205
perversion, 12, 44–45
Peters, Tom, 134
phallic thematics, 25, 32, 75–76, 98
Pleck, Elizabeth, 72
Pleck, Joseph, 72
Poe, Edgar Allan, "The Purloined Letter," 149
Prioleau, Elizabeth Stevens, 25–28, 31, 35
psychoanalysis and queer theory, 24–25, 215n16
public/private, 7–8, 14, 15, 18, 23–24, 96, 140–41, 143–52, 155–56
Pullman, George, 137
Pullman, Illinois, 137
Pynchon, Thomas, 140

Ricoeur, Paul, 185
Riesman, David, 74, 78, 84, 90
Rogin, Michael, 105
Roper, Michael, 221n26
Rotundo, Anthony E., 209n12

Santayana, George, 163
Savran, David, 82, 97
Schaub, Thomas, 77, 79
Sedgwick, Eve Kosofsky, xii, xiv, 5, 25, 41, 57, 96, 116, 118–19, 127, 130, 136, 145, 185–86, 190, 196, 210n19, 217n35, 218n43
Seelye, John, 43–44
Silicon Valley, 167, 170, 177–79, 181, 183–84, 190, 193
Simmons, Phillip E., 149, 164
Simon, Meri, 171
Sinclair, Upton, 80
Sinfield, Alan, 82, 83
Sisley, Alfred, 159, 160, 163
Slotkin, Richard, 76–77

sperm, 4, 25–26, 32, 35–36, 123
Stallybrass, Peter, 145
Stoneley, Peter, 168, 185
Sudan, xvii

Tallack, Douglas, 72, 78
Tarbell, Ida, 206
Taylor, Frederick, 70
Taylorism, 70, 71, 143, 171, 181
Thomas, Calvin, xix
Trilling, Lionel, 77, 78
Turing, Alan, 194
Tyson, Lois, 125

Updike, John, 164

Veblen, Thorstein, 71

Weber, Max, 136
White, Edmund, 205
Whyte, William H., 74, 80, 81, 83, 90
Wilson, Sloan, 65, 66, 88, 89, 90, 96, 99, 134, 135, 161, 164; *The Man in the Gray Flannel Suit*, 65–66, 71–72, 74, 85, 87–107, 133, 146–47, 154, 163, 165, 169, 170, 179, 184, 188, 201, 202, 203, 204
Woods, Gregory, 3, 123
work/home separation, 6, 136–37, 196
Wright, Frank Lloyd, 181

Yahoo!, 168, 171